Regional Monetary Policy

T0361173

With the final phase of the European Monetary Union under way concern has been raised over the regional implications of the European Central Bank's (ECB) Monetary Policy. Departing from the standard approach utilized by the ECB, this book provides a comprehensive theoretical framework to explore the ways through which money and monetary policy may affect regions.

Regional Monetary Policy examines the role that the banking system and the liquidity preference of economic agents play in the transmission of central banks' monetary policy decisions to regions within a country or countries within a currency union. This book utilizes a unique framework built upon the basic principles of the Post Keynesian monetary theory which enables the identification of a new way for money and monetary policy to have a regional impact: the behavioural effect.

This book will prove essential reading for all students of economics and politics as well as readers interested in the development of the European Union.

Carlos J. Rodríguez-Fuentes is 'Profesor Titular de Universidad' in the Department of Applied Economics at the University of La Laguna, Canary Islands, Spain.

Routledge Studies in the Modern World Economy

Regional Monetary Policy

Carlos J. Rodríguez-Fuentes

Routledge
Taylor & Francis Group

LONDON AND NEW YORK

First published 2006
by Routledge
2 Park Square, Milton Park, Abingdon, Oxon OX14 4RN

Simultaneously published in the USA and Canada
by Routledge
711 Third Avenue, New York, NY 10017

Routledge is an imprint of the Taylor & Francis Group

Transferred to Digital Printing 2006

First issued in paperback 2012

© 2006 Carlos J. Rodríguez-Fuentes

Typeset in Times New Roman by
Keyword Group

British Library Cataloguing in Publication Data
A catalogue record for this book is available from the British Library

Library of Congress Cataloging in Publication Data
A catalog record for this book has been requested

ISBN 10: 0-415-32763-6
ISBN 13: 978-0-415-65141-7

This book is dedicated to Sara, Diego and Eva

Contents

Contents

List of tables

List of tables

List of tables

List of tables

Foreword

We are delighted to be invited to write the Foreword to this volume. It brings together and extends Carlos Rodríguez-Fuentes's important and innovative work on regional finance and the differential regional impacts of monetary policy.

The contribution this book makes to our understanding extends beyond the specifically regional field. Carlos makes a much more general contribution by developing fully a Post Keynesian account of money and banking and the mechanism by which monetary policy is transmitted through the banking system. The contrast between the Post Keynesian approach and the more conventional money-macro approach is drawn out in the discussion of monetary policy. The conventional approach assumes that money is under the control of the monetary authorities, while the Post Keynesian approach stresses the active role of the banking system in the creation of money. This challenges the whole idea of thinking of monetary policy in terms of exogenous shocks.

The realism of the analysis is grounded in its application to regional economies, both within and among nations. Until recently, regional economics had been treated as of minor importance within the discipline. But, since the introduction of the euro, regional economics has enjoyed much broader application and has drawn more extensively on monetary and macroeconomic theory.

In the application to the impact of monetary policy on different regions, the role of the banking system becomes even more clear. Banks exercise their power over credit creation differentially, depending on their perceptions of region-specific risk and growth potential. But this power also depends on the stage of development of the banks concerned. Within nations, small firms in particular regions may be dependent on borrowing from local banks with less credit-creating capacity than national banks. Even more clearly, national banking systems may be at different stages of development, as well as having differing conventional behaviours, something which is very apparent within the euro-zone. This translates into a variable regional impact of monetary policy. Until recently, the subject of regional finance has been comparatively underdeveloped. But now the political importance of the euro has prompted a significant research agenda, which has almost exclusively drawn on conventional money-macro theory and competition theory. This book provides an important counterweight to this body of research, opening up another perspective, and one which we feel is both closer to the real operations of the banking system and accordingly more fruitful.

Regional analysis is normally dogged by data availability problems, which impede effective empirical analysis. Carlos's work provides some rare examples of econometric analysis of the regional impact of monetary policy for the euro-zone, Spain and the US, where regional data are less scarce. Again the analysis is all the more effective for being accompanied by a critical analysis of the extensive body of empirical work based on the conventional money-macro approach.

We feel personal pleasure in being involved in Carlos's book in this way, for he is someone we admire as a creative and careful thinker, and value greatly as a colleague and friend.

Sheila Dow and Victoria Chick
Dunblane, 27 November 2004

Acknowledgements

Many people have contributed to the writing of this book. Some of them got involved from the very beginning, when I started my research work for the Ph.D. dissertation. That was some time ago, during my stay at the Economics Department of the University of Stirling in the academic year 1992–93, under the supervision of Professor Sheila Dow. Since then, Sheila has been there for personal support and intellectual guidance. I would like to express my warmest gratitude to her for this, and also for her friendship.

Some other people whose contributions have been crucial for this book started playing a rather casual influence on my early work. This is the case of Professor Victoria Chick, whose 'Theory of the Monetary Policy' book I bought by chance at a second-hand bookshop in London well before I started thinking about my Ph.D. I can't remember exactly why I walked into that bookshop, since I was visiting London on holiday, in the summer of 1991. But the thing is that I went into the bookshop and found that book. 'What the hell are we doing in this bookshop in our holidays?' This is probably what my wife, Eva, was thinking at that moment. She now understands what I was doing there: keeping my eyes open and paying close attention to other people's thoughts; something which I have learnt from Sheila and Vicky.

To Sheila Dow I am also indebted for all the joint work we have done so far, and hope this fruitful collaboration, particularly for me, continues in the future. Vicky is also responsible for encouraging me to submit a book proposal to Routledge (that took place at the EAEPE 2002 Conference, in France). I really thank Vicky for 'pushing me'.

Many parts of the book have been presented at seminars, conferences or workshops over the last years. I thank the participants in all these events, and particularly those colleagues who made comments on the papers presented. Chapter 3 (co-authored with Sheila Dow) was originally presented at the 'International Conference on the Political Economy of Central Banking' (East London University, London, May 1996) and later published by Edward Elgar in a book edited by Philip Arestis and Malcolm Sawyer. Some parts of Chapter 4 were presented at the following conferences: the '36th European Congress of the Regional Science Association'

(Zurich, August 1996); the '39th European Congress of the Regional Science Association (ERSA)' (Dublin, August 1999); the '6th World Congress of the Regional Science Association International (RSAI)' (Switzerland, May 2000), and the 'EAEPE 2002 Conference' (Aix-en-Provence, November 2002). Some parts of Chapter 5 were presented at a workshop organized by the University of Granada and centrA (October 21st, 2004). Some of the empirical results reported in Chapter 6 have been presented at the following conferences: 'EAEPE 2003 Conference' (Maastricht, November 2003); the Workshop on 'Money, financial system and economic growth', organized by FUNCAS and CajaDuero (Salamanca, July 2004); the 'VII Encuentro de Economía Aplicada' (Vigo, June 2004), and the '44th European Congress of the Regional Science Association (ERSA)' (Porto, August 2004).

The empirical evidence provided in Chapter 6 is the result of my joint research with other colleagues. In particular, Sections 6.2 and 6.3 are co-authored with David Padrón and Antonio Olivera. Actually, Section 6.3 has been partially published in the Spanish journal *Papeles de Economía Española* (Vol. 101). Section 6.4 is co-authored with Sheila Dow, and is part of the work published in the journal *Regional Studies* (vol. 57, no. 9).

Over the last years I have met some colleagues from other Spanish universities, now also good friends, who share my interest in regional financial issues. They are Dr. Luis Castañón (University of Santiago de Compostela), Professor Santiago Carbó, Dr. Francisco Rodríguez and Dr. Rafael López (University of Granada and FUNCAS). I am particularly indebted to Santiago, a very good scholar (and better friend) who has shown as much interest in my work as I have in his.

I also thank my colleagues at the Department of Applied Economics at the University of La Laguna, particularly Pedro Gutiérrez, Dirk Godenau, José A. Rodríguez, Raúl Hernández, Candelaria Barrios and David Padrón, who have always provided support and friendship in this project.

This book could not have been written without the assistance from the professionals at Routledge. I thank Robert Langham (Senior Editor of Economics and Finance books) for all the editorial assistance and support provided during the production of this book.

I would like to express my sincere gratitude to Stephen Di Santo, who has played an important role in improving my communication skills in English during the writing of the book. His 'mathematical background' has also contributed to clarifying my own ideas without changing the original meaning, which I think is a very important condition when economists and mathematicians have to work together.

As usual, none of the people mentioned in this section are responsible for the final product.

Finally, I would also like to acknowledge the kind cooperation of the following publishers or institutions for the permission granted to include in some chapters of this book the work originally published by them:

Taylor & Francis Group Ltd:

- 'EMU and the regional impact of monetary policy', by Carlos J. Rodríguez-Fuentes and Sheila C. Dow, *Regional Studies*, (2003) vol. 37, no. 9, pp. 973–984.
- 'Regional finance: a survey', by Sheila C. Dow and Carlos J. Rodríguez-Fuentes, *Regional Studies*, (1997) vol. 31, no. 9, pp. 903–920.

Springer-Verlag GmbH & Co. KG:

- 'Credit availability and regional development', by Carlos J. Rodríguez-Fuentes, *Papers in Regional Science*, (1998) vol. 77, no. 1, pp. 63–75.

International Papers in Political Economy 1998:

- 'The political economy of monetary policy', by Sheila Dow and Carlos J. Rodríguez-Fuentes, in P. Arestis and M. Sawyer (eds) (1998) *The Political Economy of Central Banking*, Cheltenham: Edward Elgar.

Fundación de las Cajas de Ahorros (FUNCAS):

- 'Estructura financiera regional y política monetaria. Una aproximación al caso español', by Carlos J. Rodríguez-Fuentes, David Padrón-Marrero and Antonio Olivera-Herrera, *Papeles de Economía Española*, (2004) no. 101, pp. 252–261.

Carlos J. Rodríguez-Fuentes
La Laguna, December 2004

1 Introduction

1.1 Delimiting the aims and scope of the book

This book is about the regional effects of monetary policy and was partially motivated by the increasing attention that this topic is attracting in Europe over the last decade or so. I have always found it very interesting that the same national central banks that never paid much attention to this issue in the past for regions within national economies are now supporting joint-research programmes to study the cross-country differences in the responses to monetary policy shocks within the euro area.[1]

This increasing interest in Europe could probably be explained by the fact that, in January 1999, with the establishment of the third and final stage of the European Monetary Union (EMU), some European Union (EU) countries became regions within the euro area. This fact has raised some concerns over the regional implications of the European Central Bank (ECB) monetary policy and there is accordingly an increasing number of contributions addressing this issue.

This book aims to contribute to this debate by presenting a theoretical framework that explores the ways through which money and monetary policy may affect regions. Our analysis emphasizes the role that the banking system and the liquidity preference of economic agents (including banks) play in the transmission of central banks' monetary policy decisions to regions within a country, or countries within a currency union.

One peculiarity of this framework, which is built on the basic principles of the Post Keynesian monetary theory, is that it broadens the scope of the analysis of the regional effects of monetary policy by taking into account the underlying factors determining regional credit availability: the stage of banking development and the liquidity preference of financial agents (including the banking system). The consideration of these two variables allows us to identify a new way for money and monetary policy to have a regional impact: the *behavioural effect*.

Our analysis specifically suggests that monetary policy affects regional credit availability through its influence on banks' and borrowers' liquidity preference and that regional differences in terms of banking development and liquidity preference may produce higher instability in credit availability in less developed regions. This argument clearly contrasts the orthodox one, which assumes that regional credit shares mirror regional GDP shares, since money is considered to be a means of payment and, consequently, its demand is only determined by the transaction motive. This argument is sometimes extended by pointing out that peripheral regions may face a long run decrease in their credit shares because banks tend to lend in these markets less than they borrow, whereas the contrary applies to more developed regions. However, this interregional distribution of financial funds is usually seen as efficient and neutral since it assures that funds are driven toward the best alternative investment projects (which are usually located in central markets, where investment is less risky and also offers better prospects in the long run). This argument implies that, from an empirical point of view, there should be a close correspondence between both regional GDP and the credit shares, and regional GDP per capita and credit shares. However, there is some empirical evidence that shows that the relationship between regional GDP per capita and some banking variables is highly variable across some European countries (Mackay and Molyneux 1996: 758). Our empirical results also point out to the existence of a more unstable pattern of credit availability in the less developed regions in Spain.[2] We interpret the variability of such nexus as an indication that a stable relationship between monetary and real variables does not exist, as orthodox monetary theory suggests, since this relationship depends very much on behavioural responses which are difficult to predict.

Contrary to the orthodox view, we will suggest that credit instability is explained by changes in banks' liquidity preference alongside business cycles, and not only for regional differences in terms of GDP rates of growth. This constitutes the way through which monetary policy and the banking system may influence regional development: by producing unstable patterns of credit availability for some particular regions, and not a long run decrease in their credit shares.

The theoretical framework presented in this book is based on the assumption that, as the financial system develops (stage of banking development), central banks lose their ability to directly influence the money stock, so the money supply becomes increasingly endogenous to the economic process. However, and contrary to orthodox monetary theory, an endogenous money supply does not mean that regions face a horizontal money supply thanks to interregional arbitrage. An endogenous money supply means that any increase in liquidity depends more on the demand for credit (and thus borrowers' liquidity preference) and on the willingness of banks to supply credit (and thus the banks' liquidity preference) than on the central bank's direct interventions. Consequently, even at the regional level the money supply is the outcome of the willingness of the banks to create credit in response to demand, although subject to indirect influence (but not determinism!) from the central bank.

One of the consequences of the framework presented in this book is that the proper analysis of the regional impact of monetary policy should explicitly take into account the spatial differences in terms of banking development and liquidity preference, as well as the influence that monetary policy may have on such variables (the *behavioural effect*), and not only the structural differences that might produce regional asymmetric responses to exogenous monetary policy shocks (the *structural effect*).

1.2 Money is regionally neutral ... unless there are market failures

Orthodox economic theory has usually assumed that monetary policy has no role to play in economic development. Money is considered as a separate variable whose only role is to ease the exchange of goods already produced. Consequently, all that money can do is to affect the general level of prices (when it is supplied in excess for exchange purposes) but not the real output (at least in the long run). According to this view, financial factors play no role in regional development since monetary policy has no real effects and the banking system simply allocates scarce financial resources among regions. The argument runs as follows: the central bank sets the money supply in accordance with the real needs (the transaction motive in the demand for money) and then the money multiplier determines the total available supply of bank credit. Finally, the banking system passively distributes total amount of available credit among regions according to demand pressures.

This perspective offers very few exceptions where money, banks and monetary policy could influence regional development. One of these possibilities arises when the existence of segmentation in credit markets interferes in the equilibrating interregional financial flows that otherwise would exist (Roberts and Fishkind 1979, Moore and Hill 1982). However, as long as financial markets work properly, that is financial markets are fully integrated, regions would never experience financial problems since they potentially face a perfectly elastic supply of credit (see Borts 1968, Moore and Nagurney 1989). Under these conditions, there will always be equilibrating interregional financial flows which, in turn, would mean that money is of no significance at the regional level. Another possibility why monetary policy matters for regions is when national monetary policy shocks produce different responses in regions (Beare 1976).

The predominance of the above argument might have led regional scientists to generally omit the inclusion of money and monetary policy in their analysis or to belittle the power of money in explaining regional income differences. Therefore, there is a tendency to interpret money and monetary flows as mirroring regional economic differences rather than a key factor which might have played a role in their explanation.

This lack of interest in financial variables within regional economics could be explained by the following three factors.[3] First, regional economists have usually used the orthodox assumption that money and monetary policy are neutral in the determination of real income, at least in the long run. Consequently, if money does not matter at the national level, as orthodox monetary theory suggests, it does not matter at the regional level either. The second factor is that regions do not have monetary tools. If a region does not really have the chance to implement its own monetary policy, what is the point in studying these matters? Third, even if regions were to use monetary tools, their extreme openness and perfect capital mobility would leave them no possible control over their monetary conditions (the money supply would be horizontal at some interest rate level and, therefore, endogenous).

These reasons might have led regional scientists to rule out money and monetary variables in their analysis, or when they have decided to include them, to consider them endogenous, that is, determined at the national level (such as the money supply or the interest rate) and mirroring real economic differences. This explains why regional monetary analysis has usually corresponded with global monetarism theory, since regions, like small open economies in the international context, are supposed to face a horizontal supply of money at some interest which is fixed, in national or international markets.[4] Providing that financial capital flows freely from one region to another, interregional monetary flows mirror real ones unless some market failure inhibits such accommodating behaviour. All of these reasons explain why traditional models of regional income determination, such as Neo-Classical models, cumulative causation models, I-O models and multi-sector models, have excluded monetary variables. Of these traditional models, only export base and econometric models have included some kind of monetary variable in their specification.[5] Regional econometric models in turn have usually included some monetary variables in their specification, either in simple equations where regional income is linked to some national variables (such as GDP, interest rates or money supply), or in simultaneous models, where interest rates are very often included as an exogenous variable (see, for example, Czamanski 1969, Glickman 1977, 1980a, 1980b). The consequence of all of these is that, as Richardson (1973: 12–13) pointed out, traditional regional economics has not been able to make any significant contribution to discussions of national monetary policy.

The macroeconomic perspective is covered in a large empirical literature studying the regional impact of monetary policy; particularly for the United States (see, among others, Scott 1955, Lawrence 1963, Beare 1976, Fishkind 1977, Miller 1978, Garrison and Chang 1979, Mathur and Stein 1980, Chase Econometric 1981). However, most of these contributions seem to be a regional extension of the national discussion about whether or not money matters[6] (Dow and Rodríguez-Fuentes 1997: 903).

Consequently, the 'old regional macro literature' has implicitly taken for granted the neutrality of monetary policy so it has attributed the regional effects of monetary policy to either the existence of a market failure (lack of information, segmentation, money illusion, etc.) or structural differences which make the transmission mechanism differ from one region to another. Consequently, most empirical work has focused on identifying the factors which may lead to some segmentation in regional credit markets or the regional structural differences in terms of IS and LM slopes, respectively. In fact, these two approaches, along with the other contributions which have considered money as being the cause of regional business cycles, have attracted most empirical effort. Nevertheless, most of these pioneering contributions paid no attention to either the differences in regional financial structure or to the changing nature of the financial structure and the transmission mechanism of monetary policy. This latter aspect is at the centre of attention of the 'newer' contributions which have flourished because of the third stage of EMU, so the 'old literature' on the regional impact of monetary policy has been complemented with some 'newer' contributions, which are mainly concerned with the consequences which might stem from the existence of significant differences in the transmission mechanism of the European Central Bank monetary policy to the member economies of the euro area (see Dow and Rodríguez-Fuentes 1997, Rodríguez-Fuentes and Dow 2003).

1.3 When countries become regions, monetary policy suddenly matters again

When the EU entered the third stage of EMU, in January 1999, the euro-area member economies became regions from the monetary policy perspective. It was when 11 national economies of the EU lost their monetary policy identity (in favour of the ECB) that the concerns over the regional implications of the single monetary policy came to the forefront of the economic debate in Europe and elsewhere.

Since then there has been an increasing concern for studying the transmission mechanism of the ECB monetary policy within the EMU area. These concerns are grounded on the fact that empirical evidence reveals substantial differences in financial structure across countries in the euro area (De Bandt and Davis 1999, Danthine *et al*. 1999, Schmidt 1999, Bondt 2000, Maclennan *et al*. 2000, Padoa-Schioppa 2000, Kleimeier and Sander 2001, Cabral *et al*. 2002) and on the expectation that these differences will persist for long in the retail credit markets (Danthine *et al*. 1999, Padoa-Schioppa 2000, Cabral *et al*. 2002).

This evidence has led some authors to suggest that differences in financial structure among the European Monetary Union countries may produce a differential impact of the ECB's monetary policy (Kashyap and Stein 1997b, Cecchetti 1999, Bondt 2000). However, other authors have pointed out that these regional asymmetries in the monetary policy transmission mechanism are only temporary, since cross-country differences in financial structures will be removed in the future as the process of economic integration continues and economic policy coordination among euro countries increases (see Dornbusch *et al.* 1998: 52, Ehrmann 1998: 28, Arnold 1999: 22, Arnold and Vries 2000: 213, Clausen 2001: 172, Suardi 2001).

The current orthodox empirical literature on the regional effects of monetary policy approaches the issue from two different perspectives. On the one hand there is the literature studying the consequences of a common monetary policy when the currency union member economies show a low degree of business cycle synchronization (Carlino and Defina 1996, 1999, Angeloni and Dedola 1999, Ramos *et al.* 1999a). The aim of this literature is to suggest that a common monetary policy might not fit to all members of a currency union, particularly when the regions (national economies) of the currency union differ in terms of inflation and growth rates.

On the other hand there is the larger group of contributions focusing on studying the cross-country differences in the transmission mechanism of monetary policy within a currency union. Sometimes this literature is simply focused on studying whether (or not) the euro countries differ in their responses to monetary policy shocks. In other cases it also tries to provide an explanation for the cross-country differences in responses to monetary shocks. In this case, the asymmetric impact of monetary policy is usually explained by differences in economic and/or financial structure that increase the sensitivity of some regions to exogenous changes in national interest rates or business cycles (which are considered to be caused by monetary policy).

One of the constant conclusions from surveys of the empirical literature on asymmetries in the transmission mechanism of the monetary policy in Europe is that the empirical evidence is not conclusive at all. These surveys usually mention that there is a high variability in the results, both across countries and across studies. They agree that no robust conclusions can normally be extracted from the available empirical literature (Kieler and Saarenheimo 1998: 12, Guiso *et al.* 1999: 61). Some authors have even gone further and suggested that, given the complexity of the task, the econometric analysis 'will never be able to resolve this issue' (Kieler and Saarenheimo 1998: 32).

Why has current empirical work failed to deliver a robust and definitive conclusion about the regional effects of monetary policy, in Europe or elsewhere?

Honestly, it is hard to say. Everyone has his own opinion in this regard. Some authors could suggest that it is the variety of econometric techniques which are used that produces so much noise in the results. Others could say that the imperfection of data sets does not allow us to fully test theories. It could also be argued that institutional differences across countries may also be important to interpret the variability of the results. For sure all these arguments are relevant.

However, we believe there could be other explanations to this question and that the theoretical framework presented in this book can help us understand these other possibilities. In our opinion, the current orthodox empirical literature normally ignores the fact that monetary policy influence on economic activity depends on the 'behavioural responses' of economic agents, and these responses cannot always be fully anticipated by policy-makers nor completely modelled by econometricians. Economic agents are of course rational but we all know that human beings do not always follow deterministic rules. Fortunately the possibility for change is always present and the economics profession is aware of that and calls it 'structural change' (econometricians call it 'structural break').

Monetary theory therefore has to take into account that monetary policy might work differently, depending on the 'behavioural responses' by economic agents, which is reflected in their liquidity preference. However, a quick look at the current research on regional monetary policy would show that the usual explanation for the differences in responses to monetary shocks relies on macroeconomic structural differences (economic and financial structure), and very little attention is paid to the determinants of economic agent responses,[7] which certainly influences the macroeconomic structure (outcome) but are always open to change in a non-deterministic way. Thus, it is difficult to say which part of the asymmetric effect is due to structural differences and which part is due to the behaviour of the economic agents (Mazzola *et al.* 2002). This is an important issue, since the current structural differences in Europe might disappear in the future, but this would not necessarily mean that asymmetries in the transmission of monetary policy would automatically vanish: there would still be scope for asymmetries arising from differences in the behavioural responses of economic agents to monetary policy. The theoretical framework presented in this book is aimed towards emphasizing the relevance of those behavioural responses in the analysis of monetary policy.

1.4 Structure of the book

The book has seven chapters, including the Introduction (Chapter 1) and Conclusions (Chapter 7). Chapters 2 and 5 are reviews of literature which are necessary to build up Chapters 3 and 4, where our own arguments are developed.

Chapter 2 offers a review of the literature on the transmission mechanism of monetary policy. The aim of this chapter is to review the differences between different schools of economic thought with regard to the specification of the transmission mechanism. Our analysis will show that most of these differences are more of degree than of kind, as the idea of a mechanism that links real and monetary forces is commonly shared by all the participants in the debate. Actually, to a great extent the debate on the transmission mechanisms of monetary policy has been developed within the IS-LM model and, in particular, it has been focused on the slopes of the IS and LM curves.

Chapter 3 explores the meaning and role of monetary policy in a context of endogenous money, where endogenous money means a situation where, thanks to the development of the banking system, the increase in liquidity depends more on banks' and borrowers' liquidity preference than on the central bank's direct interventions. The theoretical perspective put forward in this chapter aims to challenge the view that central banks do unilaterally determine the money supply through monetary policy. This view is present in most economic textbooks, where the money supply curve is represented as vertical and any change in money stock is thus represented as a horizontal displacement of this line. This displacement is due to exogenous monetary management by the central bank. Money supply is therefore considered to be exogenous in the sense that it is unilaterally determined by the monetary authorities. Our analysis in Chapter 3 will instead suggest that, as financial systems develop, central banks lose their ability to control the money stock, since the money supply becomes endogenous to the economic process. However, our analysis will also challenge the belief that, in a context of endogenous money, monetary policy is ineffective to influence the liquidity of the economic system. On the contrary, we will assume that central banks can always influence the liquidity of the system, but it is only influence, since monetary policy is only one of many factors which are involved in the process of liquidity creation. Consequently, our conception of endogenous money in Chapter 3 will not mean that money is not important, as some orthodox economists could argue. Instead, the endogenous money approach only removes the causal role attributed to money by orthodox economists, but not necessarily its power to affect real variables nor affect the whole process of credit creation (Dow 1993a: 26).

Chapter 4 applies the notion of endogenous money developed in Chapter 3 to build up a theoretical framework that allows us to explore the way through which money and monetary policy may affect regions. The peculiarity of this framework is that it broadens the scope of the analysis by taking into account the underlying factors determining regional credit availability, specifically the stage of banking development and the liquidity preference of financial agents (including banks). Contrary to other theoretical approaches employed to study the regional effects of national monetary policies, our framework particularly pays attention to the influence of monetary policy on banks and borrowers liquidity preference, that is, 'the *behavioural effect*' and not just the effects of monetary policy on economies with divergent economic structures ('the *structural effect*').

Chapter 5 offers an analytical review of the existing literature on the regional effects of monetary policy. The chapter not only reviews the 'old literature' on the regional impact of monetary policy, that is, those early empirical contributions explicitly concerned with the regional effects of national monetary policies, but also the 'newer contributions' studying differences in the transmission mechanism of the European Central Bank monetary policy to the member economies of the euro area.

Finally, Chapter 6 presents some empirical evidence which we think might be useful to illustrate some of the issues mentioned in the book about the regional dimension of national monetary policies.

2 A dichotomized view of the economic process

The transmission channels of monetary policy

2.1 Introduction

There is a large amount of literature which deals with the transmission mechanism of monetary policy, i.e. the way monetary policy exerts its effect on economic activity.[1] The basic assumption which underlies this 'transmission mechanism view' is that a real and monetary side of the economy can be clearly distinguished, where the monetary transmission is the way through which both sides interact with each other. Furthermore, real forces of the economy are seen as determining not only the value of real variables such as the level of income and employment but also real interest rates. Interest rates are hence considered to be a 'real phenomenon' since they are determined by, on the one hand, the real forces of productivity (investment decision), and thrift (savings decision) on the other. Interest rates are thus determined in the goods market by the interaction between savings and investment schedules, being its role to equalize both decisions. Within this framework financial variables are seen as factors which may or may not help the economic system to reach its 'real equilibrium' by means of easing or speeding up the exchange of goods and services already produced. Nevertheless, monetary variables do not play any role in determining the real outcome itself, since the only role which is left for money to play is a 'negative' one, in the sense that, at best, it is considered to be responsible for determining the general level of prices (inflation) in the long run or business cycles in the short run. Within this schedule money matters, but for its potential power to disrupt the real economy.

The aim of this chapter is to review the discrepancies between different schools of economic thought with regard to the specification of the transmission mechanism. It will be shown that, for some economists, this mechanism takes on the form of a direct and simple effect which runs from changes in money supply to expenditure. On the contrary, other economists believe that the way through which monetary variables affect economy is not so clear, more complicated and indirect than monetarists sustain. This group is usually known as Keynesians.

Our analysis will show that most of these differences are more of degree than of kind, as the idea of a mechanism that links real and monetary forces is commonly shared by all the participants in the debate. Actually, to a great extent, the debate on the transmission mechanisms of monetary policy has been developed within the IS-LM model and, in particular, it has been focused on the slopes of the IS and LM curves. On the one hand, we have the monetarist view, which has tried to show that the LM curve was steep and, therefore, demonstrate the power of monetary policy to affect nominal income. On the other hand, there is the Keynesian view, which tries to demonstrate the opposite, i.e. the existence of a flat LM curve, which would mean that monetary policy was either partially or totally ineffective in affecting nominal income. In fact, the debate has mostly centred on the size and stability of the parameters of the model, not on the suitability of the IS-LM model itself, as many authors have pointed out:

> the neoclassical synthesis claims to have produced a macro model of complete generality in the sense that, given a certain set of assumptions, it can be used to prove the macroeconomic propositions of classical economists and, given a different certain set of assumptions, it can be used to validate Keynes' conclusions.
>
> (Morgan 1978: 4)

Chick (1973) emphasized this point when analyzing the theoretical differences, or, to be more precise, the absence of theoretical differences between the two schools of economic thought. Indeed, she has suggested that both schools 'are consistent with several specifications of the structural equations of IS-LM' and, therefore, differences between them only arise when some parameters of the model are constrained to be zero (Chick 1973: 19, Chick 1985: 79–98). Figure 2.1 illustrates this point.

This suggestion in turn, would partially explain why the debate between both schools of thought has been mainly developed on an empirical basis, as it has very often been argued that only by appealing to the 'truth of the

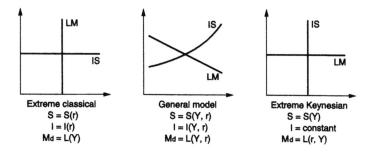

Figure 2.1 Monetarists and Keynesians on monetary policy effectiveness.

data' could a definitive answer to this debate on the value of the parameters be found. In fact, Friedman has many times suggested that 'the basic differences among economists are empirical, not theoretical' (Friedman 1970: 234), and that the only way to know which 'pudding' is best is by 'eating them' (Friedman 1956: 17). However, he has also pointed out that differences among theories ('puddings') can not always be disentangled by 'eating them' (empirical testing) since only 'imperfect figures' (data), unable to 'disentangle what is systematic and what is random and erratic', are available to researchers. This explains why both Friedman's work and that of many of his followers has focused on trying to obtain perfect figures rather than on the elaboration of the theory (Friedman 1970: 235).

The chapter is organized into five sections, apart from the introduction and the conclusion section. Sections 2.2 and 2.3 start with the monetarist and Keynesian views on monetary policy transmission, where by Keynesian is meant the neoclassical synthesis represented in the IS-LM model. Sections 2.4 and 2.5 present the New Classical and New Keynesian reactions, whereas Section 2.6 offers a brief review of recent macroeconomic developments that, in some authors' opinions, are producing a new synthesis which, 'like in the synthesis of the 1960s, melts classical with Keynesian ideas' (Goodfriend and King 1998).

2.2   The monetarist view

The monetarists' view is based on the assumption that the economy is naturally stable and, as long as markets work properly, should work at its equilibrium level. This equilibrium level is assumed to be achieved by the interaction between the production function and the supply of labour. Equilibrium therefore has nothing to do with money or monetary variables as it is assumed to be dependent on real factors endowments (capital and labour).

Within the monetarist model money is as a factor which comes into play to ease the exchange of goods and services already produced and, in so doing, it might fuel production as it speeds up the exchange. Money would therefore be, according to John Stuart Mill, just 'a machine for doing quickly and commodiously, what would be done, though less quickly and commodiously, without it.' (John Stuart Mill, as quoted in Friedman 1969: 105).

The reason why money demand is mainly considered as being determined by the transactions motive is due to its function as a means of exchange. Monetarists thus consider money, as Dow (1985: 182) has pointed out, as if it were 'a technical input' and, as such, its quantity should be supplied according to the real needs given by real production (transaction motive).

As money is (i) an asset which does not earn any interest and (ii) is only demanded for transaction purposes, any quantity of money supplied over this transaction level, which in turn is determined by the availability of capital and labour, will produce a portfolio disequilibrium. Agents will try to restore the imbalance by changing money for any other assets in order to restore their former desired portfolio (because money does not earn any interest). It is precisely this switch from money to any other asset, both financial and real, that fuels spending and, as a result, money income. The monetarist transmission mechanism is therefore a direct effect which runs from money supply shocks to money income (equation 2.1).

$$\Delta \text{ Money supply} \longrightarrow \text{portfolio changes} \longrightarrow \Delta \text{ Expenditure} \qquad (2.1)$$

The relationship shown in equation 2.1 has been empirically assessed by means of some reduced-form models, such as the so-called St. Louis Equation or VAR models. Its aim is to find empirical support for the monetarist view on the monetary transmission mechanism.[2] However, Keynesian authors have criticized this direct mechanism as a 'black box' because it only shows the correlation between money and income but is unable to provide an explanation of how money affects economy.

Further, monetarists consider that real income is relatively fixed within the short run because physical capital is fixed within this period of time. However, they also acknowledge that, within the very short run, income may overshoot its long run equilibrium level when 'money illusion' exists. Money illusion may then lead both supply of and demand for labour to grow when real wage changes. However, this possibility for income to overshoot is removed in the long run since economic agents cannot be constantly fooled by nominal shocks in the long run.[3] To monetarists then, inflation 'is always and everywhere a monetary phenomenon' and, what is more important, could be eliminated by implementing a close control of the quantity of money. Monetarism has not only given an explanation of the inflation process but also offered its definitive solution, and those two points should be considered, as Johnson has pointed out, when analyzing the political success of monetarist thought.[4]

The monetarist model may be formally summarized as follows (Morgan 1978: 19):

$$D\left(\frac{W}{P}\right) = S\left(\frac{W}{P}\right) \quad \text{(labour market)} \qquad (2.2)$$

$$Y = y(N, \bar{K}) \quad \text{(production function)} \qquad (2.3)$$

$$I(r) = S(r) \quad \text{(goods market)} \qquad (2.4)$$

$$\bar{M} = kPY \quad \text{(money market)} \qquad (2.5)$$

where equations 2.2 and 2.4 represent the equilibrium conditions in the labour and goods market, respectively. Equation 2.3 is the production function and equation 2.5 represents the money demand. W is the nominal wage, P is the price level, D and S are the demand for and supply of labour, which depend on real wages (W/P), Y and N are the level of output and employment, I and S are the investment and savings functions, which depend on the interest rate (r).

The assumptions underlying the model can be summarized as follows. First, income is fixed within the short term because both capital (K) and labour (N) are relatively fixed within the short term. Secondly, as money (M) is only held for transactions motive its demand must be specified in real rather than in nominal terms. Thirdly, money demand is stable and depends on a very small number of variables, mainly permanent income and interest rate, and its interest elasticity is low. Friedman's first specification of money demand took a form similar to equation 2.5, which did not include any interest rate, but he later considered interest rates among the parameters upon which money demand depended. He specifically put forward the money demand function[5] shown in equation 2.6:

$$\frac{M}{P} = \int \left(y, w, r_m, r_b, r_e, \frac{1}{p}\frac{dP}{dt}, \mu \right) \tag{2.6}$$

where M, P and y are the stock of money, the price level and the nominal income, respectively, w is the fraction of wealth in non-human form, r_m is the expected nominal rate of return on money, r_b is the expected nominal rate of return on fixed-value securities, r_e is the expected nominal rate of return on equities, $(1/p)(dP/dt)$ is the expected rate of change of prices of goods and hence the expected nominal rate of return on real assets, and μ is a symbol standing for whatever variables other than income may affect the utility attached to the services of money (Friedman 1970: 204).

If the above monetarist assumptions were right, then monetary policy would be the most important tool to affect expenditure and money income. Further, if output were relatively fixed within the short term then monetary policy would be responsible for business cycles when it is used for doing 'what monetary policy cannot do', that is, to maintain interest and unemployment rates below their 'natural' levels (Friedman 1969: 99). The monetarist advice for avoiding business cycles and economic instability would therefore be to use monetary policy considering 'what monetary policy can do', that is, in Friedman's own words: 'prevent money itself being a major source of economic disturbance ... and provide a stable background for the economy (price stability)'. (Friedman 1969: 105–106).

Additionally, price stability would be best achieved, following Friedman's advice, by setting a steady and low rate of monetary growth, although the latter has not been acknowledged as a necessary condition.[6]

It is worth noting that this argument is based on the assumptions that money demand is stable, depends on a few variables (permanent income and interest rates) and that its interest rate elasticity is low or insignificant.

2.3 The Keynesian view

Keynesian economists, contrary to the monetarist ones, do not think that the economy automatically works at its full employment capacity but that some economic management is usually required in order to achieve such a situation. This belief has led them to focus their attention on the role of fiscal and monetary policy for restoring market equilibrium when an insufficient level of aggregate demand exists. The Keynesian model, which is shown below, is similar to the monetarist. Differences between the two only arise when specifying the demand for money and the consumption function in order to let a speculative motive (interest rate) and wealth (Pigou's effect) play a role in money demand and consumption functions, respectively (Morgan 1978: 62).

$$I(r) = S(r, Y, W) \quad \text{(goods market)} \tag{2.7}$$

$$\frac{\bar{M}}{P} = L(r, Y) \quad \text{(money market)} \tag{2.8}$$

where I and S are the investment and savings functions, respectively, r is the interest rate, Y is the level of output, W is the nominal wage, M is the money supply, P is the price level and L represents the money demand function, which depends on both r and Y.

Within the Keynesian model the debate over the relative effectiveness of monetary policy for affecting income and employment has focused on the size and stability of the monetary multiplier (equation 2.10) with respect to the fiscal one (equation 2.9).[7] What is worth noting for our analysis here is that the monetary multiplier depends on both the interest elasticity of income and interest rate elasticity of money demand. These two factors are the variables which would determine the relative effectiveness of monetary policy to affect output.

$$dy = \frac{1}{1 - c'(1 - t') + (i'k'/l')} dg \quad \text{(fiscal)} \tag{2.9}$$

$$dy = \frac{i'/l'}{1 - c'(1 - t') + (i'k'/l')} dm \quad \text{(monetary)} \tag{2.10}$$

where dy, dg and dm represent the change in the level of output, public expenditure and stock of money, respectively, c' is the propensity to consume, i' is the interest rate elasticity of investment, k' is the income elasticity of money demand, l' is the interest rate elasticity of money demand, and t' is the tax rate.

Hence, the standard Keynesian monetary mechanism (equation 2.11) is not a direct one, which runs from money to income, but rather an indirect one whose first step is the change in interest rates due to the monetary change, while the second one would be made up of the effect that interest rates would have on expenditure (investment).[8]

$$\Delta M \rightarrow \nabla r \rightarrow \Delta investment \rightarrow \Delta real\ output + prices \qquad (2.11)$$

However, the Keynesian view also asserts that monetary policy becomes ineffective when either money demand is highly interest elastic or the income function is highly interest inelastic. In the former case (money demand is interest elastic) the first step within the Keynesian chain is broken since monetary authorities are unable to affect interest rates because of the perfect elasticity of money demand. This is the so-called 'liquidity trap' (LM curve being flat). On the other hand, when the spending function is interest inelastic, changes in interest rates will have no effect on spending, nor income, because investment is not sensitive to changes in interest rates. In this case it is the second step of the transmission chain that breaks down (IS curve being a step function). Further, the effectiveness of monetary policy to affect the

> ... real economy will depend not so much on the *absolute* ... but on the *relative* values of these two elasticities (LM and IS curves) ... The higher the interest elasticity of demand for money *relative* to the interest elasticity of demand for goods, the less the impact of open-market operations on the demand for goods.
>
> (Goodhart 1989a: 271)

Tobin (1947) already made this point as early as 1947. A summary is given in Table 2.1. The former explains why the debate on the effectiveness of monetary policy focused on empirical grounds until the mid 1970s and was concerned with the estimates of the interest rate of money demand and income function as those would determine the ability of monetary policy to affect economic activity.[9]

An extended version of the IS-LM Keynesian model is the open one, i.e. the one which lets the external sector come into play. As far as the monetary effect on income is concerned, the open version of the IS-LM model differs from the closed one in that at least one new variable has to be added to the standard 'interest rate monetary channel'. In fact, most large macroeconomic Keynesian models[10] have included in their monetary transmission mechanisms the exchange rate and other variables such as wealth or price assets, the former being considered of great importance due to the current greater links among different economies.

The inclusion of both the exchange rate and the external sector in the model partially modifies the standard analysis of the effectiveness of monetary policy and requires additional information regarding exchange

Table 2.1 Fiscal vs monetary policy effectiveness within the standard IS-LM model

Interest rate-elasticity	Effectiveness of monetary policy alone	Effectiveness of income-generating expenditures alone
(a) 'L' function perfectly inelastic, implying either 'I' function not perfectly inelastic, or 'S' function of positive elasticity, or both.	Effective	Ineffective
(b) 'L' function elasticity between zero and infinity, and either 'I' function not perfectly inelastic or 'S' function of positive elasticity, or both.	Effective	Effective
(c) (i) 'L' function perfectly elastic, regardless of other elasticities, or (ii) 'I' and 'S' functions perfectly inelastic, regardless of 'L' function	Ineffective	Effective

Source: Tobin (1947: 125).

rate regime, degree of international capital mobility, degree of substitubility among national and foreign financial assets, etc. On the one hand, it is sustained that the greater the international capital mobility and the degree of substitubility among national and foreign financial assets, the lower the ability of national monetary policy to affect local interest rates. In fact, some argue that no differences between national and international interest rates could exist since arbitrage would remove any significant difference.[11] On the other hand, it has also been pointed out that the exchange rates regime may also modify the mechanism, in the sense that a fixed regime would not allow for differences in interest rates between national and foreign rates, whereas some influence on national interest rates is acknowledged when a flexible or 'dirty floating' system exists.

The monetary chain of causation when a fixed exchange rate regime exists is shown in equation 2.12.

$$\Delta M \longrightarrow \nabla r \longrightarrow capital\ outflows \longrightarrow \nabla M \longrightarrow \Delta r \qquad (2.12)$$

In this case, the existence of a fixed exchange rate regime, along with perfect international capital mobility, removes the potential effect that national monetary policy could have on expenditure, as interest rates are not allowed to change because of the perfect arbitrage among national and international markets.[12] Hence, any reduction in interest rates (due to an exogenous increase in money supply) can only be temporary, since it would immediately lead to an infinite outflow of financial capital searching for higher interest rates anywhere else. This capital outflow would reduce the national money supply, returning interest rates to their former level. Both perfect arbitrage and fixed exchange rates guarantee that national interest rates keep in line with international ones.[13]

Equation 2.13 in turn shows the adjustment mechanism when a 'dirty float' system exists. In this case, interest changes are allowed for some variation although this will be lower than the one experienced in the closed version of the model.

$$\Delta M \longrightarrow \nabla r \longrightarrow exchange\ rate\ depreciation$$
$$\longrightarrow capital\ outflows \longrightarrow \nabla M \longrightarrow \Delta r \tag{2.13}$$

The final effect on interest rates in this case will depend on whether financial outflows due to interest rate arbitrage account for as much as the inflows due to balance of trade surplus because of the exchange rate depreciation. The open version of the IS-LM model is specified in equations 2.14 and 2.15. The two terms on the right-hand side in equation 2.14 represent the internal and external sectors, respectively. Y is the level of output, P is the price level, r is the rate of interest, and e is the exchange rate. The external variables are denoted by $*$. Finally, equation 2.15 shows the interest rate equilibrium between national and international interest rates which must hold when a fixed exchange rate and perfect capital mobility exist.

$$Y = A(r, Y) + T\left(Y, Y^*, \frac{eP^*}{P}\right) \tag{2.14}$$

$$r = r^* \tag{2.15}$$

2.4   The New Classical monetary theory

New Classical monetary economics points out that only unanticipated changes in money can affect real output although the neutrality of money is sustained in the long run (Lucas 1972: 103). The new classical argument rests upon these assumptions. First, there exists a 'natural rate' of real output and, secondly, economic agents behave optimally in light of their objectives and expectations and form their expectation in a forward-looking way, rather than on either an adaptive or backward-looking way. New classical authors additionally acknowledge that agents sometimes may not be able to differentiate between a rise in the general level of prices and a change in relative prices,[14] especially when they face unexpected or unanticipated changes in money supply. Consequently, New Classical monetary theory accepts the existence of a direct effect between monetary changes and income but only when the former is not fully anticipated by economic agents. Otherwise, the monetary effect will be on nominal variables (prices, interest rates, etc.) because economic agents would fully anticipate the effect of such a monetary increase. Economic agents behave in a 'rational way' and as such are free from money illusion. The conclusion then is that only unanticipated monetary changes will affect (destabilize) the economy, although in the long run money is still considered to be neutral.

A consequence of the above argument is that any stochastic (unanticipated) change in the quantity of money which leads to changes in price level may increase temporarily production and employment, because producers interpret the current increase in prices as a change in their relative prices and not as an increase of the whole set of prices of the system (Lucas 1972, 1973, Sargent and Wallace 1975, Barro 1976, 1977b).

Business cycles are hence seen as a monetary phenomenon because the economy, by assumption, grows at a 'natural rate'. Business cycles are viewed as simple producers' responses to the difference between expected and current price, the latter being explained by unexpected monetary shocks. Lucas' (1972, 1973) aggregate supply, which is specified in equation 2.16, shows this relationship.

$$\ln Y_t = \beta_0 + \beta_1 (\ln P_t - \ln P_{t-1}) + \varepsilon_t \tag{2.16}$$

where Y denotes real gross national product (GNP) or employment, P is the implicit GNP deflator, and ε is a sequence of independent, identically distributed random variables with zero mean (Lucas 1972: 117–118).

The sort of model that new classical economists use to test their theory could be seen as just an 'ad hoc modification' of the monetarist reduced form models which try to analyze the effect of both monetary and fiscal variables on the economy. As we have pointed out above, monetarist economists have tried to assess the greater power of money to affect income with respect to fiscal variables by means of reduced-form models which relate monetary income to fiscal and monetary variables. One of these models is the so-called St. Louis Equation (equation 2.17)

$$Y_t = \alpha + m_i M_{t-1} + e_i E_{t-1} + r_i R_{t-1} + \mu_t \tag{2.17}$$

where Y, M, E and R stand for income, money, public expenditure and public revenues, respectively, α is a constant, and μ is the error term.

Neoclassical economists have also tested their hypothesis by way of reduced-form models which are similar to the St. Louis form. One difference between the monetarist and neoclassical models is that the latter include an 'ad hoc hypothesis' whose aim is to distinguish between anticipated and unanticipated monetary shocks. Barro (1977b), for example, used this assumption when testing for the effects of monetary policy (equations 2.18 and 2.19).

$$\log\left(\frac{U}{1-U}\right) = \alpha_o + \beta_1 DMR_{t-1} + \beta_2 DMR_{t-2}$$

$$+ \beta_3 MIL_t + \beta_4 MINW_t + \mu_t \qquad (2.18)$$

$$DM_t = \beta_o + \beta_1 DM_{t-1} + \beta_2 DM_{t-2}$$

$$+ \beta_3 FEDV_t + \beta_4 UN_{t-1} + DMR_t \qquad (2.19)$$

where U stands for annual average unemployment rate, DMR is the unanticipated monetary change (residuals from equation 2.19), MIL is a measure of military conscription (military personnel), $MINW$ is minimum wage rate, μ is error term, DM is the annual average money growth rate, $FEDV$ is real expenditure of federal government, and UN is the dependent variable in equation 2.18 (Barro 1977b: 104–107).

Equation 2.19 could be interpreted as the 'ad hoc hypothesis' to discriminate between expected and unexpected monetary changes. The unanticipated change in money supply is simply identified with the random term DMR, which stands for the difference between the expected and current money supply.

The implication for monetary policy that is drawn from this model is that only unanticipated money matters, although some have also found that anticipated monetary changes also matter.[15]

2.5   The New Keynesian monetary theory

New Keynesian monetary theory focuses on the role that monetary policy plays when 'imperfect competition' is present in the economic system. It is the existence of imperfect competition in the goods, labour or financial markets which leads to some kind of price rigidity or market segmentation, making monetary policy powerful for having 'real' effects, at least in the short run under some assumptions. Unions, the existence of long run contracts and implicit contracts, and wage efficiency theory, are among the factors which would explain, for example, wage rigidity within labour markets. As Fischer points out: 'the effectiveness of monetary policy (to affect output) depends ... on the existence of nominal long-term contracts' (Fischer 1977: 194) and explains this through the following expression.

$$Y_t = \alpha + \beta(P_t - {}_{t-1}P_t) + \mu_t \qquad (2.20)$$

where α is a constant and β is a parameter, Y is the level of output, P is the logarithm of the price level, and ${}_{t-1}P_t$ is the expectation taken at the end of period $t-1$ of P_t, and μ_t is a stochastic disturbance term (Fischer 1977: 193).

Further, Fischer develops his argument from an 'expectational Phillips curve' of the Lucas form (equation 2.20), his conclusions will not differ significantly from those of the New Classical models, i.e. that only unanticipated monetary changes matter (unless there exists wage indexation). He put it as follows:

> monetary policy can affect output ... by creating a difference between the actual price and the expected price level. However, if the money supply is known to economic agents ... then the predictable effects of the money supply on prices are embodied in $_{t-1}P_t$, and monetary policy can affect output only by doing the unexpected.
>
> (Fischer 1977: 193–194)

Therefore, according to the New Keynesian theory, it is not only imperfect competition (sticky prices, both in goods and labour markets), but also the monetary 'surprise', that makes monetary policy have real effects in the short term. Consequently, in this point new Keynesians agree with the new classical position: only unanticipated monetary policy can affect output.[16]

The new Keynesians have also paid attention to the role of credit in the transmission mechanism of monetary policy. This literature is usually known as the lending or credit view and, contrary to the traditional 'money view' that sees monetary policy operating exclusively only through changes in interest rates, it maintains that monetary policy might make access to credit more difficult or expensive for some borrowers when there exist credit market imperfections.[17] According to this view, monetary policy '... will affect the level of investment, not through the interest-rate mechanism, but rather through the availability of credit' (Stiglitz and Weiss 1981: 409). Consequently, the transmission mechanism implicit in the textbook IS-LM model is rejected, since it does not take into account such capital market imperfections.[18]

The assumption that capital markets are imperfect leads to the inclusion of two additional channels in the transmission of the monetary policy, namely the balance sheet channel and the lending channel (Bernanke and Gertler 1995). A large amount of empirical evidence exists which supports the relevance of these two original channels,[19] and could be complemented with the much more recent 'capital channel' (Van den Heuvel 2002a, 2002b).

This literature is concerned with the existence of credit rationing when capital markets fail to work properly. It is therefore when capital markets are incomplete that the banking system becomes important for the transmission of the monetary policy, due to several factors. From the bank lending channel perspective, monetary policy may affect credit availability to some kinds of borrowers (those most dependent on banks) when banks do not have close substitutes for bank loans in the asset side of the bank's balance sheet. On the other hand, the 'balance sheet channel' (also known as the financial accelerator) might reinforce monetary policy through their effects on the financial structure of economic agents. Finally, the 'bank capital channel' suggests that monetary policy might also influence lending through its impact on bank equity capital (Van den Heuvel 2002a, 2002b). Overall, what this literature suggests is that banks are important for the 'transmission mechanism' of the monetary policy because they provide credit and monetary policy affects credit availability when capital markets are imperfect.

2.6   The New Neo-Classical synthesis

There is a growing argument that macroeconomics is currently moving towards a new synthesis (Goodfriend and King 1998, Clarida *et al.* 1999, Blanchard 2000, Hoover 2003), as in the 1960s. This new synthesis, which has been labelled as the New Neo-Classical Synthesis, seems to have put an end to the intellectual battles in macroeconomics which have been going on over the last decades, particularly between the flexible price model (neoclassical macroeconomics and real business cycles) and the sticky one (new Keynesian). The debate seems to be over, since the model which has emerged from this new synthesis incorporates both Keynesian and Neoclassical ideas. This point has been made by Goodfriend and King (1998), who state that the New Neo-Classical Synthesis:

> involves the systematic application of intertemporal optimization and rational expectations, which are applied to both the pricing and output decisions (Keynesian model) as well as to the consumption, investment and factor supply decisions (Classical and real business cycles) ... It also embodies the insights of monetarists[20] regarding the theory and practice of monetary policy.
>
> (Goodfriend and King 1998: 2)

The new synthesis seems to be the result of a move into a middle ground in between the two ruling orthodox paradigms in macroeconomics from the 1980s. This theoretical convergence has been possible because 'the neoclassical insistence on microfoundations has been adopted by almost all mainstream economists, and most have accepted microfoundations in the form of the representative-agent model'. Another reason is that 'Neo-Classicals have been forced to concede that without sticky prices or wages their model cannot reproduce the empirical fluctuations in the economy' (Hoover 2003: 425). Some economists argue that it is because of this convergence that some argue that 'today the ideological divide is gone. At the frontier of macroeconomic research, the field is surprisingly a-ideological' (Blanchard 2000: 39).

According to Goodfriend and King (1998: 25), the New Neo-Classical Synthesis is characterized by two central elements: (a) the introduction of intertemporal optimization and rational expectations into dynamic macro-economic models (Neo-Classical and real business cycles) and (b) the assumptions of imperfect competition and costly price adjustment (new Keynesians). The second element implies that monetary policy is not neutral in the short run since it exerts a powerful influence on aggregate demand through the changes in real interest rates. However, the influence of rational expectations and real business cycles (the first element) ensures monetary policy is neutral in the long run, so the output is supply-determined.

The macroeconomic model of the new synthesis could be represented by equations 2.21, 2.22 and 2.23 (Clarida *et al.* 1999: 1664–1668), although some other representations have also been proposed (Meyer 2001: 2–4).[21]

$$x_t = -\theta[i_t - E_t\pi_{t+1}] + g_t \tag{2.21}$$

$$\pi_t = \lambda x_t + \beta E_t\pi_{t+1} + \mu_t \tag{2.22}$$

$$i_t = (1 - \rho)[\alpha + \beta\pi_t + \gamma x] + \rho i_{t-1} + \varepsilon_t \tag{2.23}$$

where x is the output gap, π is inflation, i is the nominal interest rate, g and μ are disturbances terms, α is a constant that can be interpreted as the steady-state nominal interest rate, and ρ is a parameter that reflects the interest rate smoothing behaviour $(0 < \rho < 1)$. All the variables are expressed as a deviation from their long run levels.

Equation 2.21 is an aggregate demand (IS curve) whereas equation 2.22 is a Phillips curve. Contrary to the traditional IS-LM framework, the new model replaces the LM curve for an interest rate monetary rule (equation 2.23). The replacement of the LM curve could be seen as an improvement of the traditional IS-LM model, since it is widely accepted that 'most central banks now pay little attention to monetary policy in conducting monetary policy' (Romer 2000: 149). This explains the increasing concern for the need to produce a 'Keynesian Macroeconomics model without an LM curve'.[22]

Aside from replacing the LM for a concrete[23] monetary policy rule, there are some other aspects which differentiate this model from the traditional textbook IS-LM model.[24] First, in the new IS current output depends both on expected future output and the interest rate (Clarida *et al.* 1999: 1665). Secondly, in the new Phillips curve 'the expected future inflation enters additionally, as opposed to expected current inflation. The implication of this is that inflation depends entirely on current and expected future economic conditions' (Clarida *et al.* 1999: 1667).

It is worth pointing out that within this model the influence of monetary policy on economic activity depends entirely on the existence of 'distortions' (namely price rigidities) which give rise to 'small variations in the average markup[25] over time' due to monetary policy shocks (changes in the short-term interest rates) (Goodfriend and King 1998: 31–32). It is also acknowledged that monetary policy cannot affect the steady-state level of the markup. Some authors have also mentioned that in the new synthesis monetary policy works not only through changes in the short-term interest rates (as in the traditional IS-LM model) but also through 'beliefs about how the central bank will set the interest rate in the future, since households and firms are forward looking' (Clarida *et al.* 1999: 1668). The objective of monetary policy within this model is to adjust interest rates to the current state of the economy with the aim of maximizing welfare. The maximization of welfare is achieved when central banks succeed in minimizing the squared deviations of both output and inflation from their target levels (Clarida *et al.* 1999: 1668–1669). Consequently, monetary policy is designed to remove any signs or expectations of inflationary pressures in the short to medium term and so contribute to the normal or natural development of the economy (Goodfriend 2004: 36–38), which is independent of any monetary factors in the long run (monetary neutrality).

2.7 Conclusions

This chapter has presented a brief review of how monetary policy affects the economy according to some monetary theories. In particular, the chapter has paid attention to the monetarist, Keynesian, New Classical and New Keynesian perspectives. The chapter has also considered the more recent contributions by the so-called New Neo-Classical Synthesis.

Our analysis suggested that according to both monetarists and new classical economists, monetary policy is neutral since for those two schools money is just a veil which has nothing to do with the real economy. Monetarist and new classical economists believe that money can only cause inflation in the long run or economic instability (business cycles) in the short run.

On the contrary, Keynesians and new Keynesians have insisted on the idea that money may affect economic activity, at least in the short run and under some assumptions. This idea is also central in the New Neo-Classical Synthesis, since their followers maintain that even though there is little trade off between inflation and real activity in the long run, monetary policy can have important real effects in the short run due to temporary nominal rigidities in the economy (Goodfriend and King 1998: 2).

Despite the theoretical differences between these different schools in terms of how monetary policy works, they seem to share a common assumption: monetary policy only matters when there are distortions in the economy. These distortions take the form of imperfect competition, information, nominal rigidities, etc. Without such an assumption monetary policy should be neutral, since money would only act as a medium of exchange, as the oil which lubricates the machine. However, the oil is not considered to be an integral part of the machine itself.

In the next two chapters we will elaborate a theoretical framework where the monetary policy is seen as an integral part of the economic system. From this perspective the monetary policy will not be limited to a passive response to economic developments, since it might well play a crucial role in determining the long-run equilibrium values of real variables. The theoretical framework developed in Chapters 2 and 3 will be primarily based on the Post Keynesian monetary theory.

3 Beyond transmission mechanisms

3.1 Introduction

This chapter explores the meaning and role of monetary policy in a context of endogenous money, where endogenous money means a situation where, thanks to the development of the banking system, the increase in liquidity depends more on banks' and borrowers' liquidity preference than on the central bank's direct interventions.

The theoretical perspective put forward in this chapter aims to challenge the view that central banks do unilaterally determine the money supply through monetary policy. This view is present in most economic textbooks, where the money supply curve is represented as vertical and any change in money stock is thus seen as a horizontal displacement of this line. This displacement is due to exogenous monetary management by the central bank. Money supply is therefore considered to be exogenous in the sense that it is unilaterally determined by the monetary authorities.

The chapter will instead suggest that, as financial systems develop, central banks lose their ability to control money stock, since the money supply becomes endogenous to the economic process. However, our analysis will also challenge the belief that, in an endogenous money context, monetary policy is ineffective to influence the liquidity of the economic system and its only role consists of setting the level of interest rates over which banks mark-up their loan applications. On the contrary, we will assume that central banks can always influence the liquidity of the system, but it is only influence, since monetary policy is only one of many factors which are involved in the process of liquidity creation. Our analysis shares the view expressed by Chick and Dow (2002), who see monetary authorities as having certain influence on both interest rates and bank behaviour, but without absolute power to determine both.

Consequently, an endogenous money approach will not mean that money is not important, as some orthodox economists could argue. Instead, the endogenous money approach only removes the causal role attributed to money by orthodox economists, but not necessarily its power to affect real variables nor to affect the whole process of credit creation (Dow 1993a: 26).

The chapter has six sections. Since our analysis is built on the principles of the Post Keynesian monetary theory, Section 3.2 offers a brief review of their view on money and monetary policy. Section 3.3 goes on to explore the meaning of and possibilities for monetary policy in a context of endogenous money. Section 3.4 addresses the influence of monetary policy on liquidity while Section 3.5 concentrates on monetary policy non-neutrality. Finally, Section 3.6 offers some conclusions.

3.2 The Post Keynesian view on money and monetary policy

One of the relevant characteristics of Post Keynesian monetary theory is that 'money is integral to the capitalist process' (Dow 1993a: 1). This particular characteristic means that, contrary to other schools of economic thought (see Chapter 2), no clear distinction between real and monetary forces is made. This feature points out the difference between general equilibrium models and Post Keynesians with regard to the way money enters the economic system. Within walrasian general economic models money only plays a single role: to lubricate exchange. Money does not play any real role in the determination of real variables; money only matters in the determination of the level of prices. Real forces determine real variables and monetary ones determine nominal ones. It is because of this dichotomy that money is usually introduced, exogenously, into the analysis only once the output has been already specified.[1] This explanation is sometimes reinforced by suggesting that early societies were barter economies and money appeared in society to solve problems associated with barter (barter is both costly and time-consuming). However, some authors have suggested that 'early societies were not barter economies, that markets did not spring forth from barter, and that money was not invented to facilitate exchange' (Wray 1990: 4).

It is because money is introduced (exogenously) 'at the end of the real process' that a 'transmission mechanism' must be found in order to explain what role money will play within these models. The discussion then turns into whether this mechanism is either direct or indirect, as we have seen in Chapter 2, but not on the very distinction between real and monetary sides of the economy. That is the reason why some authors have argued that 'the difference between Keynesians and monetarists lies in their policy recommendations, not in their theories' (Chick 1973: 1).

On the contrary, Post Keynesians do not need to specify a 'transmission mechanism' to link the real and monetary sides of the economy because 'money and monetary institutions are an inseparable part of the real sector of the real world' (Davidson 1978a: 213–214). That link is not needed, since, as some authors have pointed out, money

> does not enter the system like manna from heaven, nor is it dropped
> from a helicopter, nor does it come from the application of additional
> resources to the production of the money commodity
>
> (Davidson 1978a: 226)

According to Davidson, money enters into the system through two
different ways. These ways are 'the income-generating process (the finance
motive)' and the 'portfolio-change process' (Davidson 1978a: 226–227,
Davidson 1988: 163–166). In the 'income-generating process' money
appears at the beginning of the production process because 'production
takes time and purchase of inputs has to be financed prior to the sale of the
output' (Arestis 1992: 180). Since money, and particularly credit, bridges
the financial gap which arises in the production process, then investment is
no longer constrained by a shortage of saving.[2] But, in this case, money
also plays another important role: to reduce the uncertainty attached to
the investment process itself. Davidson put it as follows,

> In the absence of money contracts, it is unlikely that entrepreneurs,
> facing a statistically unpredictable and unknowable future, would
> undertake large and long-lived complex production processes
>
> (Davidson 1988: 154).

In the 'portfolio-change process' money comes through 'fiscal and open-
market operations initiated by the monetary authorities' (Arestis 1992: 180).
Money, in this case, is seen as exogenous to the extent that monetary change
comes from the central bank. However, monetary change in the 'income-
generating process' is endogenous because it is the private sector which
commands this increase in the money supply (providing that both borrowers
and lenders 'agree' in their expectations). On the one hand, we have the
borrowers (credit demand) who are willing to run into debt because they
'expect' an increase in their demand. On the other hand, there is the banking system (the supply side) which, depending on whether it shares this
optimism, may be willing to meet all the increase in the demand for credit.
The issue regarding whether the banking system meets all the increase
in the demand for credit remains as a point of disagreement within the
Post Keynesian school. The source of disagreement does not lie in the
'impossibility' of the banking system to expand lending because of a lack of
reserves but in its willingness to do it because of its liquidity preference.[3]
Post Keynesians also differ from orthodox economists in their methodological roots. To post Keynesians, 'it is impossible to establish any one set of
axioms which is broad enough to support an adequate theoretical structure',
and this explains why it has been suggested that 'any problem requires to
be analyzed from a variety of angles (historical, political, sociological,

and psychological)' (Dow 1993a: 12–14). In other words, economic analysis must be context-specific because only this kind of analysis is able to take into account all these specific aspects. Further, only in a context-specific analysis can the role played by institutions in the economic process be introduced, and 'institutions, economic and political, are of paramount importance in shaping economic events' for post Keynesians (Arestis 1992: 88–89).

Post Keynesians consider the IS-LM model as a misleading representation of the economic process because it assumes that monetary and real sectors are independent (IS and LM curves are independent). However, Davidson (1978b: 52–57, 1978a: Chapter 7) has noted that once we consider the finance motive within the demand for money, the IS and LM curves are not independent anymore and, therefore, the debate about their relative slopes becomes misleading. Secondly, post Keynesians consider money to be endogenous and not exogenous, as is assumed within the IS-LM model. Finally, the IS-LM model is not context-specific, like other general models. This final observation is worth noting because, as suggested in the former chapter, most of the debate on the effectiveness of monetary policy has been reduced to the simple estimates of the IS and LM slopes. However, Chick (1986, 1988) has suggested that the effectiveness of monetary policy may depend very much on the stage of development of the banking system itself. Therefore, the relevant question for post Keynesians is not 'whether' monetary policy is effective or not, but 'when' and under which 'institutional setting' it becomes effective. This issue has been particularly addressed by Chick in her stages of banking development (Table 3.1).

During the first stage banks are merely intermediaries in the sense that lending is limited by their deposits. The cash drain from lending is high in this stage. Deposits are used as a means of saving rather than a means of payment. It is when deposits begin to be used as a means of payment that we move on to the second stage. In this stage reserves rather than deposits constrain lending and the banking multiplier begins to apply.

Stage three is characterized by the extended use of interbank lending. This in turn allows some banks to lend more than what their reserve position allows. At this stage the bank multiplier works faster than it did in stage two.

Stage four appears when monetary authorities begin to act as a 'lender of last resort' in order to preserve financial stability of the banking system. It is at this stage when the causation between reserves and lending reverses. Hence, whereas for lower stages bank lending may be constrained by scarce bank reserves, here the causation between those variables works the other way round since central banks will always supply reserves to demand from banks. If central banks are to fulfil this lender of last resort function they have to supply reserves, at a penalty price if they want, but they have to. This is why it is said that rather than a 'lender of last resort function', what central banks offer is a 'lender of first resort function' (Chick 1988: 6).

Table 3.1 Chick's stages of banking development: implications for monetary policy effectiveness

Stage of banking development	Banking system characteristics	Degree of monetary policy effectiveness
Stage 1	Banks are intermediaries between savers and investors. Investment is limited by saving; lending is limited by deposits	Traditional monetary policy is more effective to control lending as this depends very much on banking reserves. Banking multiplier is less than 1
Stage 2	Claims on deposits are widely used as means of payment. Deposit multiplier applies (bank reserves determine lending)	Banking multiplier greater than 1, and determined by banks
Stage 3	Interbank lending arises but, as a whole, deposit multiplier still applies	Banking multiplier works faster
Stage 4	Central Monetary Authorities act as 'lender of last resort'. Banks are less constrained by their reserve positions. It is banks' liquidity preference and not reserves which determines lending. The former causality between reserves and lending is thus reversed	From here on, it is banks' willingness and not banks' reserves that determines how much credit is given. However, monetary policy may still exert some effect on lending as it may affect banks' behaviour
Stage 5	Liability management and increased competition among banks characterize this stage. Banks seek lending opportunities rather than wait for them to come	(Same as Stage 4)
Stage 6	Securitization and other banking practices (off-balance-sheet operations) make banks less vulnerable	Monetary policy is ineffective because lending and, therefore, monetary expansion, relies on banks' and borrowers' liquidity preference. Monetary policy may, however, affect these behavioural parameters

Source: Adapted from Chick (1986, 1988).

From this point bank lending will start to depend more on banks' willingness to supply credit than on banks' reserves position.

Finally, in stages five and six the former tendency for bank lending to depend more on banks' behaviour rather than on banks' reserves is reinforced, due to factors such as: liability management, increased financial competition, securitization, etc. All these factors free bank lending from the reserve constraint, which in turn makes it difficult for monetary authorities to have strict control on bank lending and the supply of liquidity to the system. The supply of liquidity has become endogenous in the sense that it does not depend on exogenous injections of money on behalf of the central bank but it mainly depends on banks' and borrowers' willingness to lend and borrow, respectively.

Time, uncertainty and money are three other key variables which very much define Post Keynesian monetary theory. These three variables have also been explicitly considered in other theoretical approaches, but their meaning in Post Keynesian theory is quite different. It is precisely here where major differences between the Post Keynesian and other theoretical approaches to money are to be found.

As regards the variable time, post Keynesians usually consider time to be 'historical' rather than 'logical'. Time is therefore irreversible and implies that 'economic decisions taken in the present will require actions which cannot be completed until some future day (or days)' (Davidson 1992: 15).

On the other hand, uncertainty is clearly distinguished from predictable risk to the extent that to post Keynesians risk can be measured by recurring to the calculus of probabilities but uncertainty can not.[4] The assumption here is that decisions taken today can affect, in an unpredictable way, the economic environment (the parameters of the model) and, therefore, no probability can be applied. It is recognized that

> errors, surprises and disappointments are part of the human condition ... (therefore) economic agents in a Keynes world will take actions that would be considered irrational in a neoclassical world, e.g. the holding of money over periods of calendar time for liquidity motives.
>
> (Davidson 1992: 17)

On the contrary, in neoclassical models it is assumed that, providing economic agents are rational, future events can be fully anticipated, at least within a probability distribution. However, many authors have insisted on the idea that uncertainty and risk are not the same thing. Keynes for example pointed out the differences between these two concepts as follows:

> By 'uncertain' knowledge, let me explain, I do not mean to distinguish what is known for certain from what is only probable. The game of roulette is not subject, in this sense, to uncertainty ... The sense in

which I am using the term is that in which the prospect of a European war is uncertain, or the price of copper and the rate of interest rate twenty years hence, or the obsolescence of a new invention, or the position of private wealth-owners in the social system in 1970. About these matters there is no scientific basis on which to form any calculable probability whatever. We simply do not know.

(Keynes 1973a: 113–114)

With regard to money, post Keynesians have stressed, above all, its function as a store of value, because it is this fact that explains why a monetary economy works in a very different way to a barter one, i.e. an economy where Say's Law does not apply any more. In a barter economy, such as

monasteries, nunneries, prisons, or even an Israeli Kibbutz ... a central authority directs and plans both the production and payments in terms of real goods distributed to the inputs according to some predetermined rules accepted by the members of the community. There is never any involuntary unemployment of monks, nuns, prisoners, ... Say's Law prevails. This is the world of neoclassical analysis.

(Davidson 1992: 37)

However, the existence of money permits that not all the money paid out to inputs in the production process will be spent on the products of industry because part of these earnings can be transferred to the future (savings in liquid assets, e.g. money). In this case, when money enters as a store of wealth, Say's Law does not apply any more and possibly involuntary unemployment in the economy arises.

Even more important than the recognition of the relevance of time, uncertainty and money is the close relation which exists among them (Dow 1993a: Chapter 2, Davidson 1978a). To be short, we could state that money exists because production takes time and the future is uncertain and unknowable. Historical time causes any investment decision to be made under uncertainty. The problem that investors have to face is the calculation of the profitability of the 'position' that they want to take (Davidson 1982–1983, Davidson 1992: 48–50). This calculation entails the estimation of, among many other things, that we, the economists, include in the ceteris paribus condition, the stream of cash flows (wages, raw materials, interest payments, etc.) till the investment process begins to deliver its products, the expected price of our product, the level of demand, etc. The investor then faces an uncertain decision because all these expected variables, and many others not considered in the initial moment, can change in the future. The decision can be considered as a 'crucial experiment' (Shackle 1955) in the sense that no past experience is relevant to the future[5] and decisions taken now can change the future in a totally unexpected way. Once uncertainty is introduced in the analysis money follows naturally because money is a way to cope with uncertainty. On the one hand, because it helps put a limit on production costs when forward contracts are used in the production process for the hiring of inputs (Davidson 1992: 42). On the other hand, because money is also a way to transfer purchasing power to the future (saving). This is so because people are confident that money will be always 'universally accepted in the discharge of contracts' (Davidson 1992: 43). Therefore, money can be seen as a way to cope with uncertainty. As Keynes pointed out, if it is not because of uncertainty, 'why should anyone outside a lunatic asylum wish to use money as a store of wealth?' when there are many other financial assets which earn interest (Keynes 1973a: 115–116).

As we suggested earlier, the endogeneity of money supply is another characteristic which defines the post Keynesian monetary theory.[6] Although the roots of the concept can be found in Keynes' writings, especially in his *Treatise of Money*, the concept itself has further been developed by post Keynesians.[7]

Post Keynesians see money supply as being determined endogenously to the system. However, mainstream economics considers money to be exogenous to the economic system, i.e. money supply is under the control of central banks through, mainly, their open market operations and mechanism of reserve requirement.[8] As real variables are considered to be determined by only real factors and money is only seen as a medium of exchange, the only role which is left for money is to determine the general level of prices (inflation). At most money can influence real variables when there is a 'failure' in the market process. For example, in the New Classical model, money plays a real role when agents cannot anticipate changes in money supply ('imperfect information' is present). Within the New Keynesian model, money affects output when either there is 'imperfect competition', which leads to price rigidity[9], or 'imperfect information', which leads to credit rationing. However, if these imperfections would not exist, money would be neutral. It is this assumed neutrality of money, along with the assumption that money supply is under the control of monetary authorities, which explains why, within these models, the discussion on monetary policy is reduced to three main points: first, the determination of the channels through which monetary changes affect nominal income; second, which is the 'right quantity' of money to be supplied according to the needs of the 'real economy'; and finally, which are the best instruments to control the liquidity of the system?

Nonetheless, post Keynesians do not share this view because a clear distinction between real and monetary sides of the economy is not acknowledged by them. On the contrary, as we have already noted, money is considered to be integral to the economic process. Money does not enter at the end but at the very beginning of the production process (Lavoie 1984: 773). Credit is what finances or bridges the time–financial gap which arises in each new investment, e.g. between the very moment we invest (and make outpayments in advance of the expected profitability of our investment) and the time where our investment begins to deliver products to be sold in the market. The monetary authorities and the banking system play a central role in this process because they can provide these credit needs in advance. This argument leads to another post Keynesian assumption: that it is not a shortage of savings what can constraint investment but a shortage of liquidity and finance (Davidson 1992: 51).

Post Keynesians consider that money supply is 'credit-driven' and 'demand-determined'. Money is credit-driven because money is seen as the outcome of the production process (Lavoie 1984: 775, Arestis 1992: 182). Money then cannot be the cause of changes in any economic magnitude because it is an outcome (Arestis 1992: 203). The causation chain then is reversed[10] in comparison to the standard view. Causation does not run from money to nominal income but from income to money, since money-growth occurs prior to income-growth simply because money is credit-driven and the demand for credit depends both on current income and expected income. However, Wray (1992c) points out that 'the reverse causation argument does not mean that spending must increase before the money supply expands' because in the real world 'it may be difficult to establish empirically the relations between money and spending' for two main reasons: first, there is a wide variety of liabilities that function as money and, secondly, money is created not only to finance spending, but also to finance purchases of financial assets and other things that do not show up in GNP (Wray 1992c: 299).

On the other hand, money supply is considered demand-determined[11] because 'commercial banks are rarely constrained in terms of their reserves' (Arestis 1992: 201). The lender of last resort function of the central banks, access to the discount window, financial innovation, asset and liability management, access to international financial markets, etc., are some of the factors mentioned to explain why 'banks do not passively await deposits so they can issue loans' (Wray 1990: 73), but instead first make loans and, afterwards, worry about their reserves.[12]

Even though post Keynesian economists share the belief that money supply is endogenous, i.e. 'that the rate of money supply growth and, more important, credit availability are fundamentally determined by demand side pressures within financial markets' (Pollin 1991: 367), the degree of its endogeneity remains a controversial point. Two different views have been identified regarding this point, namely the 'accommodative endogeneity' and the 'structural endogeneity' (Pollin 1991: 367).

The 'accommodative endogeneity' view is identified with authors like Kaldor (1986) and Moore (1988a). Moore maintains that it is not true that central banks can choose whether to control interest rates or monetary aggregates directly. They cannot do so because an 'elastic supply of credit money in the short run is a necessary precondition of the perpetuation of system liquidity' (Moore 1988a: xi), and system liquidity must be guaranteed in order to avoid financial distortions. Therefore, he goes on:

> The supply of credit money responds endogenously to changes in the demand for bank credit. The supply of credit money is governed by the amount of credit granted (financial asset purchased) by banking institutions. Modern commercial banks are price setters and quantity takers in both their retail deposit and loan markets. As a result at every moment of time the money supply function should be viewed as *horizontal*.[13] It follows that the total quantity of money is both credit-driven and demand-determined.
>
> (Moore 1988a: xii)

One of the implications which can be drawn from this 'horizontality' of the money supply is that central banks do not exogenously determine the quantity of credit money in existence, and therefore,

> the entire literature of monetary control and monetary policy, IS-LM analysis, the Keynesian and the money multiplier, liquidity preference, interest rate determination, the influence of public sector deficits on the level of domestic interest rates, growth theory, and even the theory of inflation must be comprehensively reconsidered and rewritten. All models that treat money as exogenous ... are either misspecified or incomplete.
>
> (Moore 1988a: xiv)

However, and contrary to Moore's horizontalist view, 'structuralist' post Keynesians argue that banks do not fully meet all credit demands (Lavoie 1984, Wray 1990, Dow 1993a and 1996b, Davidson 1994, Rousseas 1986, Chick and Dow 2002). These authors do not agree with Moore's argument because 'in his model, there is no room for liquidity preference in the determination of interest rates' (Wray 1989b). Additionally, as Dow has suggested, for borrowers such as small firms and developing countries, 'it is not the general case that the banks are price setters and quantity takers' (Dow 1996b). What all these authors come to say it is that, perhaps, Moore has become too horizontal,[14] because money supply is more likely to be horizontal during expansions and (more) vertical during recessions (Wray 1990, Dow 1993a, particularly Chapter 3).

Another implication that follows from the above is that the analysis of the effects of the monetary policy on economy is no longer reduced to the calculus of monetary multipliers, nor is it possible to be evaluated in a pure theoretical ground because the issue will depend itself on factors which can only be made explicit in a specific context. Chick summarizes the point in the following way:

> In monetary theory ... the main theme is the effects on the economy of variations in the quantity of money. The literature is extensive but inconclusive, ... Perhaps it is inconclusive because the effect of a change in the quantity of money is contingent upon the state of the economy at the time of the change and upon who issues the money and in exchange for what.
>
> (Chick 1992: 159–160)

And she expands on the argument by pointing out that:

> A change in the quantity of money, however, never occurs in isolation: it always comes into the system in exchange, as half of some transaction, and its effects depend partly on what the other half is. An expansion of government-issued money may result from an increase in the government's purchases of new goods and services, a direct stimulus to demand, or from an exchange for interest-bearing debt outstanding, in which case the effects are more roundabout. Bank money is expanded through increases in bank lending, so the effect of the change depends partly on what the borrower does with the proceeds of his loan.
>
> (Chick 1992: 160)

The above argument means that when analyzing the effectiveness of monetary policy the point is not then to determine *whether* monetary policy is effective or not but *when* and *why* it has been effective. We believe that the '*whether matter*' only fits in a world where money is considered to be fully exogenous. That is to say, a world where, due to the low stage of development of the financial system, the monetary authorities have a tighter control over the level of liquidity of the economy. Under these particular circumstances, some exogenous monetary management could be implemented by central banks if they wanted to. This possibly explains why the impact of monetary policy on economy has been mainly addressed either by means of correlating money growth with output, or by looking at the effects that monetary changes have on some financial variables (interest rates, credit, exchange rate, etc.). If, for instance, these estimates showed money to have a strong effect on real variables, we should then conclude that money does affect output. The answer to the '*whether matter*' would be: yes, money does affect output.

However, one wonders whether this would still be the relevant question to address if, as we suggested earlier in this section, money were not exogenous to the economic system. What would happen then if the supply of liquidity depended more on banks' and borrowers' liquidity preference rather than on exogenous monetary authority interventions? Further, if money were endogenous to the economic system, how should we understand the correlation between money and output? Would monetary growth be explained by exogenous central bank interventions alone? Would monetary authorities really be open to exogenously modify such a relationship? Furthermore, if money is credit-driven, how could we determine the real effect of any monetary increase without having additional information regarding the final use of credit, for example. Perhaps all these points would explain why empirical literature fails to offer a definitive answer to the debate of whether money affects output. Perhaps the issue, as we suggested above, is not to determine whether or not, but why and when monetary policy has been able to affect economic activity.

Another implication that follows from the above argument is that a redefinition of the precise meaning of monetary policy is required. Although for lower stages of banking development the textbook monetary policy concept may apply, as we move on to further stages this concept does not apply any more. Additionally, central banks lose their ability to strictly control the liquidity of the system by means of open market operations at further stages of banking development, but instead rely more on the 'expectational effect' that their policies may have on banks' and borrowers' liquidity preference. Monetary policy should be understood as a wider concept rather than a narrow one which only considers open market operations and reserve requirement instruments. Hence, variables such as financial regulation should also be included within this wider concept of monetary policy. We address this issue in the following section.

3.3 A reconsideration of the meaning and role of monetary policy

The New Palgrave: A Dictionary of Economics defines monetary policy as follows:

> The term *monetary policy* refers to actions taken by central banks to affect monetary and other financial conditions in pursuit of the broader objectives of sustainable growth of real output, high employment, and price stability.
>
> (Lindsey and Wallich 1998: 508)

It would be difficult to argue with this very general definition of monetary policy. Differences do, however, arise among economists when trying to expand on this definition. Orthodox monetary theory sees monetary policy as a simple combination of day-to-day interventions within financial markets. Hence, monetary policy is usually understood as injections (or withdrawals) of cash (outside money) in primary money markets, either through open market operations or changes in the reserve requirement ratio. In its simplest form, monetary policy is then understood as shifts or displacements of the LM curve within the IS-LM model, due to exogenous changes in the money supply which, in turn, are due to central bank interventions.

Discussions of the practicalities of monetary policy soon become heavily conditioned by the type of banking system under discussion. Chick (1986) has extensively studied the different stages through which most banking systems proceed during their development. She demonstrates that the form of monetary policy which is appropriate and feasible depends on the stage of development of the banking system. In particular, she points out that the capacity for monetary authorities to exert direct control over monetary aggregates declines dramatically once a lender-of-last-resort facility is introduced. Then the central bank cannot determine the volume of reserves, nor credit and deposits.

If money is supplied by commercial banks which have a considerable degree of latitude in determining credit levels, how much of the LM curve shift can be attributed exclusively to the actions of the monetary authorities? Would such a thing as a monetary policy exist if the money supply were endogenous? The argument we wish to develop here is that monetary policy cannot, in modern banking systems, be understood as the effecting of discrete changes in the money supply (either directly, or indirectly, through interest rate control). Nevertheless, this does not remove the possibility of effective monetary policy. But monetary policy needs to be understood as a much more complex intervention in a process within which money is endogenously generated. Further, the possibilities for monetary policy extend beyond manipulation of the traditional instruments (open market operations, etc.) to encompass such elements as bank regulation and supervision.

What we are suggesting here is that, as financial and banking systems develop and money supply becomes endogenous, the very concept of monetary policy should also change in order to take into account such major changes. Even though it is difficult for monetary authorities to control liquidity, central banks still intervene in markets through open market operations. We believe this kind of intervention is neither their only tool nor the most effective way to affect liquidity. As banking systems develop, monetary policies rely much more on indirect mechanisms than on direct ones; central bankers themselves are perfectly aware of their own limitations in affecting liquidity without risking financial instability. In other words, at higher stages of banking development, central banks are perfectly aware of the limits of the traditional textbook monetary policy rules, so that in practice they choose to affect liquidity through a variety of means, including influencing the mood of the market and bank supervision.

This view of monetary policy is to be distinguished from the more standard one, which considers that monetary policy always works in the same way regardless of institutional factors, such as the degree of financial development. In fact, traditional monetary analysis has usually drawn a line between monetary and financial or regulation policy.[15] Monetary policy is concerned with monetary control whereas financial regulation deals with financial stability. Furthermore, orthodox economists consider financial regulation as a 'negative' factor that makes financial intermediation more expensive or less efficient. It is sometimes argued that bank regulation (or over-regulation) has been responsible for periods characterized by 'missing money' or 'credit crunch' which, in turn, has made monetary control more difficult to achieve.[16] Some others have claimed that central bank regulation may be seen as a 'tax on transactions intermediated through banks' (Wills 1982: 249). Prudential financial regulation is thus never seen as being either an integral part of the monetary policy itself or as a 'positive' factor which may encourage lending by providing confidence into the workings of the financial system.

But the existence of a regulatory burden on banks' capital level, banks' portfolios, shares, etc. may give confidence to the consumers of financial services as they perceive that such a system is being backed by monetary authorities (Dow 1993a: 20–21). Indeed the development of banking can be seen in terms of the creation of confidence in the banking system, which in turn allowed banks to grow while maintaining increasingly small reserve ratios. In other words, prudential regulation has made a positive contribution to the growth of banking, without which it is not clear that banks could now function effectively. Modern banking systems generate a money stock which is primarily inside money, i.e. money which is the liability of the banking system, with only fractional backing by outside money. The confidence in inside money reflects a confidence not only in the outside money (bank reserves) but also in the panoply of regulation and supervision which facilitates a backing by only fractional reserves.

It is also useful to consider the balance between regulation for monetary control purposes and prudential regulation. The first form of regulation is likely to exert a larger effect when the banking system is less developed. The latter however will become more important for the more developed banking systems. This does not mean that central banks need to refuse the use of monetary control at higher stages of banking development but rather that they should use both kind of policies to control liquidity, since banks may bypass direct monetary controls. That is, as the financial system develops, monetary control relies more on the effects of central bank interventions on banks' and borrowers' behaviour than on simple monetary restraints. J.C.R. Dow and Saville (1990) point out the relationship between monetary policy and regulation policy:

> Though the two kinds of official involvements (monetary policy and prudential supervision) have different aims, these are not completely distinct. Prudential supervision does not aim to affect the course of the monetary aggregates, ... but it could do so [they are referring to

the British monetary experience since 1971], and perhaps at times has done so.

(J.C.R. Dow and Saville 1990: 163)

Further:

> To some extent, then, the purposes of monetary policy and banking supervision run together; and it is worth considering whether the procedures of banking supervision could properly assist monetary policy more actively.

(J.C.R. Dow and Saville 1990: 168)

By monetary policy then we would distinguish two different, but interrelated, ways through which central banks may affect the liquidity of the system (Figure 3.1). The first channel for monetary policy is a direct channel which would apply at lower stages of banking development and would fit well within the standard IS-LM view. The direct effects work through the banking multiplier model which assumes exogenous and complete control of money by central banks. This concept would match

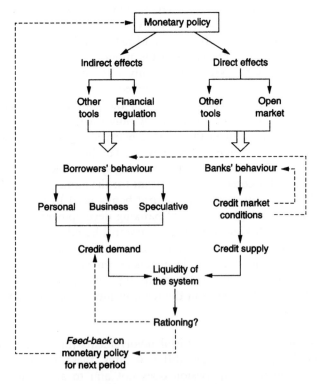

Figure 3.1 Monetary policy influence on liquidity.

with the most restrictive view of monetary policy and would only work in banking systems at low stages of development. However, as banking systems develop, this concept of monetary policy becomes less operative as central banks experience a reduced capacity to control liquidity.[17]

It is when central banks lose their power to exert a perfect control on liquidity that they try to exert their influence through alternative means. We have labelled this action as the indirect channel and it would mainly apply to a highly developed banking system. At this stage, central banks affect liquidity through their influence on agents' (borrowers and lenders) financial behaviour rather than through the standard banking multiplier model. From this perspective, then, monetary policy would affect the liquidity of the system by means of changes in behavioural parameters that have always been considered as fixed. In fact, some have acknowledged this point. For example, Kaldor (1986) pointed out that:

> the major effect of changes in interest rates is to be found 'in their repercussions on the behaviour of financial institutions' rather than that of private individuals.
>
> (Kaldor 1986: 13)

Chick (1985: 90–91) has also acknowledged that monetary authorities have relied, to some extent, on the 'expectational effect' that an exogenous monetary intervention may have on agents' expectations and that a change in interest rates is not essential to the transmission of monetary policy. There is in any case an issue in terms of the capacity of the central bank to affect market interest rates. J.C.R. Dow and Saville (1990: Chapter 4) point out that when reserve requirements are low changes in the cost of borrowed reserves have such a minor effect on bank costs that its influence on market rates is necessarily diffuse. Changes in bank rate are taken by the market primarily as a signal. But, depending on the current mood of the market, and the market's perception of the behaviour of the central banks, the signal may or may not be taken seriously. Successful efforts to influence market rates must thus be endogenous to current behaviour and expectations in the market.

Monetary policy influence on liquidity cannot be seen as being deterministic because the 'same monetary policy' may produce different expectational responses on behalf of economic agents.[18] This argument gathers force the more developed the banking system and the more the reliance on indirect channels of influence. Direct interventions would mainly work through changes in interest rates and bank reserves. However, the effectiveness of these two factors to slow down the demand for and supply of credit would depend both on the nature of borrowers and on the ability of the banking system to extend credit beyond their deposit base.

The effect of interest rates on the demand for credit will depend on how interest elastic the demand is: the more interest elastic, the stronger the effect. However, what is worth considering are the differences in terms of interest elasticity between, on the one hand, the demand for credit for productive purposes and, on the other hand, the demand for credit to finance speculation. In this regard we would argue that, as both speculative and personal demand for credit are less interest elastic than corporate demand, it would be this latter which is most likely to be squeezed from credit markets when a rise in interest rates is being pursued.[20] This squeeze however is more likely to apply to small firms since these may be more dependent on bank finance.[21]

Regarding the quantitative effect, i.e. the change in credit availability, it is worth noting that the issue regarding whether tight monetary policies are able to reduce credit demand will depend on the stage of banking development. The lower the stage, the more central banks are able to constrain credit expansion by pursuing tight monetary policies. As long as banks may have ways either to avoid monetary control by innovating or alternative sources of liquidity, and thus their credit no longer depends on bank reserves, then the credit constraint is not likely to work unless it affects banks' expectations and thus banks' lending policy. However, the final effect will be mediated by the banks' behavioural response. It is on these variables that indirect monetary instruments, such as prudential regulation, exert their effects.

The issue of whether monetary policy so considered is able to affect the liquidity of the system will thus depend on variables such as:

- the interest rate elasticity of demand for credit, since this will determine whether higher interest rates may reduce credit demand or not;
- the stage of banking development, as this will determine whether monetary constraints may directly constrain bank lending expansion;
- banks' and borrowers' response to such monetary changes, since these will determine whether banks decide to meet all credit demand increases or not. These responses will finally depend on how monetary policy affects banks' and borrowers' liquidity preference (willingness to assume risks) and agents' expectations.

Monetary policy could then be considered as an exogenous variable which is incorporated into the decision-making process of the private sector. It is exogenous in the sense that its changes are related to decisions taken by central banks. But, at the same time, monetary policy may be considered as an endogenous variable because once its future lines are known these are incorporated into the decision-making process of private agents. Hence, the announcement of future monetary policy intentions may affect current financial behaviour (the 'announcement effect') and so exert its effect on the economy through behavioural rather than structural parameters. Future monetary restraints may slow down current demand for credit because of a general increase in liquidity preference. It is this interrelationship, which has been labelled as the 'identification problem' of money demand, which makes it difficult (if not useless) to draw the distinction between exogenous and endogenous variables which is usually made in economic analysis.

3.4 Monetary policy and credit availability

We suggested earlier that, for orthodox economists, money supply is exogenous to the system and so determined by central banks. Post Keynesians, on the contrary, consider the money supply to be credit-driven and demand-determined, i.e. endogenous to the system. Some economists have therefore argued that, as long as money supply is credit-driven and demand-determined, monetary policy becomes ineffective in terms of controlling the money stock. This argument is reinforced by the fact that the most extreme endogenous position, the horizontalist one,[22] considers banks as simple *price setters* and *quantity takers* in retail credit markets, i.e., banks set prices and demand establishes the quantity to supply. This horizontalist position argues that the money supply is demand-determined and therefore all that monetary authorities can do is to set the general level of interest rates at which banks would supply, at a marked-up interest rate, as much credit as creditors demand.

This perfect endogeneity has sometimes been understood by orthodox economists that money does not matter. For orthodox theorists, any exogenous variable is automatically significant as a cause of disturbance from equilibrium; once a variable is endogenous it loses causal force. However, this extreme horizontalist position is not widely shared by all post Keynesians economists,[23] since for some it is not enough to say that 'demand creates its own supply, but it must be explained how the private sector commands the money supply it wants?' (Chick 1973: 88).

While we share the endogenous money approach we will argue that some factors put limits on the endogeneity of the money supply and, furthermore, that some of these limits will come both from the activities of a monetary authority, which tries to control the liquidity of the system, as well as from the banks themselves, which may also put limits on their credit extension. Our argument will be that monetary policy does matter even if money is endogenous. As Wray (1992a: 1163–1164) put it[24]:

> banks do not fully accommodate the demand for flows of credit even if their expectations move in the same direction as those of borrowers. ... This does not mean that we must accept the textbook 'deposit multiplier' or the orthodox position that the central bank controls the quantity of money. However, the central bank can make it very difficult for banks to extend their balance sheets if it so chooses.
>
> (Wray 1992a: 1163–1164)

In principle we will assume money supply to be horizontal at some level of interest rates. In so doing, it must be emphasized that the money supply schedule employed here is itself the outcome of a process over time, unlike the orthodox money supply schedule which represents a range of simultaneous possibilities. This distinction is central to the analysis of Arestis and Howells (1996) which unpacks the money supply curve into a shifting series of credit demand and supply curves.

It has been argued by several authors that the horizontal cannot be extended indefinitely, but instead that there must be some point (M1 in Figure 3.2), beyond which 'banks might require higher interest rates to compensate for greater perceived risk as balance sheets expand' (Wray 1992a: 1160).

This point would be where, following Minsky's analysis,

> the internal workings of the banking mechanism or central bank action to constrain inflation will result in the supply of finance becoming less than infinitely elastic – perhaps even approach to zero elasticity.
>
> (Minsky 1982: 107)

The point where the money supply approaches zero elasticity is labelled M2 in Figure 3.2.

But what are the factors that determine changes in money supply? We follow Minsky's work on financial instability[25] in order to explain why the two turning points (M1 and M2) are likely to exist and why they are also likely to move (backward and forward) along with business cycles. Let's first start by analysing the factors determining these turning points in the money supply curve. Bank lending expansion is likely to arise during economic upturns, since it is then that economic optimism fuels both demand for and supply of credit as new business opportunities arise. It is during economic upturns that the number of people willing to run into debt grows and this in turn may make credit demand more interest inelastic. Hence, banks not only face a growing demand for credit but also a less elastic one. Banks can

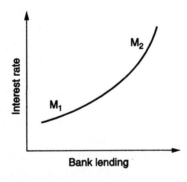

Figure 3.2 Lending expansion.

thus charge higher interest rates without any fear of loss of market share. It could be argued that growing competition both between banks and between banks and non-bank financial intermediaries would drive prices (interest rates) down. Even though competitive pressures that may put bounds to interest rates rising, it is likely that, sooner or later, interest rates will rise and that this policy will be followed by all institutions simultaneously.[26]

As bank lending increases, banks become less liquid and borrowers become less credit worthy than before (personal indebtedness has already increased and this might affect personal creditworthiness). On the other hand, as demand for bank lending increases it is likely that riskier and more speculative projects come into banks' portfolios. Furthermore, lending expansion may also drive banks to accept new customers whose risk is difficult and costly to assess. This factor would in turn explain why banks may begin to ration credit, not only by raising interest rates but also by asking for higher collateral requirements from their new customers.

The effect of higher interest may well displace some projects (investments) which cannot sustain higher rates within the very short term; for example, long term projects which demand low interest rates until they begin to produce cash flow to pay off debts. Only those projects with higher profit expectations within the very short term will be able to afford these higher financial costs. Since some of these projects are likely to be speculative, these activities then displace productive activity from financial markets.

One important by-product of these displacements is that the demand for credit will become more interest-inelastic, so that higher interest rates will have a weaker effect on the demand for credit. At this point banks may decide to ration credit themselves despite the fact that the demand is still going up. In addition, as banks' lending portfolios increase, banks' fears about their own financial stability may arise, driving banks into more prudent and conservative behaviour as regards their lending policies.

Another factor which may halt the lending-expansion process is the running of both tight monetary and banking-supervision policies. These factors may affect lending expansion since it would make it more expensive and difficult for banks to extend lending further and, what is more important, may affect banks' attitude towards lending (banks' liquidity preference). We are not arguing that central banks can control liquidity by means of quantitative ratios which make the provision of credit by commercial banks more difficult. Instead, we agree with J.C.R. Dow and Saville (1990), who clearly stated that central banks' power is more a *qualitative* than a *quantitative* matter. They put the argument in the following way:

> Banks are older than central banks, and if central banks were abolished, banks would undoubtedly survive. ... One or more large banks could indeed in principle provide the services now provided by the central

bank, so that the extreme position in which the banking system became completely independent in this respect is not inconceivable. ... That situation is not, in practice, likely to arise. For the game is essentially a political one: the central bank could always control the banks in other ways, as all parties are aware.

(J.C.R. Dow and Saville: 1990: 148–149)

It is the combination of all these factors, both quantitative and qualitative, that explains the increasing slope of the money supply as bank lending expands. The extension of lending may finally stop when both central and commercial banks begin to implement restrictive policies to slow down credit expansion at any cost.

So far we have concentrated our analysis in studying how a bank lending expansion may entail an upward-sloping money supply function, even when money is endogenous. However, there is another feature of the process that we would like to stress here: the different path that this process may take along economic business cycles. Both M1 and M2 cannot be considered as fixed points but are likely to move, either forward or backward, along with economic upturns and downturns. We explicitly suggest that money supply is likely to be more elastic in upturns than in downturns and that this differential behaviour is explained by changes in the overall liquidity preference of the economy (Figure 3.3). It is worth noting that these changes are mainly due to changes in financial behaviour which have the capacity to change the functioning of the whole financial system:

individual actions which are rational in themselves generate outcomes which act against the collective interest. ... In an expansion, the supply of money may increase to such an extent that ... fuels the speculative expansion ... An extreme euphoria followed by collapse may even

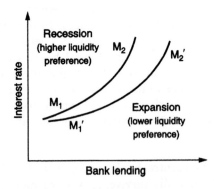

Figure 3.3 Lending expansion: recession and expansion.

irrevocably destroy the confidence in the outside money ... which had allowed the financial system to function as it did. In the aftermath of the bursting of the speculative bubble, the supply of credit is inelastic relative to demand ... (and this) inelasticity of supply with respect to demand is so great as to force bankruptcies and impede investment plans, thus contributing to the contraction of output and employment.

(Dow 1993a: 39–40)

In terms of Figures 3.2 and 3.3, point M_1 moves because of the higher (lower) banks' liquidity preference during downturns (upturns). The more confident banks are (the lower its liquidity preference is), the later they will begin to charge higher interest rates on new loans. Point M_2 in turn is also able to move because of central banks' interventions. The tighter the monetary conditions the central bank establishes, the more likely it is that commercial banks will begin to cut back on their lending expansion.

Overall this argument suggests that money supply is 'sometimes horizontal' and, depending on some factors, 'sometimes vertical' (Wray 1990: 91–93). Table 3.2 summarizes the relationship between the endogenous/exogenous character of money and the elasticity/inelasticity of money supply, as well as the effect that monetary policy, banking development and liquidity preference may have on such variables. Table 3.2 shows that, at lower stages of banking development there can only exist an elastic supply of liquidity when central banks are implementing a loose monetary policy and both banks' and borrowers' liquidity preference is low. In all other cases, an inelastic supply of liquidity is likely to exist, either because central banks are pursuing tight monetary policies which makes banks' reserves scarce, or because banks or borrowers are unwilling to lend and borrow, respectively. However, a high stage of bank development does not necessarily mean that an elastic supply of liquidity exists, but it rather reinforces the fact that liquidity expansion relies much more on banks' and borrowers' liquidity preference than for lower stages of banking development.

3.5 Monetary policy non-neutrality

We have suggested that monetary theory has traditionally drawn a sharp distinction between real and monetary variables. This distinction has led most economists to study how these two relate to each other, in the form of the monetary transmission mechanism. Real economic variables are usually assumed to depend only on real factors such as physical capital and labour, whereas money is seen as just a device to ease the exchange of goods and services already produced. Therefore, the only role which is left for money to play is to determine the general level of prices. Providing the system is working properly, monetary flows should thus mirror real flows. From this point of view money (and by implication monetary

Table 3.2 Endogeneity of money and liquidity expansion

Degree of endogeneity	Monetary policy	Stage of bank development	Liquidity preference		Liquidity expansion
			Bank	Borrower	
Exogenous	Tight	Low	Regardless	Regardless	Inelastic
Exogenous	Loose	Low	Low	Low	Elastic
Exogenous	Loose	Low	High	Low	Inelastic[a]
Exogenous	Loose	Low	Low	High	Inelastic[b]
Exogenous	Loose	Low	High	High	Inelastic[c]
Endogenous	Regardless[d]	High	Low	Low	Elastic
Endogenous	Regardless[d]	High	High	Low	Inelastic[a]
Endogenous	Regardless[d]	High	Low	High	Inelastic[b]
Endogenous	Regardless[d]	High	High	High	Inelastic[c]

[a] Banks may decide not to lend despite having funds available because of their high liquidity preference. Instead they would prefer less-risky investments such as public bonds, large companies rather than small ones, etc. Some credit rationing may exist.

[b] Even though banks are willing to lend, borrowers may decide not to borrow because of their unwillingness to invest. High economic instability, low profitability, higher risks, etc., may explain this kind of conservative behaviour.

[c] In this case both borrowers and lenders are unwilling to run into debt and to lend, respectively. Banks decide not to lend nor borrowers to borrow. This situation would be what Dow (1992d) labelled as 'defensive financial behaviour'; a situation where the low availability of credit is explained by both a weak supply and demand for credit.

[d] Once the banking system reaches some level of development, monetary authorities lose their power to control liquidity perfectly. However, monetary authorities may still exert some effect on liquidity of the system by affecting banks' and borrowers' financial behaviours. Hence, monetary and financial policy may play this role at this stage and these influences should be considered.

Source: Dow and Rodríguez-Fuentes (1998: 12).

policy) is considered to be neutral because a change in its quantity only changes 'the level of prices in an economy, and not the level of its real outputs' (Patinkin 1998: 639). Furthermore, 'money is said to be super-neutral – or long run neutral – if changes in the steady-rate of growth of the money supply do not affect the growth path of real economic variables' (Patinkin 1998: 641). The neutrality of money simply means that economic agents are free of 'money illusion' or, more formally, that demand functions 'are homogeneous of degree zero in the money prices and in the initial quantity of financial assets, including money' (Patinkin 1998: 639).

However, some economists have recognized that money need not be neutral, at least within the very short term. For example, some have pointed out that an increase in the price level, which is always seen as a monetary phenomenon, may have a stimulating effect on production since this 'keeps alive a spirit of industry in the nation' (Hume 1752: 39–40, as quoted in Patinkin 1998: 640). Others have relied on the redistributive effects that such a monetary change could produce, for example, the redistributive effects that inflation may cause between lenders and borrowers, and the redistributive effects that high interest rates may have on profits, wages and personal indebtedness.[27]

Monetarists, in turn, have recognized that money may not be neutral in the short run although they claim its neutrality in the very long run. But rational expectation theorists have pointed out that this effect of money on output and employment within the short run only happens when the monetary change is unforeseen by economic agents. Otherwise, only prices will be affected. That is, only a non-systematic (unanticipated) monetary policy is able to affect output within the short run. However, in the long run money is neutral.

Price stickiness, either in nominal interest rates or wages, is often noted as another source of monetary non-neutrality. Indeed, much of the standard Keynesian view on monetary effects has relied on such price stickiness. This approach underpins New Keynesian theories of non-neutrality, which have explored the role of asymmetric, or otherwise imperfect, information in generating market failure. In particular, asymmetric information is seen as causing credit rationing, where capital markets are not sufficiently perfect to provide substitutes for bank credit. However, if information were full, costless, complete and available to all agents, money would be neutral.

The implications of these arguments are that, as long as there are market imperfections, money is non-neutral and monetary policy is important (Laidler 1990: 21). This is why most of the empirical literature dealing with the issue of whether money is neutral has looked at one or more of the following issues:

- how different economic sectors respond to exogenous monetary shocks;
- the degree to which anticipations of monetary changes matters;
- whether credit markets are rationed.

Unfortunately, this approach is rather misleading because it only fits in a theoretical framework which splits economic activity into real and monetary variables. The starting point is a world of exogenous money where real variables are determined only by real factors and money determines prices. The question then is, under what conditions would an exogenous change in the money supply have real effects? Money would be neutral within this model if it were unable to affect real variables.[28] It is only from this particular perspective that the issue regarding monetary neutrality (non-neutrality) makes some sense.

If money were not exogenously introduced into the system but endogenously created by the banking system to finance economic activity, how could we address the issue of whether money is neutral? In particular, how could we discuss the effects of a money supply increase without first discussing the expenditure plans which generated the demand for credit, and the bank behaviour which led to the demand being met? If these factors are introduced,[29] then the issue is no longer restricted to whether money is neutral or not but when and why it has been so. The issue is not then to determine whether the banknotes dropped from the helicopter affect output and employment. 'It matters who receives the money' (Dow and Earl 1982: 255). Only by assuming that what is going on in the *real economy* is strictly independent on what is going on in the *helicopter* could we safely analyze the matter of whether money is neutral or not. Otherwise the relevant question to be addressed would be a more specific one: why the money dropped in this place has not produced the same effect as the one dropped a little further away.

What we are suggesting here is that the issue of the money neutrality is related to the issue of how money enters into the economy. If we assume that money is endogenous to the system, then the issue of its neutrality does not make sense any more since the question regarding whether money helps to increase production or employment will depend on factors such as (i) what money is used for and (ii) the response of investors, banks, savers, etc. to monetary changes. Hence, the pure analysis of the neutrality of money which ignores these considerations can only make sense in a theoretical framework which assumes the banking system to play a passive (neutral) role in the economic process. It cannot make sense in a framework which assumes money to be endogenously supplied by the system:

> There always has been a conflict between those who see banks as the operators of a safe and secure payments mechanism and those who see banks as an essential institution for the capital development of the economy. The first group views banking and financial intermediation as essentially passive processes by which a predetermined amount of savings is allocated among alternative uses. The second group views banking and financial intermediation as active agents in the economy that, by financing investment, force resources to be used to put investment in place, thereby fostering the development of the economy.
>
> (Minsky 1993: 82)

There are two different dimensions within the neutrality/non-neutrality debate: a quantitative and a qualitative one. The quantitative dimension, which we shall call the *structural effect*, would mainly apply to an economy where money is exogenously determined and would be concerned with the effect that exogenous monetary changes may have on different sectors, level of employment, output, etc. We have named this the quantitative effect because it can be quantified through the calculus of simple elasticities. This, in turn, helps to explain why most research has paid so much attention to this dimension. Nevertheless, a focus on this dimension can only explain at best one half of the process. The other half, we suggest, would be explained by what we have labelled as the *qualitative* dimension of the process.

The qualitative dimension highlights what we call the *behavioural effect* and would instead fit in a world of endogenous money. Here, the question to be addressed is how economic and current monetary conditions[30] may affect agents' financial behaviour and how those, in turn, may affect economic activity (employment and output). In other words, the question is how financial behaviour affects the real economy, bearing in mind that this behaviour is determined both by financial variables (monetary policy and financial regulation) and real variables (economic expectations, etc.) and neither a clear-cut nor a one-way causal relationship between the two can be established. It is clear that the behavioural effect can not be completely deterministically quantified.

3.6 Conclusions

The aim of this chapter has been to clarify the meaning of the concept of monetary policy when money is endogenous to the economic process. It has been argued that, as the financial system develops and therefore money creation becomes endogenous, the concept of monetary policy has to be widened in order to include the factors which may affect banks' and borrowers' behaviour, since these will determine credit expansion/destruction. Accordingly it is not possible to draw a clear distinction between monetary policy and financial regulation, since the latter is probably the most important determinant of credit expansion in financially developed economies.

Regarding the endogenous character of money, we suggested that an endogenous money supply does not necessarily mean that the demand for money is passively accommodated, nor that money loses its causal power. But, by the same token, if money is generated endogenously, its causal role is suffused within the overall economic process.

We have argued here that, under certain conditions, money supply may become inelastic even though money is endogenous: for example, when there exists high liquidity preference among borrowers and lenders. Furthermore, it was suggested that the money supply is likely to be more elastic during expansions rather than during downturns. That is, the pattern of credit expansion follows a cyclical pattern, as do changes in liquidity preference.

As far as the analysis of the effects of monetary policy on economic activity is concerned, we pointed out that the debate over whether *money matters vs doesn't matter* only makes sense if (i) there is a sharp distinction between the real and monetary sides of the economy and (ii) money is perfectly exogenous to the system. Only this distinction would allow us to analyze what happens to the real side when we introduce an exogenous change in the money supply. Only by assuming that economic activity depends on real factors such as labour, physical capital, etc., and monetary flows simply mirror real ones, can it be assured that money and monetary policy are neutral with respect to output and employment. Otherwise, the issue regarding whether money is neutral would not make any sense, just as it would not make sense to consider whether labour or physical capital, for example, were neutral.

If such a clear distinction between real and monetary sides of the economy are not drawn, then efforts should be put into studying *when and how* rather than *whether* monetary policy is neutral or not. Whether monetary policy is neutral or not could only be addressed from a theoretical standpoint which, by assuming money to be exogenous to the economic process, tries to determine the long run effect of an exogenous increase in the money supply. However, if money were not exogenous then this matter would not be relevant. Then the issue to analyze would rather be how exogenous monetary interventions in financial markets affect the liquidity of the system and thereby economic activity.

We also argued that two dimensions have to be distinguished when analyzing the effects of monetary policy on economic activity: a *structural* dimension and a *behavioural* dimension. The first is concerned with the effects of exogenous monetary changes on different economic variables. The second dimension is related to the effect that such changes may have on agents' behaviour. The more developed the financial system is, the more relevant this second factor will be.

Bearing this in mind, it is clear that the issue to study is no longer whether exogenous monetary changes affect output or not but when and how they do, especially in financially developed economies. This is so because the final effect of any monetary change will depend on the final use given to the new money which is supplied. This is what Chick (1973: 132) has labelled as the second half of the monetary transaction. In this sense, an endogenous money supply perspective would mean that the place in which, and time at which, the 'helicopter' throws the money is of crucial importance when analyzing its effects.

The view that monetary policy enters into an endogenous process, where its effects are context-dependent, therefore clears the way for analysis of what that monetary policy should consist of in particular contexts. This in turn requires understanding, not only of the structure of the banking system and of the economy as a whole, but also of the determinants of behaviour. In particular, this approach draws attention to the fact that behaviour is conditional on an institutional structure which emerged as a result of past behaviour. In other words, modern banking systems function on the foundation of confidence, which is the product of institutional arrangements, and experience of central bank behaviour, built up over many years. Minsky's work highlights the interdependence between financial behaviour, the state of confidence, and output and employment. What we have argued here is that this interdependence should be borne in mind when designing monetary policy. Specifically, this requires attention to bank regulation and supervision, with a view to maintaining financial stability, as a central plank of monetary policy.

4 The regional effects of monetary policy
A theoretical framework

4.1 Introduction

This chapter presents a theoretical framework, built on the principles of the Post Keynesian theory of regional finance (Chick and Dow 1988, Dow 1990, 1993a, Dow and Rodriguez-Fuentes 1997), which allows us to explore the way through which money and monetary policy may affect regions. One peculiarity of this framework is that it broadens the scope of the analysis by taking into account the underlying factors determining regional credit availability, specifically the stage of banking development and the liquidity preference of financial agents (including banks).

The framework presented in this chapter explicitly acknowledges that central banks lose their ability to directly influence the money stock as financial systems develop, thus money supply becomes increasingly endogenous to the economic process. An endogenous money supply means that any increase in liquidity depends more on the demand for credit (and thus borrowers' liquidity preference) and on the willingness of banks to supply credit (and thus the banks' liquidity preference) than on the central bank's direct interventions.

Contrary to other theoretical approaches employed to study the regional effects of national monetary policies, our framework pays particular attention to the influence of monetary policy on banks' and borrowers' liquidity preference, that is, 'the behavioural effect' and not just the effects of monetary policy on economies with divergent economic structures ('the structural effect'). Nevertheless, behaviour not only reflects economic structure but also influences its evolution. Consequently our theoretical framework considers the interdependencies between economic structure, financial structure, economic conditions and financial behaviour. In our opinion this framework offers a more satisfactory basis for analyzing the regional impact of monetary policy than the orthodox approach, which relies on exogenous factors for explanation.

The chapter has been structured in two sections. Section 4.2 studies the effects that exogenous monetary shocks may have on economies with different economic structures. As will be seen, this section only focuses on what we have labelled as the *structural effect* of monetary policy. Section 4.3 extends the analysis and includes not only the effects due to differences in economic structure, but also those due to differences in economic responses to monetary policy decisions: the *behavioural effect*. The chapter ends with the conclusion section.

4.2   The regional impact of monetary policy with exogenous money: the structural effect

Most of the literature dealing with the regional impact of monetary policy could be considered as a 'regional extension' of the more general discussion on the transmission mechanism of monetary policy. In practical terms, the regional literature has mainly focused on studying those regional differences where national monetary policy may have a different impact across regions within a country. In particular, the literature has concentrated on studying the relevant factors of the transmission mechanism, particularly those pointed out by both Keynesian and monetarist authors.

Monetarists identify the regional impact of monetary policy with different regional responses to business cycles since they take for granted that business cycles are due to monetary shocks. The monetarist argument relies on two assumptions. The first one is that monetary policy is responsible for fluctuations (business cycles) in the short run. The second one is that some regions might be more affected than others by these business cycles, which is usually explained by regional differences in terms of income or wealth elasticity of the demand for regional products (see, for example, Beare 1976). However, if the fluctuations created by exogenous monetary shocks were evenly distributed across regions, then such regional effects of the monetary policy would not exist. Monetary policy would therefore be neutral at the regional level, since no region would improve its relative position with respect to the rest. Everyone benefits or no one does, depending on whether the monetary policy causes a temporary upturn (expansion) or downturn (recession). However, the monetarists also suggest that these gains (or losses) would be only temporary, since in the long run real growth depends only on real factors, i.e. money is neutral. The monetarists have tried to test their assumptions by means of estimating some kind of reduced-form model where the regional income depends on monetary policy. The purpose here has been to prove that money and income are highly correlated also at the regional level, and that changes in regional nominal income are explained by changes in the national money supply. This reasoning is presented in the papers by Beare (1976), Cohen and Maeshiro (1977), Toal (1977) and Kozlowski (1991), among others. However, it is not free from criticisms.[1]

Traditional Keynesians in contrast have denied the existence of a direct relationship between money and income. They argue that such a relationship between money and income, either at the national or regional level, is rather indirect and mainly works through the effect that changes in interest rates have on the different components of the aggregate demand. Here the regional effect of monetary policy depends on the existence of regional differences in the responses of the aggregate demand components (consumption, investment, exports and imports) to changes in interest rates.[2] These authors suggest that the regional impact of monetary policy is reduced to the study of the regional differences in terms of consumption (durable and non-durable) and investment (fixed, construction, etc.) responses to changes in national interest rates. The potential regional effect that changes in exchange rate could have on regional exports and imports is sometimes included.[3] Other authors have pointed out that some regional differential impact of monetary policy may exist when regional credit markets are segmented, either because of imperfect or asymmetric information, and this in turn impedes a proper allocation of financial resources.[4]

The fact is that for monetarists and Keynesians the regional impact of monetary policy is reduced to either the existence of structural differences, which cause a higher response to national monetary policy shocks (monetarists) or a higher response of some of the regional aggregate demand components to changes in interest rates (Keynesians). Independent of the reason why, the fact is that regions that are structurally more different with respect to the national average would be the ones most likely to suffer from differential effects of national monetary policy.[5] It is clear then that the main difference between monetarists and Keynesians (Neo-Classical synthesis) is rooted in their diverging views of the transmission channels of monetary policy, which were reviewed in Chapter 2. Even so, both schools share two important points. Firstly, they assume the money supply is exogenous, that is, unilaterally determined by the central bank's interventions. Secondly, their explanations of the regional impact of monetary policy are primarily based on the existence of structural economic differences among regions of a national economy (structural differences in terms of regional sensitivity to business cycles, or structural differences in terms of regional sensitivity to changes in national interest rates).[6] Figure 4.1 shows the argument which we have labelled as structural,

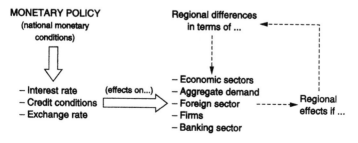

Figure 4.1 Structural effect of monetary policy.

since its applicability is strongly linked to the existence of regional structural differences.

According to the *structural effect*, national monetary policies may have a regional differential effect only if regional differences in terms of economic structure exist. Otherwise all regions would be equally affected by national monetary policies, either positively (expansion) or negatively (recession).

Two objections arise from this argument. First, there is nothing specific to monetary policy. If monetary policy affects regions differently because of their structural differences, the same could also be claimed for any other national economic policy. In fact, as many authors have pointed out,[7] any policy, either strictly economic or not, has a regional dimension since it may affect economic activity, either directly or indirectly, intentionally or not, and economic activity, in turn, is not evenly distributed along the spatial surface. We are not neglecting the possibility that a single monetary policy may affect some economies differently, particularly those with strong structural differences.[8] Instead, we are suggesting that the 'real cause' of the regional impact of monetary policy in this analysis is not money itself, but regional structural differences which have nothing to do with monetary policy.

The second objection to this argument is that it only applies to a context where the national money supply is considered exogenous. However, if money is created endogenously, monetary policy may have an impact on banks' and borrowers' liquidity preference, and thus on credit creation. This is what we have called the *behavioural effect*, which is explored further in the next section.

4.3   The regional impact of monetary policy with endogenous money: the structural and behavioural effects

As we suggested earlier, most of the literature on the regional impact of monetary policy concludes that, while money is exogenous at the national level, it is endogenous at the regional one. That is, national monetary authorities control national money supply which, thanks to interregional arbitrage and perfect capital mobility (as a result of financial market integration), then flows freely among regions according to regional differences in demand pressures.

This argument, which is illustrated in Figure 4.2, is embodied in the small open economy version of the IS-LM model, although this time the reasoning is applied to a regional setting (see, for example, Roberts and Fishkind 1979, Moore and Hill 1982, Harrigan and McGregor 1987). Regions having higher demands for credit will experience financial inflows, since they will be willing to pay higher interest rates for financial resources. Regions having lower demand relative to its supply will experience financial outflows, since they cannot compete with higher interest rates offered in faster-growing regions which demand more financial resources. These interregional

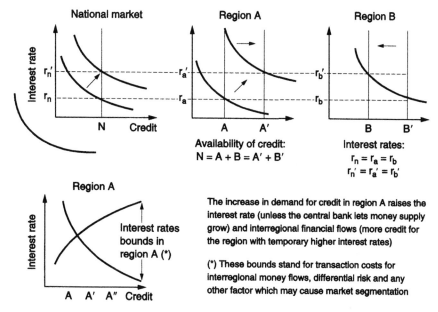

Figure 4.2 Standard regional finance literature.

financial flows will equalize regional interest rates. Regional differentials in interest rates may only persist in the long run if markets fail to work properly,[9] or if regional differences exist in terms of perceived risk or transactions costs. In the latter, the market will allow for such differences and add some mark-up on the normal interest rate. Within the very short term there could also be some differentials as financial flows to (from) other regions may take time. In this case differentials in interest rates could last until financial funds are driven in (out) of the region. Both national demand and supply determine interest rates and total amount of credit available. The supply of credit is perfectly inelastic, since it is assumed that banks can only lend a fixed amount of credit, providing the central bank does not relax its monetary policy. The total amount of available credit is then divided among regions (regions A and B in our figure) according to their demands for credit. Under these circumstances, and assuming that there exists perfect interregional capital mobility, if one region experiences an increase in its demand for credit relative to its supply, this would drive regional interest rates above the national average, leading financial institutions to drive financial resources (credits) into the region to make profits (a positive differential in interest rates). However, as total available credit is fixed, banks can only lend more in one region (region A) if they lend less somewhere else (region B). Regional supply in A will increase, driving interest rates down, whereas the reverse happens in B. Equilibrium is therefore again achieved at higher interest rates, unless the central bank lets national supply increase, with A (B) having a higher (lower) amount of credit available than before.

The former argument has led some authors to conclude that, providing there is perfect interregional capital mobility, no financial constraint can ever arise at a regional level since regions face a horizontal supply of funds at some level in interest rates. This statement has also led to the interpretation that money supply is endogenous at the regional level so small open regions have no monetary identity (see Dow 1993a, Chapter 8).

However, in our work the term endogenous money does not necessarily mean that regions face a horizontal money supply, thanks to interregional arbitrage, but rather that the money supply at the national level, just as at the regional level, is the outcome of the willingness of the banks to create credit in response to demand, albeit subject to indirect influence from the central bank. Contrary to 'horizontalist' Post Keynesians (Moore 1988a), who consider that endogenous money means a perfectly elastic supply of credit, both at the national or regional level, our analysis makes a case for the 'structuralist' post Keynesian monetary theory. 'Structuralist' post Keynesians emphasize the significance of the particular financial structure (of banks and of firms) which has evolved in a particular economy, with reference to the stage of banking development. It also emphasizes how financial behaviour, given that structure, can vary over time as economic conditions change, and over space in line with the real characteristics of a particular economy.[10]

Our argument is graphically shown in Figure 4.3, whereas Figure 4.4 explains how both regional supply of and demand for credit are influenced by changes in the regional stage of bank development and liquidity preference.

Contrary to the belief that small open regions face a horizontal money supply (see Figure 4.2), our analysis considers the possibility for regions to face an upward-sloping supply for credit, either because banks can not provide more credit due to reserve constraints (low stage of banking development) or because banks and borrowers are not willing to provide or demand credit (high liquidity preference).[11] Consequently, the question to address is not how to divide a given amount of credit among different regions but instead to determine why banks lend within some regions more than in others, that is, why some regions face a nearly inelastic supply of credit whereas others face a more elastic one.

Another important aspect which distinguishes our analysis from the standard regional finance literature (Figure 4.2) is that more credit for one particular region does not necessarily mean less credit available for the rest. According to Chick's theory of stages of banking development (Chick 1986, 1988), as the banking system develops, the supply of credit becomes less constrained by reserves.[12] This point is worth considering since it completely changes the focus of the discussion on regional finance. If the relevant issue

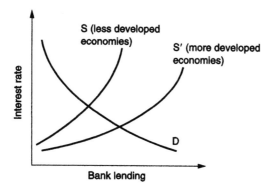

Figure 4.3 A Post Keynesian view of regional finance.

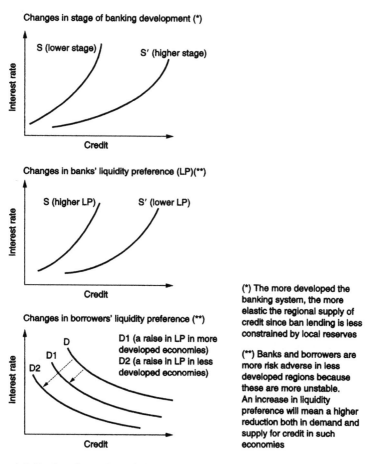

Figure 4.4 Regional supply and demand for credit and changes in stage of banking development and liquidity preference.

were how to divide a given amount of credit regionally, the increasing of credit availability in one region might be achieved by expanding the national money supply, so the given amount of credit would automatically rise. This could explain why some authors have called for regional monetary policies to be implemented, as this would allow regional monetary authorities to let regional monetary supply grow according to their interests. However, if the issue were not how to divide a fixed amount of credit among regions but how to increase banks' willingness to lend in some regions, the managing of a regional monetary policy could not work since the decision regarding credit availability depends on the interaction between local banks' and borrowers' liquidity preference.

The following considerations are necessary when studying the determinants of credit availability. From a theoretical perspective, the relevant question is to study the determinants of credit availability: a) banks' ability and willingness to extend credit, b) borrowers' liquidity preference, and c) the influence that monetary policy and the central bank may have on the two aforementioned points. Borrowers' liquidity preference would determine the increase in demand for credit. Both banks' ability and willingness to provide credit and monetary policy would determine how much credit demand can be met by banks. From a regional perspective, the relevant question is to study the spatial differences in terms of banking development and liquidity preference, as well as the influence that monetary policy may have on such variables.

The stage of banking development influences the money supply through its influence on banks' ability to lend. More developed banking systems are able to extend more credit than less-developed systems, regardless of their deposit base. The earlier stage of bank development, the more applicable the money multiplier model is. This fact would imply that regions having banking systems in earlier stages of development and regional borrowers more dependent on these banks for credit, would be more constrained by, say, low saving or deposit ratios than others. Thus, local banks characterized by an earlier stage of development, compared to national or international banks, will find themselves at a competitive disadvantage, including a lesser capacity to create credit.

Liquidity preference affects not only banks' willingness to lend within the region, but also savers' and borrowers' behaviour. Thus, higher liquidity preference may reduce the supply of credit in some regions by encouraging savers to adopt more liquid portfolios, which may produce an outflow of financial resources from peripheral to central regions. However, higher liquidity preference may also reduce the regional demand for funds to the extent that investors are less willing to accept additional debt due to uncertain expectations. Liquidity preference is normally discussed in temporal terms, and indeed the greater volatility over time in peripheral regional economies, and the lesser protection, in the form of wealth, from fluctuations, will also cause greater volatility in liquidity preference over

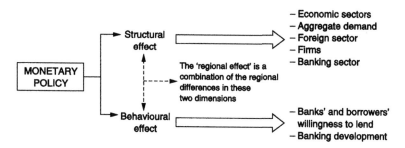

Figure 4.5 Structural and behavioural effects.

time for these regions. But there may also be secular regional differences in liquidity preference. Peripheral regions on average over time will display higher liquidity preference than central regions because of their greater vulnerability to instability.[13] Therefore, regional differences in terms of stages of banking development and liquidity preference may produce higher instability in the credit availability in some regions[14] (see Dow and Rodriguez-Fuentes 1997).

The introduction of these two variables, the stage of banking development and liquidity preference, means that the analysis of the regional impact of monetary policy cannot be restricted to the so-called 'asymmetric shocks', but should also pay close attention to the influence of monetary policy on financial behaviour. This result is shown in Figure 4.5, which clearly contrasts with Figure 4.1, where only the structural differences were included.

4.3.1 Banking development and liquidity preference

We have mentioned that banking development and liquidity preference are two important determinants in the supply of credit. This section explores further the influence of these two variables on regional credit availability.

When the banking system is at a low stage of development, national money supply can be considered to be exogenous, since central banks perfectly control the liquidity of the system and, consequently, bank credit is limited by reserves. Under these circumstances, the financial problem becomes one of how the resulting fixed amount of credit (given by the banking multiplier) is distributed among different regions. Regional credit is therefore limited by regional deposits or bank reserves, the variations in the quantity of outside money which is supplied by the central bank, the interregional monetary flows and the changes in financial regulation (such as reserve requirements, capital ratio, etc.). This situation coincides with the regional monetary multiplier model.[15] Within this framework, the monetary policy affects some particular regions through its influence on the total amount of bank credit (and its cost) which is available (through the banking multiplier). The differential regional effect of monetary policy would arise if the reduction in total credit were not evenly distributed among regions, for example when peripheral markets experienced higher cuts in lending when monetary policy tightens, or when higher interest rates had stronger effects on particular regions (due to the higher interest rate elasticity of their sectors). With regard to the reduction in credit, it is likely to expect some regional differences, since cuts in lending policy by banks are likely to affect some regions more than others. For example, those markets considered as 'peripheral' by financial institutions will first experience a reduction in credit availability. The problem here is to define a 'peripheral market' for a financial institution, although it would not be too risky to say that they are likely to be located in regional peripheral economies. This question could be empirically addressed by studying the regional pattern for credit distribution over the business cycle and, particularly, by studying whether empirical evidence suggests a more unstable pattern for credit availability between central and peripheral regions alongside business cycles.

A second question which requires studying is the different impact of changes in interest rates across regions. In this case, regional differences arise not only because sectors' sensitivity to changes in interest rate may vary across regions, but also because of a higher concentration of small businesses in some regions.[16]

This scenario would be quite different under a more developed banking system. Credit supply would depend more on banks' and borrowers' liquidity preferences instead of on bank reserves exclusively. Consequently, if a bank decided to lend more in one region this would not necessarily mean less available credit for the remaining regions (this would only apply in a situation where banks can only provide as much credit as the banking multiplier allows them to do). A bank could provide more credit in one region if it succeeds in getting more resources to lend from external sources, such as national or international financial markets or from their central offices outside the region, or by means of managing its assets and liabilities (securitization and off-balance-sheet operations).

The analysis would also vary depending on the institutional structure of the banking system. We will consider two different scenarios in this regard. The first one considers the existence of institutional segmentation in the banking system (regional branch banking system), so some regions might differ from others in terms of their respective financial structures. The second one considers the existence of a national branch banking system which operates nationwide (national branch banking system).

The supply of credit in a regional branch banking system is less elastic in those regions with both a lower deposit base and lower stage of banking development. That is, when monetary authorities try to slow down the growth of credit, these regions are likely to experience higher cuts in their credit availability. Consequently, in these regions the traditional monetary multiplier is likely to apply.

However, when a national branch banking system exists, local branches in one region could also borrow from their central offices to obtain funds at no cost and then lend them in the regional market at a mark-up. Consequently, a low regional deposit ratio does not necessarily mean low availability of credit. In addition, a perfectly elastic regional supply of funds can be assumed, as in both the open version of the IS-LM model and the 'horizontalist' post Keynesian view. Even though local banks can get extra funds to lend in the region, they still may decide not to lend if they are unsure of the investment prospects. In this case, it is the banks' liquidity preference that determines the credit creation process. From a regional point of view the relevant question is to study whether banks' lending policies (liquidity preference) vary across regions and whether monetary policy effects on banks' liquidity preference can reinforce such regional differences. What we are suggesting here is that the more conservative practices in terms of lending that certain banks show in some regions, particularly during downturns, might also be a response to tighter monetary conditions pursued by the central bank, and not only to the worsening of the regional economic prospects. Let us suppose that the central bank considers current credit growth to be too high for the long term stability of the financial system. It would then try to slow down credit growth through a wide set of measures. Such measures may include higher interest rates applied at the discount window, quantity limits for outstanding credit, changes in reserve requirements, financial regulation[17] or even the use of moral persuasion. Under these 'tighter circumstances', banks may find it to be more difficult to extend credit endlessly and borrowers would face increased borrowing costs. We are not arguing that banks' lending is limited by their reserves position, since this would only apply in an exogenous money approach. Banks' reserves cannot constrain lending because banks can overcome such restraints on lending by recurring to either their innovative power (asset and liability management, off-balance sheet operations, etc.), to the discount window (since central banks would always supply whatever quantity is needed to maintain financial confidence[18]), or look for liquidity in external markets (international financial markets), etc. In this sense we could consider that modern banking systems would never be constrained as long as their lending policy is concerned. However, as Rousseas (1986) has pointed out, all these operations take time and hence it is likely that, within the very short term, some banks may find it more difficult or even impossible to carry on with their lending policy.[19]

In addition, it seems unlikely that these restrictive practices which are being put in to practice by central banks do not affect banks' behaviour. Banks know that central banks' actions exert an important psychological effect on the market.[20] Secondly, if commercial banks also share central banks' fears of the negative effect that extension of lending could have on financial stability of the financial system, they would be the first ones interested in following the central banks' advice, since their business relies on the confidence which promotes such stability. Hence, the overall effect could lower banks' willingness to lend, i.e. a higher liquidity preference on behalf of the banking system under these circumstances. The more conservative lending policy would be a response to monetary changes introduced by the central bank, rather than a low deposit or reserve position.

The relevant issue from a regional perspective is to determine whether a higher bank's liquidity preference leads to an even cut in lending policies across regions, or whether the credit contraction concentrates in particular regions. If such differences exist, then it is also necessary to determine why banks seem to be more conservative in some regions.

The problem we face here is how to empirically measure banks' liquidity preference. Some economists sort out the issue by comparing bank lending and deposits by regions, the difference between the two being understood as a rough measure of such concept. Hence, higher deposits relative to credit would mean that banks were driving financial resources out of that region because of the lack of confidence attached to it, or because of the lack of profitable investment alternatives in comparison to other regions. This interpretation would fit in an 'exogenous money view', which sees banks as 'passive agents' which can only lend what has already been deposited before.

However, the previous argument can only be applied in specific situations, namely where bank lending is limited by bank reserves (monetary multiplier). It cannot be used in a scenario where commercial banks normally lend first and afterwards look for their reserves.[21] In this latter context (where the monetary multiplier does not apply), high deposits relative to credit could be seen either as a high banks' liquidity preference (which leads banks to not meet some regional credit demands) or as a situation, where regional demand for credit is weak (banks can not provide credit because borrowers are not willing to run into debt). As a consequence of the interdependence between the supply of and demand for credit, it is difficult to interpret the information given by ratios such as deposit/credit at the regional level or to put forward economic policy solutions for the situation, since the nature of the problem has not been clearly identified.[22] Thus, if the problem were due to the existence of a weak demand for credit, this situation could be reversed by encouraging borrowers to borrow and invest in profitable projects.[23] However, if the problem were due to the existence of a high bank liquidity preference, policy makers should act by helping banks to provide more credit to regional investors (by providing incentives to lend regionally, by establishing some regional differentials in terms of financial regulation, by monitoring regional investment projects and in doing so help banks in their credit-risk assessments, etc.).

What happens in reality is that these two effects, the existence of both a weak demand and supply of credit, are interdependent because both banks' and borrowers' liquidity preference tend to move in the same direction as they are affected by the same underlying factors. Therefore, it is likely that for some regions both supply and demand for credit tend to decrease in downturns because of the lower economic expectations and, therefore, this complicates the identification of the existence (or absence) of credit rationing. This also may result in incorrect interpretations of ratios such as credit/deposit, since they show what the result of this interdependence has been but reveal nothing about the underlying factors which led demand or supply to increase (decrease). This situation might well apply to peripheral regions, which, due to their intrinsic economic instability (because of their low economic diversification or higher dependence on business cycles, lower economic development, etc.) may experience a more unstable pattern of credit availability than the one for the more developed ones. This economic instability might consequently reinforce the growth of credit during expansions as well as its destruction during recessions. Therefore, the question is not that the less developed regions face a long run decline in their credit shares, but a more unstable pattern of credit availability alongside business cycles, whereby unstable pattern means greater fluctuations in regional credit both in expansion and recession. This more unstable pattern reflects changes in regional liquidity preference (both from banks and borrowers) and may have important consequences for regional economic activity. The credit expansion during upturns may foster speculative activities and hence squeeze non-speculative activities from credit markets. The credit contraction during downturns may drive some regional investors not to go ahead with their plans, and banks to not meet some regional demands for credit.

Some economists argue that this 'discriminatory effect' is the proof that the financial system works properly, i.e. driving scarce financial resources away from risk, allocating them to the 'best' investment alternative, thus improving the overall efficiency of the system as a whole because, at the end of the day, this is what matters. However, this argument does not answer the question of whether this 'efficient argument' is a suitable policy for promoting economic growth and, in the case that it was, how the gains of such a process should be distributed between losers and winners. This is worth noting, since our argument states that one of the factors which may cause instability in credit extension to peripheral economies is 'monetary policy', which, in turn, is often implemented to achieve inflation goals claimed by central and more developed regions.

But, apart from banks' liquidity preference, the availability of credit also depends on borrowers' willingness to run into debt (liquidity preference) since banks can only provide credit when someone is asking for it. Banks could not lend if nobody was interested in borrowing under any conditions. Therefore, the availability of credit is the result of the interaction between the demand and supply of credit. The next section concentrates on studying the implications of changes in both borrowers' and savers' liquidity preference for regional credit availability.

4.3.2   *Borrowers' and savers' liquidity preference*

With regard to the influence of borrowers' liquidity preference on regional credit availability, it is important to consider the effect that monetary policy may have on borrowers' investment plans, who are highly sensitive to changes in interest rates (high interest rates elasticity demands). The investment decisions with a low short term profitability (or higher maturity) might not survive in a context of higher interest rates when other riskier short term projects that compete for funds are expected to yield higher returns.[24] This 'price effect' is likely to slow down the growth of credit demand but may also have varying consequences across sectors and regions. For example, the 'adverse selection' effect is likely to affect small businesses differently to large ones. For larger firms higher interest rates could have a weaker effect on their financial costs since they have access to other financial sources than bank credit (such as bond markets, international financial markets, etc.). Large firms also have stronger bargaining power in the credit market, can offer higher collateral and provide standard information which reduces the cost of the credit scoring process. These arguments are usually employed to support the hypothesis that, if a credit rationing is to exist, it is more likely that small-sized firms will be affected.

Business size is not the only characteristic which influences credit availability. Business specialization might also matter. For instance, for firms operating in markets where any increase in cost could be easily translated to the selling price, higher interest rates (higher financial costs) would have a weaker effect on their 'balance sheets' in comparison with those firms which are facing more price-elastic demands for their products.

The foregoing implies that changes in interest rates (caused by monetary policy) may have different effects on regions, depending on factors such as the spatial distribution of investment projects returns (low vs high returns), maturities (short or long term project), business size (small vs large firms) and specialization, populations' attitudes towards risk (personal liquidity preference), personal wealth,[25] etc.

Another important and neglected issue in the literature is the effect that monetary policy could have on savers' behaviour and, particularly, on their portfolio preferences. If raising interest rates would lead regional savers to change their portfolios into safer and more liquid positions, and if risk-free and more liquid assets were not available within the region, then monetary policy might cause financial outflows, since regional savers would try to look for safer and more liquid financial assets elsewhere.

4.3.3   *Beyond the structural effect of monetary policy*

The introduction of the stages of banking development and (banks', borrowers' and savers') liquidity preference means that the analysis of the

Table 4.1 Relevant variables for analyzing the regional impact of monetary policy: structural and behavioural effects

Structural effect	
Sectoral-mix	• Sectors' sensitivity to business cycles: interest rate elasticity
Aggregate demand-mix	• Consumption (durable and non-durable) and investment (fixed capital, construction, etc.) responses to changes in: interest rates, national income and credit restrictions
	• Export and import responses to: exchange rates, interest rates, credit restrictions. Regional differences in degree of openness to trade, marginal and average propensity to export and import, export specialization and import composition
Business structure	• Firms' size: differences in terms of sources of finance, costs and availability of bank credit, collateral, etc.
Degree of competition	• Internal competition: degree of segmentation in regional financial markets (information costs gathering, administrative and risk evaluation costs, regional financial assets and intermediaries, isolation and distance from 'financial centres', etc.)
Behavioural effect	
Regional supply of funds	• Banks' ability to expand credit (banking development) and liquidity preference
	• Central banks' financial regulation and monetary policy influences
	• Savers' portfolio preferences
Regional demand of funds	• Borrowers' willingness to borrow (invest), liquidity preference, firms' size (dependence on bank lending, bargaining power, etc.)

Source: Rodríguez-Fuentes (1997b: 174) and Rodríguez-Fuentes and Dow (2003: 976).

regional impact of monetary policy cannot be restricted to the structural effect, but should also pay close attention to the influence of monetary policy on financial behaviour. The two sets of effects shown in Table 4.1, structural and behavioural, provide a framework for studying the factors determining regional differences in credit availability. A second aim of this framework is to ease the identification of the processes underlying the real and financial structural effects of the orthodox approach, as well as to extend the analysis to incorporate associated behavioural differences.

Table 4.1 provides guidance as to the kind of regional data that would be useful in order to conduct a full regional analysis of the effects of monetary policy; a significant barrier to (sub-national) regional analysis is that much of this information is not readily available; although when regions are understood as nations, as in the EMU debate, this problem is greatly diminished.

The structural effect applies to the orthodox view that sees monetary policy as an exogenous force applied to an existing (arbitrarily disparate) economic or financial structure. The structural effect suggests that monetary policy would affect regions differently because these are structurally different to the economy for which the monetary policy is actually being designed. For example, it is sometimes argued that national monetary policy does not suit those regions whose business cycles are not fully synchronized with the national economy, or that the central bank has set the official interest rate too low for the more inflationary regions. However, this argument only applies to a world of exogenous money where the central bank's role is to determine the quantity of exogenous money that fits to real needs of exchange. Nevertheless, this view ignores the influence that central banks' monetary policy decisions may have on banks' and borrowers' liquidity preference, which, as suggested earlier, have important consequences for regional credit availability in more financially developed economies. In this particular setting monetary policy could help by facilitating lending but could never assure that banks automatically expand regional credit when more outside money is supplied, nor borrowers to go ahead with their investment plans even though banks are ready to provide funds.

A further question is to determine how useful a regional monetary policy would be to achieve such goals. On this issue most researchers agree that a true regional monetary policy would be of little help, since regions would not succeed in effectively controlling their money supply because they are very small open economies (this is the 'global monetarism' proposition applied to a regional setting).[26]

However, the aim of the more general framework considered here is to go beyond the common duality between structure and behaviour. Our framework is therefore aimed to consider the interdependencies between behaviour and structure, particularly in the credit market, where the structure of the banking market influences financial behaviour. Thus, it acknowledges that behaviour reflects economic structure but also influences its evolution. Once we accept that the supply of money at a national as well as regional level is endogenous, then the volume of credit is understood to depend primarily on private banks' behaviour with respect to borrowers in different regions rather than on central banks' interventions. In this context central banks could still exert some effect on private banks' behaviour but the question then would be how deterministic this influence is.

In this scenario monetary policy could not be too loose in the sense that the central bank is causing banks to create 'too much' credit. The causality has then been reversed: borrowers decide to borrow, and banks may decide to fund them. The central bank sets a price for reserves borrowed at the margin, which undoubtedly influences banks' portfolio decisions. But it is only influence; other important factors are banks' and borrowers' expectations about returns on different assets located in different regions, and the default risk attached to each. These all take on a regional dimension because expectations formed under uncertainty rely on conventional judgement, e.g. about the relative health of the regional economy, and because both the real economic structure and the financial structure of the banking system and of firms generally differ from region to region.

4.3.4 Some implications for empirical research

The foregoing argument has important consequences for the empirical analysis of the regional effects of national monetary policies.

One implication is that the empirical analysis can not be restricted to the economic or financial structural differences which might make one particular monetary policy unsuitable for some regions (the *structural effect*), but also the behavioural responses of economic agents to changes in monetary policy (the *behavioural effect*), as well as their consequences for the economic and financial structure in the long run.

It is not enough then to restrict the empirical analysis to the measurement of the differential effect that national monetary variables, such as interest rates, money and credit, exchange rates, etc., could exert on regional economies which strongly differ from the 'national average' in structural terms (economic sectors, investment, consumption, exports, imports, etc.). The analysis must also take into account the influence of monetary policy on banks' and borrower's willingness to lend and borrow since these are the final determinants of the variation in regional lending.

Another implication is about the universal validity of the results. Many empirical approaches to the regional impact of monetary policy look at the *ceteris paribus* effects that either changes in national money supply or interest rates have on regional income or employment. Most of them address this issue by studying correlations among these variables along periods of tight and loose monetary policy in order to determine whether tight monetary policies produced higher contractions in some regions. Apart from the tricky issue of how to identify periods of tight or easy monetary policy when money is endogenous,[27] the problem with these empirical approaches is how to isolate the effect of the monetary policy from the other policies' influences implemented at the same time (fiscal, labour, industrial, etc.) and, furthermore, how to isolate the effect of the monetary policy under 'some particular given institutional conditions' (expectations, legal framework, etc.) or, alternatively, the effect of 'another kind of monetary policy' under these same institutional conditions. Actually, an increase in the money supply could come from very different sources, for example, from a government purchase, from an open market operation initiated by the central bank, from an expansionary bank's lending policy, etc. Therefore, the empirical analysis should also address the following issue: does a 'certain monetary policy' (labelled as M1 in Figure 4.6) always produce the E1 effect,

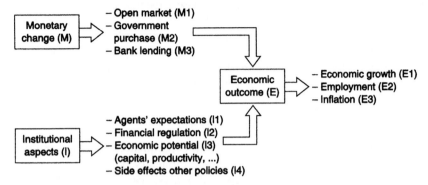

Figure 4.6 Limits attached to empirical testing.

regardless of the institutional setting (labelled as I in Figure 4.6)? Alternatively, does a monetary change always have the same effect regardless of the way this change comes about (see Figure 4.6).

The former argument implies that empirical work on the effects of monetary policy should not be restricted to the analysis of correlations between national monetary variables and some regional indicators, because these correlations tell us what the relationship between them has been in the past under particular circumstances but say nothing about the causal relationships involved in the process. For instance, a strong correlation could exist between, on the one hand, credit (or money) and, on the other, regional income in one particular economy over one particular period of time. This relationship could say that, for example, when the national money supply went up by 20 percent regional income rose by 7 percent while prices grew by 13 percent. However, if, as we have suggested, the increase in credit (or money), rather than being the result of a deliberate and exogenous increase of outside money by the central bank, were the result of an increase in the regional demand for credit which was partially (or totally[28]) met by banks, then how should that relationship be understood? Should we understand it as a fixed relationship which always applies or, on the contrary, the breakdown of the monetary increase between real and nominal effects depends on other factors which are not included in such a deterministic relationship? A second issue is whether a 'truthful and fixed relationship' between money and income exists, or whether this relationship depends very much on 'the way money comes into economy', as Chick has pointed out. That is, does it matter whether the monetary expansion comes from either an increase in the government's purchases of goods and services (direct effect on demand), or in exchange for outstanding interest-bearing debt (open market operation), or an expansion on bank lending (Chick 1992: 160)? We believe that this is a critical point for the analysis, because if the way money comes into existence matters, then the relevant question to answer is not *whether* the monetary policy affects regional output or not, but to explain *when* and *why* the monetary increase affected regional income in the past.

The foregoing clearly complicates the development of any empirical test since theory suggests the inclusion of variables that are complex to measure in a very deterministic way, such as banks' and borrowers' liquidity preference. The traditional view assumes the following: (i) economic growth only depends on real factors, (ii) money being exogenously and perfectly controlled by central banks, with financial intermediaries playing a total passive role in the process, and therefore, (iii) money causing inflation in the long run when it is supplied in excess of real needs, or business cycles when central banks surprise economic agents in the short run. Perhaps it is easier to translate this view onto empirical grounds under these assumptions, but it does not provide a comprehensive understanding of how monetary policy works in a world where it is credit that determines money supply and credit depends on borrowers' and lenders' expectations, rather than on central banks' unilateral decisions.

4.4 Conclusions

This chapter has presented a theoretical framework to explore the ways through which monetary policy can affect regions.

One peculiarity of the analysis presented in this chapter is that it explicitly takes into account the potential regional differences in terms of banking development and liquidity preference of financial agents (including banks). As has been suggested, the inclusion of these two variables has relevant implications for our analysis. One implication is that, as financial systems develop, central banks lose their ability to directly influence the money stock since the increase in liquidity depends more on the demand for credit (and thus borrowers' liquidity preference) and on the willingness of banks to supply credit (and thus the banks' liquidity preference) than on the central bank's direct interventions. However, even at this stage central banks can still influence both banks' and borrowers' decisions; so there is still scope for monetary policy to affect regions differently.

Another important implication we would like to mention here is of an empirical nature. Whereas most empirical works concentrate on studying the differences in economic or financial structure which might cause national monetary policy to affect regions differently, our theoretical framework suggests emphasizing the factors which determine regional credit availability. Consequently, the relevant issue is not to study regional differences in response to exogenous monetary shocks, nor how a given amount of credit is distributed among regions by the banking system. These might be the right issues to address where the banking multiplier applies (low level of banking development), but not when the supply of credit increasingly depends on banks' and borrowers' financial decisions (high level of banking development). Under this scenario, we suggested that the relevant issue is to study the influence of monetary policy on banks' and borrowers' liquidity preferences, that is, the *behavioural effect*, and not only its effects on economies with divergent economic structures (the *structural effect*).

5 Monetary policy, financial flows and credit markets

A survey of the regional literature

5.1 Introduction

This chapter surveys the existing literature concerning the regional effects of monetary policy. The chapter is structured into three main sections. Section 5.2 deals with the 'old' literature on the regional impact of monetary policy, that is, those early empirical contributions explicitly concerned with the regional effects of national monetary policies. Section 5.3 focuses on a more heterogeneous group of contributions, ranging from regional monetary multipliers to the regional credit markets literature. Finally, Section 5.4 includes more recent contributions which study the differences in the transmission mechanism of the European Central Bank monetary policy to the member economies of the euro area. The chapter ends with the conclusion section.

5.2 The 'old' literature on the regional impact of monetary policy

This section reviews the traditional literature that has explicitly dealt with the issue of the regional effects of national monetary policies. The papers included in this survey have been grouped into three different blocks (Table 5.1). As will be seen, most literature reviewed in this section could be considered as a regional extension of that dealing with how national monetary changes affect real economy. Therefore, the same two ruling views, monetarists and Neo-Classical Keynesian, on how monetary policy affects economy will also be distinguished at the regional level.

The monetarists look for evidence of the power of money and monetary policy to cause business cycles at the regional level. On the contrary, Neo-Classical Keynesians instead try to demonstrate that this direct monetarist effect of money on income does not seem to be reliable at the regional level either, because they believe that monetary policy affects the economy in a rather indirect way. This belief explains why they have also chosen to develop large regional structural models, mostly regional base models of growth, in order to test such an indirect effect. The monetarist models are

Table 5.1 'Old' literature on the regional impact of monetary policy

Reduced-form models	Beare (1976), Cohen and Maeshiro (1977), Toal (1977), Mathur and Stein (1980, 1982, 1983), Garrison and Kort (1983), Kozlowski (1991)
Large regional macro models	Fishkind (1977), Deiss (1978), Miller (1978), Garrison and Chang (1979), Chase Econometric (1981), Goodhart (1989a)
Diffusion of open market operations	Scott (1955), Lawrence (1963), Bryan (1967), Ruffin (1968), Barth et al. (1975), Thurston (1976), McPheters (1976)

Source: Dow and Rodríguez-Fuentes (1997: 904).

reviewed in Section 2.1, whereas Section 2.2 deals with the Keynesian ones. The third group of papers are those that focus on how open market operations may have different regional impacts. This literature is reviewed in Section 2.3.

5.2.1   *Reduced-form models*

Beare (1976) was one of the first works which empirically addressed the issue of the regional impact of monetary policy. Although there were earlier contributions, such as Scott (1955), and Lawrence (1963), Beare's contribution received much more attention since it represented a 'further' step in the development of the monetarist view on business cycles. Hence, the underlying 'theoretical roots' of Beare's work are to be found in earlier papers by Friedman and Meiselman (1963) and Andersen and Jordan (1968). These papers not only set up the basis of the so-called 'St. Louis equation', but they also provided a 'theoretical frame' where most of the monetarist argument on the impact of monetary policy, either national or regional, has developed.

The monetarist's argument has been that business cycles are mainly due to monetary shocks, and so empirical work was developed to support such a hypothesis. Beare's departing point also was aimed to test monetarist theory on business cycles. However, Beare decided to apply monetarist theory to a regional setting since he suggested that

> if money contributes at least to some extent to fluctuations in national activity levels, then it must also contribute to fluctuations in the activity levels of the different regions of a national economy
>
> (Beare 1976: 57)

In order to test this hypothesis Beare estimates a monetarist reduced-form model, the St. Louis equation, to the Prairie Provinces of Canada (Manitoba, Saskatchewan and Alberta). Beare's model was therefore a simple extension of the St. Louis equation to a regional setting. The model, shown below, was tested with annual data from 1956 to 1971, and was specified both in nominal and real terms.

$$E_i = \alpha + \beta_0 M + \beta_1 A_i \tag{5.1}$$

where E stands for expenditure on products of the i-th region, M for national money supply, and A for autonomous expenditure on products of the i-th region. The variables which were chosen to carry out the estimation were Personal Income Before Taxes, as a measure of E, and, 'after some experimentation', Total Net Income of Farm Operators from Farming Operations as a proxy for autonomous expenditure (A).[1]

Beare concluded that his model confirmed the monetarist hypothesis, i.e. the importance of money in the determination of regional income. However, one might wonder whether his results really do support the monetarist hypothesis. Indeed, what Beare presents in his paper are the results of the model in real terms for the three individual regions (Manitoba, Saskatchewan and Alberta) and in nominal terms for the three together (Prairies). And, according to the individual significance of the parameters in the model, t-ratios, the variable M/p (real money holdings) seems to have a strong effect on E_i/p in almost every case. That is, money seems to affect regional real income, at least for the regions and period of time chosen by Beare. However, the monetarist view, if we are right, states that money only causes business cycles within the short term, and inflation in the long run. Money is neutral in the long run.

Beare justified the impact of money on regional income on the ground of the existence of regional differences in terms of income or wealth elasticity of demand for their products. However, to lead his conclusion towards a monetarist field, he states that, although 'the initial effects of a monetary change are principally on real output rates,...the long run effects are principally (and perhaps totally) felt on price level' (Beare 1976: 58). Perhaps, what Beare means is that the 15 year period between 1956 and 1971 is not long enough for monetarist 'money neutrality' to be tested.

Cohen and Maeshiro's (1977) paper also aimed at testing the monetarist view of business cycles at the regional level. They did so by estimating the following two models for the US regions for the period 1948–1971.

$$GSP_t = f(MON_t, MON_{t-1}) \tag{5.2}$$

$$MON_t = f(GDP_t, GDP_{t-1}) \tag{5.3}$$

where GSP is Gross State Product and MON stands for State Money Holdings.

According to the authors' conclusions, their model supported the monetarist view, i.e. equation (5.1) was a better fit than equation (5.2).

Leaving aside any theoretical discussion regarding the 'theoretical content' of both equations, one might raise doubts about the reliability of the data used in the estimation. For example, the variable *MON*, which stands for State Monetary Holding, was obtained by adding the state currency holdings to the demand deposit holdings, being the former 'determined by applying the annual average national currency-demand deposits adjusted ratio to state demand deposits' (Cohen and Maeshiro 1977: 674). Although this procedure is frequently used when it comes to the estimation of regional variables, especially financial ones, we should bear in mind what the limits of these estimations are, and what implications for the analysis follow. For example, one implication of this approach could be that no regional differences in terms of liquidity preference are allowed to exist. Furthermore, if we do not allow regional differences in liquidity preference to exist, we are implicitly assuming that money only plays a transaction role. If money were then only demanded for a transaction motive, regional money holdings should be in line with regional shares in national Gross Domestic Product (GDP). And, finally, if regional money holdings are supposed to 'mirror' regional shares in GDP, aren't we implicitly assuming money neutrality? Furthermore, if we are assuming no influence of money on regional GDP because the former is worked out from the latter, how can we possibly demonstrate money being non-neutral? What we are suggesting here is that, sometimes, our conclusions are very much determined by our assumptions. If the former argument is right, then what does the 'empirical truth of the data' mean?

The paper by Kozlowski (1991) takes a different approach to those used by Beare and Cohen and Maeshiro. Rather than prove the suitability of a reduced-form model to test the monetarist view of the regional business cycle, Kozlowski tried to show that when a national monetary variable is incorporated in regional models of leading indicators, their forecasting performance is highly improved. In so doing he compared the performance of four leading indicator models for Detroit, South Carolina, Toledo and Wisconsin, with and without a national monetary indicator (M2). The results showed that when M2 was included in the models the forecasting performance was improved.

Although this paper does not address directly the issue of the role of money in the regional business cycle, we believe that the idea that national money supply should be considered in regional models, because it is one of the causes of regional business cycles, is implicit in it.

Within the monetarist vs Keynesian debate over the explanation of the regional business cycles, there have been also some contributions which have pointed out the dangers and limits of following simple reduced-form approaches, such as those from the St. Louis equation. The three papers by Mathur and Stein (1980, 1982, 1983) belong to this category.

As a response to the extended use of reduced-form models in economics in order to test theoretical hypothesis, Mathur and Stein (1980, 1982, 1983) pointed out the limits surrounding this kind of empirical approximation. Mathur and Stein were mainly concerned with the bias problem which arises when using such reduced-form models. They support their hypothesis both theoretically and empirically. Empirically they tested a reduced-form model similar to that of Beare (1976). Their model (Mathur and Stein 1980) was as follows.

$$\Delta Y_{it} = \alpha_{i0} + \beta_{i1} \Delta G_t + \beta_{i2} \Delta T_t + \beta_{i3} \Delta \overline{M}_t + e_{it} \qquad (5.4)$$

where Y is total personal income, G is high-employment government expenditure, T is high-employment receipts, $\overline{M}$ is national demand deposits plus currency in circulation, and e is the random error term. The subscripts i and t indicate region and time-period, respectively. The model was estimated for eight US regions during two sample periods, 1952:I to 1968:II and 1952:I to 1976:IV.

The results obtained by Mathur and Stein were in a monetarist line, i.e. monetary multipliers were highly significant in comparison to the fiscal ones. However, and this is the point the authors wanted to make with their paper, both multipliers showed high instability. It is this instability that led the authors to be sceptical regarding the use of reduced-form models at the regional level.

Garrison and Kort's (1983) paper, on the contrary, was a response to both Beare's monetarist explanation of the regional business cycle and the scepticism shown by Mathur and Stein concerning the use of reduced-form models. In order to demonstrate both the power of fiscal variables in the explanation of regional business cycles and the usefulness of the reduced-form models, they estimated the following model by states in the US for the period 1960:I to 1978:IV.

$$\Delta N_{it} = \alpha_{i0} + \beta_{i1} \Delta E_t + \beta_{i2} \Delta R_t + \beta_{i3} \Delta M_t + \beta_{i4} T + e_{it} \qquad (5.5)$$

where N is the total non-agricultural employment, T is a time variable for trend influences and rising productivity, E is the high-employment budget expenditure, R is the high-employment budget receipts, M is the national money supply (M1), and e stands for a random error term. The subscripts i and t stand for region and time-period, respectively.

The results confirmed that both money and fiscal variables influence real activity. They also argued that the instability found by Mathur and Stein (1980, 1982) was due to the misselection of both the independent variable and the temporal period. However, these criticisms were going to be rejected again by Mathur and Stein (1983).

Apart from criticisms about the usefulness of the use of reduced-form models (Mathur and Stein 1980, 1982), most of the approximations reviewed so far include some 'black boxes' regarding the explanation of the relationship between money and output. The general standpoint in all these monetarist models has been that, as economic growth depends on real factors, any monetary change, which is assumed to be exogenous to the system, is only able to distress economic activity, either creating instability in the short run (business cycle) or inflation in the long run. Others, on the contrary, have sustained that fiscal variables are also important in the explanation of the business cycle.

The solution to this debate was supposed to be found by recurring to empirical evidence. But empirical evidence, as Beare's (1976) and Garrison and Kort's (1983) papers show, has left the debate open because it has given support to both explanations. It is our view that these controversial results could be explained by several factors, among which we would mention the following:

a) As Mathur and Stein (1980, 1982, 1983) have pointed out, reduced-form models are not able to discriminate between the two sides of the debate.
b) There are differences in data and econometric tools used in each paper.
c) There does not exist a theory of general applicability; the suitability of each theory depends very much on institutional factors which differ from case to case, and might swing the empirical pendulum from one extreme of the debate to the other.

But a more fundamental issue arises if money is not exogenous to the economic system, as both monetarist and Neo-Classical Keynesians suggest, but is the result of a complex process of interaction between monetary authorities' interventions and private agents' responses to those interventions. If that were the case, how should the correlation between money and income be understood? In fact, money and income would then show a strong correlation over the cycle because credit is what finances production and money is credit-driven. From this theoretical point of view, money, rather than being the cause, would be the effect of the cycle and the correlation between money and income, either at a national or regional level, would have a different interpretation to the one given by either monetarist or Neo-Classical Keynesian models.

Furthermore, even if money were the single cause of economic instability, it would remain difficult to put into practice the monetarist proposal of controlling money supply in order to avoid business cycles if money were no longer under the control of the monetary authorities.

5.2.2　*Large regional macro models*

Although monetarists have mainly addressed the issue regarding the regional impact of monetary policy by means of some kind of reduced-form model, Keynesians have instead chosen to develop some kind of large regional macro model. Among the latter we would distinguish two different kinds. One type aimed to assess the 'side effect' that some national financial variables, mainly interest rates, have exerted on regional income. Although these papers have explicitly considered the issue of how national financial conditions have affected regional growth, they have not directly addressed the matter of the regional impact of monetary policy.[2] The other type dealt directly with the issue of the regional impact of monetary policy, either from a monetarist or Keynesian point of view.[3] Large regional macro models built on Keynesian assumptions have mainly recognized two different ways through which national monetary policies have affected regional economies. The first channel has been through the effect that money has on national income, as the latter is considered as one, if not the single, determinant of regional income. The second effect has been the one which national interest rates could have on regional expenditure. Some of these ways are explicitly considered in the papers by Fishkind (1977) and Garrison and Chang (1979), as will be shown below.

Monetarist models have instead taken a different account of the process, being more concerned with how national monetary policy has affected the regional distribution of money and, therefore, how monetary policy may affect regional business cycles. This is the approach taken, for example, by R.J. Miller (1978). In what follows, some brief comments on both kinds of models will be offered.

Fishkind (1977) developed a short run export-base model for a state economy (Indiana, US) which was estimated for the period 1958–1973. The model is not fully presented in the paper, although the author states that it is composed of 34 equations, 17 of which are stochastic ones. The first of these 17 stochastic equations is presented in the paper, the remainder being highly interdependent.

$$QB_t = f(GNP_t, YCB_t) \tag{5.6}$$

where QB is the state's basic output, GNP is the gross national product, and YCB is the yield on corporate bonds.

According to Fishkind, the model contains the three channels of monetary policy: (i) the cost of capital, which is included in the housing investment equation; (ii) the availability of capital, also included in the housing investment function; and (iii) the wealth effect.

In order to test the differential effect of the US national monetary policy on the Indiana economy, Fishkind compares the behaviour of some regional economic indicators (Gross Product, Personal Income, Total Employment, Unemployment Rate and Transfer Payments) with the national ones during periods of tight (1969–1970) and easy (1971–1972) monetary policy.[4] The results showed that during 'tight monetary policy' periods, the Indiana economy experienced slower growth than the national one. However, during 'easy money' times, Indiana grew at the same rate as the national one. This asymmetrical behaviour of Indiana was explained, according to Fishkind's conclusions, by the differences in terms of the relative composition of the state economy.

Garrison and Chang (1979) also estimated a regional Keynesian model which was built on the export-base theory.[5] The model was as follows:

$$YMFG_{it} = f(M_t, \ldots M_{t-n}, E_t, \ldots E_{t-n}, R_t, \ldots R_{t-n}) \qquad (5.7)$$

$$YB_{it} = YMFG_{it} + YAGR_{it} + YMIN_{it} \qquad (5.8)$$

$$YN_{it} = g(YB_{it}, \ldots, YB_{it-n}) \qquad (5.9)$$

$$Y_{it} = YB_{it} + YN_{it} \qquad (5.10)$$

where *YMFG*, *YAGR* and *YMIN* are the regional manufacturing, agrarian and mining earnings, respectively. *YN* is the regional non-basic income, *Y* is the total regional income, *M* stands for the national money supply (M1), *E* for high-employment federal expenditures and *R* for high-employment revenues.

The model was applied to eight US regions with quarterly data for the period 1969:I to 1976:I and, in light of the empirical results, Garrison and Chang concluded that, in line with Keynesian theory, both monetary and fiscal variables influence economic activity.

They also worked out the elasticities of manufacturing income with respect to *M*, *E* and *R*, and found that regions with higher concentrations in durable-good manufacturing experienced a larger response to changes in all variables. Therefore, they concluded, monetary and fiscal policy are likely to have different regional effects due to the regional differences in economic structure. Regions having a higher concentration of durable-goods manu-facturing will be more affected than those where agriculture and mining are more important.

Chase Econometric Associates (1981), by means of the estimation of a regional model for eight US regions, four rural and four urban, arrived at the same results as Garrison and Chang (1979). That is, that urban regions seem to be more affected by tight monetary policies than rural ones. This result is explained by the regional differences in elasticities between different economic sectors. Unfortunately, the model is not shown in the paper. The only thing we know about it from the paper is that it was composed of 164 equations, 114 identities and 38 exogenous variables. Two exercises were carried out with the model. First, the effect of a tight monetary policy was simulated. Secondly, the effect of a redistribution of credit from urban to rural regions was carried out. Both exercises gave support to the results already mentioned, i.e. tight monetary policy affected urban regions more than rural ones.

R.J. Miller's (1978) book offers a monetarist view on the regional impact of monetary policy. He put forward a 'short-run two-region macroeconomic static multiplier model' which, combining the global monetarist approach to the balance of payments and a regional specification of the money supply, allowed him to test the channels through which monetary policy affects regional economies. His model, as he states, goes further than the global monetarism literature because of the inclusion of a regional money supply mechanism (R.J. Miller 1978: 32–34). The model was expressed as follows:

$$\sum e_i = \sum Y_i^o - \sum E_i(Y_i^o - t_i^x(Y_i^o), P, r) - \sum G_i = 0 \tag{5.11}$$

$$\sum b_i = 1/P\left[\sum(B_i^s(Y_i^o, P, r) - B_i^{so}) - \sum(B_i^d(Y_i^o, P, r) - B_i^{do})\right.$$

$$\left. - \sum Z_i - \sum D_i\right] = 0 \tag{5.12}$$

$$\sum m_i = 1/P\left[\sum k_i(T_i + a_{i1} F^1 + a_{i2} F^2 - F_i^3) + \sum M_i^o\right]$$

$$+ \sum M_i(Y_i^o, P, r) = 0 \tag{5.13}$$

$$N_i^d\left(\frac{W_i}{P}\right) = N_i^s\left(\frac{W_i}{P}\right) \tag{5.14}$$

$$\frac{T_i}{P} = e_i + b_i = -m_i \tag{5.15}$$

where equations 5.11 to 5.15 represent, respectively, the commodity, bond, money and labour markets and the regional balance of payments, where e_i is the net interregional transactions in goods and services for region i, Y_i is the real regional product of the region, E_i is total real expenditure by the private sector (consumption and investment), G_i is the real government expenditure, P is the price level in the national economy, r is national interest rate, t^x is the tax function in the region, B^s is the desired nominal bond supply in region, B^{so} is the initial nominal bond supply position in region, B^d is the desired nominal bond demand in region, B^{do} is the initial nominal bond demand position in region, Z_i is the exogenous nominal net flow demand for bond in region, D_i is the nominal flow supply of inside money in region, b_i is the net interregional transactions for bonds in region, m_i is the net interregional transaction in real money balances, M_i is the desired stock of real money in region, M^o is the initial level of the real money stock in region, k_i is the regional money multiplier, F^1 is the central bank's net open market purchases of bonds, F^2 is the float item,[5] F^3 is the flow of deposits from the private sector of region-i to the government's deposit accounts at the central bank, N^d is the demand for labour services in region, N^s is the supply of labour services, W is the wage, and T is the regional balance of payments for region.

The data requirements of the model make it quite difficult to obtain an empirical estimation. In fact, what Miller did was some comparative static analysis in order to see what the regional effects of open market operations were. The conclusions were that open market operations were not neutral once the regional dimension was introduced, being the effects on each region depending on parameters such as: (i) price; (ii) interest rate elasticities of the expenditure; (iii) money demand functions in each region; (iv) their relative size in terms of their relative share in the total money stock; (v) value of regional multipliers, etc. However, what Miller means by monetary nonneutrality was not that money could affect regional output, because his model is a full-employment economy. What he really means by monetary policy non-neutrality is the possibility that monetary changes could affect either prices or interest rates, not regional output (R.J. Miller 1978: 72–74, 136).

R.J. Miller also developed another model in his book which was aimed to assess empirically the issue of the regional impact of the US monetary policy. The model is a two-region reduced-form monetarist model whose main structure is shown below.

$$\Delta SNE_t = c_1 + a_{11}\,DDNE_{t-1} + a_{12}\,DDROC_{t-1} + b_{11}\,\Delta USG_t$$

$$+ b_{12}\,\Delta FF_t + b_{13}\,\Delta FGS_t + b_{14}\,\Delta OA_t + b_{15}\,\Delta OL_t \tag{5.16}$$

$$\Delta SROC_t = c_2 + a_{21}\,DDNE_{t-1} + a_{22}\,DDROC_{t-1} + b_{21}\,\Delta USG_t$$

$$+ b_{22}\,\Delta FF_t + b_{23}\,\Delta FGS_t + b_{24}\,\Delta OA_t + b_{25}\,\Delta OL_t \tag{5.17}$$

$$KNE_t = c_3 + d_{11}\,KNE_{t-1} + d_{12}\,KNE_{t-2} + d_{13}\,KNE_{t-3} \tag{5.18}$$

$$KROC_t = c_4 + d_{21}\,KROC_{t-1} + d_{22}\,KROC_{t-2} + d_{23}\,KROC_{t-3} \tag{5.19}$$

$$\Delta YNE_t = c_5 + e_{10}\,\Delta MNE_t + e_{11}\,\Delta MNE_{t-1} + e_{12}\,\Delta MNE_{t-2}$$

$$+ e_{13}\,\Delta MNE_{t-3} \tag{5.20}$$

$$\Delta YROC_t = c_6 + e_{20}\,\Delta MROC_t + e_{21}\,\Delta MROC_{t-1} + e_{22}\,\Delta MROC_{t-2}$$

$$+ e_{23}\,\Delta MROC_{t-3} \tag{5.21}$$

$$DDNE_t = c_7 + f_{11}\,YNE_t + g_{11}\,Q2 + g_{12}\,Q3 + g_{13}\,Q4 \tag{5.22}$$

$$DDROC_t = c_8 + f_{21}\,YROC_t + g_{21}\,Q2 + g_{22}\,Q3 + g_{23}\,Q4 \tag{5.23}$$

where *SNE* is the stock of net source base to the Northeast region, *SROC* the stock of net source base to the rest of the country, *DDNE* the level of demand deposits in Northeast region, *DDROC* the level of demand deposits in the rest of the country, *KNE* the money multiplier for the Northeast, *KROC* the money multiplier for the rest of the country, *YNE* is the personal income in the Northeast region, *YROC* is the personal income in the rest of the country, *MNE* is the money supply (M1) in the Northeast region, *MROC* is the money supply (M1) in the rest of the country, *DDNE* is the level of demand deposits in the Northeast region, *DDROC* is the level of demand deposits in the rest of the country, *USG* is the Federal Reserve's holdings of government securities, *FF* is the federal reserve float, *FGS* is the gold stock, *OA* are other assets at the FED, *OL* are other liabilities at the FED, and *Q2, Q3* and *Q4* stand for quarterly dummies.

Miller's explanation of the workings of the model is as follows. The process begins with equations (5.16) and (5.17), with an exogenous monetary policy manipulation by the central monetary authority, the FED. This monetary manipulation changes the flow of net source to a region which is, in turn, amplified by the multiplier process (equations 5.18 and 5.19). This change in a region's money supply generates changes in a region's level of economic activity (equations 5.20 and 5.21). This change in a region's level of economic activity influences interregional economic relationships (interregional trade of goods and services) which, in turn, generate new inter-regional monetary flows (equations 5.22 and 5.23). These monetary flows change the region's net source base and, therefore, the process starts again.

The model was estimated for the period 1969–1975 using quarterly data for two regions: the Northeast region and the rest of the country. The Northeast region grouped the reserve districts of Boston, New York, Philadelphia and Cleveland. According to Miller's own conclusions:

> the regional pattern of monetary policy... supported a rate of growth in nominal personal income in the rest of the country which was greater than the rate of growth in nominal personal income in the northeast region

> (R.J. Miller 1978: 142)

However, just one page before this statement was made, he had also recognized that,

> the explanatory power of these reduced form equations [his empirical model] was inadequate, ... and [this low significance] suggested the need for additional explanatory variables, such as fiscal explanatory variables

> (R.J. Miller 1978: 141)

So far we have reviewed some works which have tried to assess empirically the issue of the regional impact of monetary policy. We have mainly focused our attention on those points which, we consider, conform to the main contribution made by each author. Many differences could be distinguished among the papers under review. Some of them have adopted some kind of reduced-form model, whereas others have chosen some kind of 'large' regional macroeconomic model. Differences have also arisen in the results. Some of them have given empirical support to the monetarist view of the (regional) business cycle. Others have proved that fiscal variables also matter.

In spite of these differences, there are also common points among all of them. We would underline two main ones. First, the money supply is considered as being perfectly exogenous to the system. That is, the central monetary authorities can exert a perfect control on money supply through open market operations. Second, the analysis has tried to isolate periods of tight monetary policy and see what the performance of regional economies has been by comparison with the national one.

However we find both hypotheses unsatisfactory. With regard to the second one, how could we possibly isolate the effect of monetary policy on income from the effect that all the other policies being implemented are having (fiscal, industrial, labour, regional, etc.)? That is, how could we develop a 'ceteris paribus' analysis? On the other hand, is money really so exogenous to the system? And if so, does it mean that financial intermediaries only play a neutral role in the transmission of monetary changes? That is, aren't financial intermediaries able to constrain (expand) lending, up to some extent, regardless of what the central bank does? Clearly, all these questions would modify the whole analysis and the conclusions of all the papers reviewed so far, and we strongly believe that they are very relevant indeed.

5.2.3   Spatial diffusion of open market operations

The third group contained in Table 5.1 is made up by those papers which have tried to assess the regional impact of monetary policy by looking at the 'regional lags' which may arise in the process of transmission of open market operations from central to peripheral money markets. This is a literature which is very much tied up to the US experience of the 1950s and 1960s regarding the relative effectiveness of open market operations and reserve requirement as the FED's instruments of monetary control. The debate was over the advantages and disadvantages of using one or another instrument. Those in favour of the use of open market operations claimed that open market operations were more flexible, easily applied and readily tuned. Those against open market operations claimed that reserve requirement changes exerted their effect over all components (regional FED districts) of the banking system, whereas open market operations were transmitted from central to non-central markets more slowly (McPheters 1976: 1009). The debate then went over the empirical side in order to test both the existence and length of these regional lags in adjusting to monetary changes.

One of the earlier papers in addressing the issue empirically was that by Scott (1955) which tried to estimate the lag in the transmission of open market operation from New York to the rest of the country. The period of study was 1951:6 to 1953:5 and the analysis consisted of comparing the time-pattern of free reserves by both FED districts and groups of banks. The hypothesis to be tested was whether tight monetary policy was first felt in central districts and after some lags in peripheral ones. Free reserves were then used as an inverse index of the effectiveness of restrictive monetary policy. The results indicated that there were important lags in the transmission of open market operations from central markets to the rest of the country.[7] That is, country reserves seemed to be less sensitive to the general decreasing trend followed by central reserve banks.

However, what Scott did not test was whether this comparison in sensitivity in country banks' free reserves was only explained by tight monetary policies or, on the contrary, the time pattern of free reserves was also influenced by other factors than the tight monetary policy. For example, different patterns in free reserves by banks could also be explained by both banks' and borrowers' differences in liquidity preference. That is, a bank could have a higher free-reserves ratio, either because it has decided not to lend or because their customers have decided not to borrow. On the contrary, Scott's argument ran as follows: (i) open market operations determine banks' reserves; (ii) banks maintain a fixed free reserves ratio; (iii) banks transmit tight monetary policy by reducing lending when their free-reserves are running out; (iv) those banks whose free reserves do not follow the general pattern are supposed to be isolated from tight monetary policies. However, our argument above suggests that the latter could also be explained by factors other than monetary policy.

Lawrence's (1963) paper was an attempt to distinguish between those two effects on regional banks' reserves: (i) changes due to general credit policies; and (ii) changes due to the local economic environment. Lawrence studied the US case for the period 1953–1961 and his main conclusions were that 'banks which serve primarily nonfarm business borrowers and depositors experience the greatest decline in reserve positions in periods of monetary restraint' (Lawrence 1963: 129–130).

One general criticism which applies to all these papers is that they all refer to the US case and, for this, their conclusions are only applicable to this particular institutional setting which clearly differs from the one in most other countries. Another criticism would be that what is meant by monetary policy (open market operations) is a very narrow concept since central banks dispose of many other monetary instruments to control liquidity (regulation, moral persuasion, etc.).

5.3   The regional finance literature

Apart from this literature, which has directly dealt with the issue of the regional impact of monetary policy, we will also survey some papers whose main aims focused on other regional financial matters. Table 5.2 offers a classification of such literature.

This is certainly a very broad literature and, because of this, we have decided to group it in three different categories. However, we are fully aware that what has been classified under one particular label may well possibly fall in more than one category to the extent that some papers have addressed

Table 5.2 Regional finance literature

Regional monetary multipliers	Dow (1982), Moore *et al.* (1985)
Interregional financial flow of funds	Gilbert (1937–1938), Hartland (1949), Bowsher *et al.* (1957), Lieberson and Schwirian (1962), Lees (1969), Alvarez-Llano and Andreu (1978), Fernández and Andreu (1978), Castells and Sicart (1980), Banco de Bilbao (1980), Short and Nicholas (1981), Carlino and Lang (1989)
Regional financial markets	
(a) Interest rate differentials	Henderson (1944), Carr (1960), Edwards (1964), Davis and Banks (1965), Schaaf (1966), Meyer (1967), Winger (1969), Straszheim (1971), Peterson (1973), Cebula and Zaharoff (1974), James (1976), Ostas (1977), Rockoff (1977), Hendershott and Kidwell (1978), Aspinwall (1979), Keleher (1979), Hutchinson and McKillop (1990), McKillop and Hutchinson (1990), D'Amico *et al.* (1990), Faini *et al.* (1993)
(b) Regional credit availability	Dreese (1974), Keleher (1977a), Roberts and Fishkind (1979), Moore and Hill (1982), Allen and Price (1984), Kannan (1987), Dow (1987a, 1987b, 1987c, 1988, 1990, 1992d, 1993b), Harrigan and McGregor (1987), Chick and Dow (1988), Moore and Nagurney (1989), Samolyk (1989, 1991, 1994), Hutchinson and McKillop (1990), Mckillop and Hutchinson (1990), Hughes (1991, 1992), Bias (1992), Amos (1992), Amos and Wingender (1993), Greenwald *et al.* (1993), Fainni *et al.* (1993), Messori (1993), Porteous (1995), Chick (1993a), Dow and Rodríguez-Fuentes (1997), Rodríguez-Fuentes (1998) and Rodríguez-Fuentes and Dow (2003)

Source: Dow and Rodríguez-Fuentes (1997: 904).

more than a single matter. Nevertheless, we have tried to classify the papers according to the main contribution made by each author.

First there is the literature whose focus is on how monetary multipliers are modified when monetary analysis includes interregional financial and trade flows. Another group is made up of the literature which focused its efforts on describing, rather than on explaining, interregional financial flows. Far more interesting is the literature which deals with the issue of regional financial markets. As far as this question is concerned, we have split our survey into two sections. The first one deals with the issue of regional interest rate differentials whereas the second one addresses a far more relevant literature, e.g. the one that looks at the factors determining regional availability of credit.

Although all these papers share common interests in regional financial matters, they clearly differ in their theoretical backgrounds, ranging from Neo-Classical explanations of regional differentials in interest rates to the New Keynesian literature of credit rationing, or the Post Keynesian literature on money and credit.

5.3.1 Regional monetary multipliers

The aim of this literature is to show how the standard national monetary multiplier model is modified when introducing the regional dimension, that is when the effect those interregional economic relationships (goods and financial flows) have on regional monetary base are considered. The main modification is that, when the monetary multiplier model is applied in a regional setting, a new source of base-reserves growth appears in comparison to the national case. In a regional setting, apart from open market operations and reserve requirement changes, the regional monetary base is also able to change due to the existence of real flows between regions which generate monetary flows, i.e. interregional exports (imports) either of goods and services or financial capital.

Moore *et al.* (1985) worked out the regional monetary multiplier which took the following expression (Moore *et al.* 1985: 32):

$$m = \frac{1+k}{1 - F_r(1-r)(1-i_0) + k + t} \tag{5.24}$$

where k stands for the ratio currency to demand deposits, t is the ratio of time deposits to demand deposits, r is the reserve ratio requirement, F_r is the portion of loanable funds which remain in the region when spent by regional bank borrowers, and i_0 is the portion of loanable funds invested outside the region. F_r and i_0 are the two factors which are new in the regional monetary multiplier. It is easy to see that the higher F_r (the lower i_0) the larger the regional multiplier. In the extreme case of $F_r = 1$ and $i_0 = 0$, the regional multiplier becomes the national one.

Even though the monetary multiplier model assumes perfect exogeneity of the money supply, it also introduces some interesting points which are worth considering from a regional point of view. We would mention two main ones. First, the monetary multiplier model allows behavioural parameters to have a role in the transmission of monetary changes. Behavioural parameters such as banks' and borrowers' liquidity preference which could lead regions experiencing higher liquidity preference to have the lower multipliers. Secondly, although it has been suggested that the monetary multiplier model does not match with the current stage of banking development in most developed economies,[8] perhaps it may well apply to some particular regions, particularly those having lower levels of banking development. These two considerations might open some room for monetary multiplier analysis in the regional level.

5.3.2   *Interregional financial flows*

The literature on interregional financial flows is much more concerned with the description and estimation of interregional financial flows rather than with its explanation. Perhaps the lack of regional data on financial matters is the reason for this emphasis on description rather than explanation.

There have been some attempts to estimate flows of fund between regions in different countries. Bowsher *et al.* (1957) and Lees (1969) have done it for the US case; Castells and Sicart (1980) and Banco de Bilbao (1980) for Spain; and Short and Nicholas (1981) for the UK regions. There have also been some other papers which by means of the use of money flows between regions have tried to assess intercity relationships (Lieberson and Schwirian 1962, Carlino and Lang 1989).

Nevertheless, an investigation of the methodology employed in most of these papers leads to doubts about the usefulness of most of these regional estimations. For example, a very common hypothesis which is used when it comes to estimating either regional currency, deposits or lending, is to divide the national currency according to regional GDP shares and, in the case of deposits and credits, according to personal disposable income by regions. Of course we are aware of both the difficulties surrounding any regional estimation and of the usefulness of having such information. We are not saying that most of these estimations are not useful at all. What we are suggesting instead is that we have to be aware of the limits of such estimations. For example, to assume the hypothesis mentioned above implies, from our point of view, two additional assumptions. First, it is being implicitly assumed that monetary flows mirror real ones, that is, that money is mainly demanded by the transaction motive. Secondly, it is also being assumed that no regional differences exist in terms of, for example, liquidity preference. That is, two regions having the same share in GDP will have the same currency, regardless of the differences in liquidity preference which could arise between them.

5.3.3 Regional credit markets

Within this block we have distinguished two groups. The first one deals with the issue of interest rate differentials. The other is much more concerned with the issue of regional credit markets and the factors determining regional credit availability.

5.3.3.1 Differentials in regional interest rates

Most of this literature refers to the US case. In fact, all papers except those by Hutchinson and McKillop (1990) and Faini *et al.* (1993), address the issue in the US during the 20th century, some papers even going back up to the end of the 19th century (such as Rockoff 1977). This is not surprising at all if we take into account the lack of regional financial data (and specifically on interest rates) in countries other than the US.

Within the US empirical literature we would distinguish three different approaches to the matter of the interregional differentials in interest rates.

The first group studied the topic from an 'efficiency market approach', that is, trying to see what the relationship between regional and national interest rates is like. Keleher's (1979) paper belongs to this category. Keleher estimated the following model for both the mortgage (new and existing homes) and business loan market (long and short term bank loans by size, and revolving credit bank loan by size) in the US. The periods of estimation were 1965:1 to 1977:12 for mortgages and 1967:1 to 1976:4 for bank loans.

$$i_{reg} = \alpha + \beta\, i_{us} + \mu \tag{5.25}$$

where i_{reg} is regional interest rate, i_{us} is the national interest rate, and μ is the random error.

Keleher concluded that regional financial markets were integrated because β_1 was significant and close to 1, and that interregional differentials in interest rates, which were accounted in the model through the constant (α), existed because of the regional differences in costs, risks and homogeneity of financial assets.

However, an interesting hypothesis, which was not tested by Keleher, would have been to study the behaviour of the constant term (α) over the business cycle. Indeed, it would have been interesting to see whether this term, which could be seen as the 'regional mark-up' in interest rates applied by banks, remained constant over the cycle, or if, on the contrary, it moved up and down along with the business cycle. Another interesting hypothesis to be tested would be to see whether significant differences in this mark-up exist for different agents, e.g. small and large businesses, etc.

The second of the groups we have distinguished is made up by those papers which have tried to test the sensitivity of interregional financial flows to regional differentials in interest rates. Cebula and Zaharoff (1974) tested the following model for the US regions for the period 1950–1971 in order to check whether regional financial flows were sensitive to differential in interest rates.

$$D_i = \alpha + \beta(r_i - r_j) + \mu \tag{5.26}$$

where D_i is the change in volume of total deposits in district i over period, r_i is the average rate of return on loans in district i, r_j is the average rate of return on loans in district j, and μ is the random error. The results confirmed the insensitivity of D_i to $(r_i - r_j)$, although, in the authors' view, this does not mean that markets are segmented, but that there are differences in risks and costs between regions which would remove any chance of making profitable transfers of funds between them.

The third and largest group of papers looked for reasons to explain regional interest differentials. Among the factors outlined we would point out the following:

- factors related to market structure such as concentration ratios, number of institutions, ceiling on interest rates, etc.;
- demand factors such as regional pressure on financial resources;
- risk factors, both on the demand (probability of delinquent payment) and supply (risk of bank failure[9]);
- cost factors;
- distance from central monetary markets.

In an early paper, Schaaf (1966) explained regional differences in mortgage rates in terms of risk, distance and demand pressure. The model was estimated for the period 1964–1974, and is shown below.

$$r = f(L, M, S) \tag{5.27}$$

where r is the mortgage yield, L is the loan-value ratio (risk measure), M is miles from Boston, and S is the state saving per average annual dwelling unit constructed (demand pressure factor).

Winger (1969) would later criticize the risk measure used by Schaaf (1966). According to this author, 'different lenders may not respond alike to the same risk options because they may differ in their assets preferences or in the regulatory constraints surrounding their operation' (Winger 1969: 662). He also added that regional differences in risks are a consequence of regional growth disparities.

The point made by Winger on the concept and measurement of risk is worth noting because it seems that anything which cannot be explained by empirical models is very often 'packed' under the label 'differential risk'.

This, in turn, has led to considering regional financial markets (either mortgage or loan markets) as if they were perfect, in the sense that they have been able to evaluate regional differences in costs and risks when allocating resources. However, it will be useful to think about how to measure risk and, further, whether risk is similar to uncertainty, and whether the latter would also have to be included in the analysis of the regional differentials in interest rates and credit rationing.

Another point made by Winger regarding the 'regulatory constraints' which could be affecting lenders' behaviour was also extremely important. For example, Ostas (1977) re-estimated Schaaf's (1966) model in order to include the effects of 'state usury ceilings' on mortgage market. The model was estimated for 1970–1972 and the results showed that 'usury ceilings' were the most powerful variable in the model.[10]

The model by Aspinwall (1979) was aimed to test the power of market concentration on regional mortgage interest rates and was estimated for the first months of 1965. The model included the following variables.

$$R = f(F, H, Y, L, B) \tag{5.28}$$

where R is the rate of interest, F is the number of mortgage lending institutions, H is change in number of households 1950–60, C is a concentration measure, Y is the median family income, L is the ratio of loan to dwelling price, and B is the log of average number of deposit accounts per commercial bank.

The results confirmed the power of variables related to market structure (F and C) and regional income (Y and H) in explaining regional interest rates. However, risk variable (L) did not seem to be significant.

The papers by Hutchinson and McKillop (1990), McKillop and Hutchinson (1990), D'Amico *et al.* (1990) and Faini *et al.* (1993), are among the few which have dealt with the issue of differential in regional interest from an empirical side in countries other than the US. Hutchinson and MacKillop (1990) and McKillop and Hutchinson (1990) addressed the issue for the UK and Northern Ireland cases, whereas the other two papers paid attention to the Italian case.

McKillop and Hutchinson (1990) found some evidence regarding the existence of different interest rates applied on loans to SMEs. As regards large businesses they concluded that no evidence of such regional differences existed and that this fact could be explained by the increased competition among banks for this segment of the market. As long as personal financing was concerned, and contrary to what theory would have suggested (higher interest rates in isolated regions), they concluded that

> the interest rates charged are, with one or two exceptions, either approximately equal across these three regions [England and Wales, Scotland and Northern Ireland] or highest in England and Wales
>
> (McKillop and Hutchinson 1990: 29)

However, they also pointed out that these comparisons focusing on interest rates alone 'omits important aspects of the lending process relating to bank charges and collateral requirements' (McKillop and Hutchinson 1990: 29) because these may vary across regions. It was because of this that the authors decided to look at the regional differences in bank charges and fees as they make up the 'true cost' of funds. Once these regional differences in bank charges and fees were included, some regional differences in the 'true cost' were found among the three regions (McKillop and Hutchinson 1990: 30–31). It still must be noted that the same authors also concluded in another paper that 'there is no evidence of a regional constraint nor of an interest rate structure significantly higher [for the Northern Ireland financial sector] than that which prevails at the national level [UK]' (Hutchinson and McKillop 1990: 430). The evidence would therefore seem inconclusive. However, it would be interesting to spell out further what is meant by 'significantly' higher, since sometimes regional differences in interest rates are explained as simple regional differential risks. If this were the case, then what had to be explained is how these risk differentials are accounted for and, further, whether banks are able to fully measure them or if instead they simply either add some mark-up when they simply do not know.

D'Amico *et al.* (1990) and Faini *et al.* (1993) also found some evidence of differential in interest rates between the Northern and Southern Italian regions. In particular, D'Amico *et al.* (1990) concluded that differentials in interest rates were due to differences in GDP per capita and to the particular composition of lenders (by size and sector). Those two variables accounted for almost 90 percent of the variability in interregional interest rates in Italy for the period 1969–1988. Other variables reflecting risk, such as the bad loan to total loans ratio, and concentration, such as the Herfindal concentration index, resulted in minor significance. The model estimated by them was:[11]

$$LR = f(COMP, GDP, BL, HERF, DUAG) \qquad (5.29)$$

where *LR* is the average lending rate charged by branches located in province, *COMP* is a composition effect which takes into consideration borrowers' size and economic sector, *GDP* is Gross Domestic Product per capita in each province, *BL* is the ratio of bad loans to total loans reported by local branches, *HERF* is the Herfindal index for each province, and *DUAG* is a dummy variable for the province of Agrimento (Sicilia).

5.3.3.2   Regional credit availability

Although most of the papers included in this section have a common concern, the analysis of the factors which determine regional credit availability, they clearly differ in the way they have approached the topic itself.

In order to organize our presentation we will distinguish, apart from the seminal papers by Roberts and Fishkind (1979), Moore and Hill (1982), Harrigan and McGregor (1987) and Dow (1987c), which set up the basis for the debate, three approaches which have tried to develop the topic from very different theoretical backgrounds. These three approaches could be roughly identified with the Neo-Classical general equilibrium models, the New Keynesian literature on credit rationing and, finally, the Post Keynesian literature on regional money and credit.

PERFECT CAPITAL MARKETS

The first of the approaches mentioned above, that is, the one which has tried to assess the issue through the development of some kind of general equilibrium model, is, certainly, the least extended among the scholars. This is so because money and financial flows are considered of minor, if any, relevance for regional economic growth, as it is assumed that financial resources perfectly flow from one to another region in order to fund the best investment alternative. The papers by Moore and Nagurney (1989) and, up to some point, Hughes (1991, 1992) would fit in this 'general equilibrium' category. For example, Moore and Nagurney assume that the interplay between the regional supply of funds, which is generally determined by a multiplier process, and the regional demand for funds, which is seen as mainly depending on interest rates, will create some 'equilibrium state' where:

> the supply interest rate at supply markets plus the transaction cost between a pair of supply and demand markets cannot exceed the demand interest rate at the demand market, if there is a positive monetary flow between this pair of supply and demand market
> (Moore and Nagurney 1989: 401)

Hence, so long as regional credit markets work properly there will exist equilibrating interregional financial flows between regions which, in turn, makes money of no relevance at the regional level. The only chance for money to play a role arises when 'something' exists which makes markets work incorrectly. The Neo-Classical view of the process could be summed up as follows: let the market work alone and money will be allocated in the 'best place'.

CREDIT MARKET SEGMENTATION: EARLY CONTRIBUTIONS

However, as we earlier suggested, this has not been the way in which most research on this topic has developed. Indeed, rather than assuming perfect interregional financial flows, most of the research has been concerned with the identification of the factors which does not allow markets to work in a

'Neo-Classical way'. This was certainly the path followed by those early seminal papers cited above.

Roberts and Fishkind's (1979) paper was inspired by Lösch's study of spatial fluctuations in interest rates (Lösch 1954), and tried to identify the factors which could lead to segmentation in regional credit markets. They identified three main factors which could explain regional segmentation. The first of them was related to the availability of information by regional agents. Roberts and Fishkind considered that, as knowledge and information about financial conditions outside the region are only available at some costs, these costs could lead to some regional segmentation in credit markets so long as they could remove the possibility of profitable financial arbitrage between regional and national financial markets. Additionally, the more isolated a region is, the higher the costs of obtaining information are; isolated regions are the most likely to suffer from segmentation in their credit markets. The second factor pointed out by Roberts and Fishkind was the existence of non-homogeneous financial assets among regions. Non-homogeneity of financial assets makes comparisons between them difficult to assess. Hence, the non-homogeneity of financial assets in terms of liquidity, maturity or risk, could also be another factor explaining segmentation in regional financial markets. Thirdly, they also considered that regional differences in liquidity preferences and risk aversion could lead to differences in terms of interest sensitivity of both supply and demand for assets. The foregoing led the authors to five conclusions (Roberts and Fishkind 1979: 20–22):

- Regional interest rates may be different from the national ones (either higher or lower).
- Regional interest rates vary around national ones between two bands which stand for regional differences in costs.
- The more isolated a region, the wider their bands and, therefore, the higher its regional variability in interest rates. The wider bands would be explained by the higher transaction costs, lower availability and more costly information on financial conditions that the higher isolation implies.
- The more isolated the region, the more inelastic both supply and demand for regional assets. With regard to the demand side this inelasticity would reflect local borrowers' higher dependency on banking funds, both because these are likely to be mostly personal and small businesses, and because of their isolation from central financial markets. The higher inelasticity of supply could reflect higher banks' 'perceived risk' or costlier 'risk-assessment' for 'peripheral markets' (isolated regions).
- Regional differences in IS and LM elasticities would lead to different regional impacts of monetary policy.

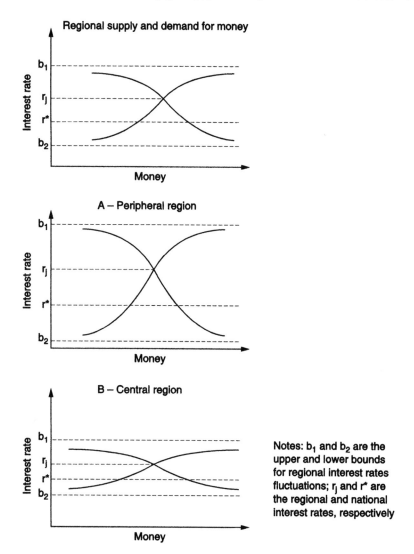

Figure 5.1 Roberts and Fishkind's analysis.

Apart from their theoretical analysis, Roberts and Fishkind also quoted some empirical evidence (Ebner 1976) which supported the hypothesis of regional segmentation in financial markets.[12]

Moore and Hill (1982) added a new factor to the three ones pointed out by Roberts and Fishkind which could lead to some kind of regional segmentation within regional credit markets: the distinction between small and large borrowers and lenders.

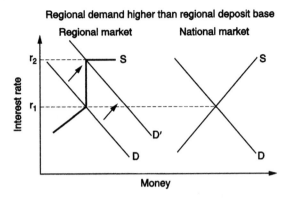

Figure 5.2 Moore and Hill's analysis.

Moore and Hill's (1982) analysis considers regional supply of funds as determined by a regional bank multiplier process and, therefore, limited for the regional deposit base. The demand for funds is considered to operate quite independently of the regional supply. They consider that the excess of demand could only be met if banks lend more locally or if they get more funds from outside the region. However, they noted that this arbitrage between local and national markets would be less than perfect because some local borrowers and lenders (small business and household sector and, possibly, some local banks) do not have access to national markets (lack of information).

The arbitrage between local and national financial markets was also developed by Harrigan and McGregor (1987) in a more straightforward way, but retaining the main ideas already put forward by both Roberts and Fishkind's (1979) and Moore and Hill's (1982) papers. The issue of the regional segmentation of credit markets has also been addressed from an empirical point of view (Hutchinson and McKillop 1990, McKillop and Hutchinson 1990, Amos 1992, Bias 1992).

As suggested earlier, McKillop and Hutchinson (1990) and Hutchinson and McKillop (1990) addressed this matter in the UK case, and found some evidence regarding regional differentials in both interest rates and fees (McKillop and Hutchinson 1990: 29–31). But they also addressed another issue: whether a credit constraint existed for the Northern Ireland economy with respect to the UK case. Their analysis proceeded by comparing the assets and liabilities of the Northern Ireland clearing banks and the British banks for the years 1977, 1980, 1982, 1985 and 1987. The hypothesis to be tested was that Northern Ireland banks had a proportionately lower deposit base, higher liquidity and lower bank advances, with respect to the British banks. They concluded that there was 'no evidence of an overall limit on the regional supply of credit' and, accordingly, that the Northern Ireland financial sector was a part of an integrated market in spite of being distant from the central market, and having particular political and financial characteristics (Hutchinson and McKillop 1990: 428–430).

Bias (1992) found some evidence of regional segmentation in US financial markets. By means of the estimation of the following equation, Bias tries to demonstrate that regional differences in terms of interest rate sensitivity exist and, therefore, regional segmentation in financial markets. The model was estimated for 12 US states for the period 1967–1986.

$$\frac{M_i}{P_i} = f(Realfed, Drate, Realbase, Population, e_i) \tag{5.30}$$

where M_i/P_i stands for regional[13] M1 supply, *Realfed* for FED's stock of treasury securities (open market operations), *Drate* for discount rate, *Realbase* is a proxy for regional basic-income (manufacturing and mining sectors) and e_i is a random error. *Population* entered as a scale variable to retain the regional size, and all variables were deflated. The results showed regional differences in terms of both *Realfed* and *Drate*, and this was interpreted by Bias as proof of regional segmentation in financial markets (Bias 1992: 331–332).

The paper by Dow (1987c) added three new points to Moore and Hill's analysis. One point was the interdependent character of demand for and supply of credit. Dow suggested that regional monetary base, apart from open market operations and interregional financial flows, could also be influenced by regional demand for credit. That is:

$$B = B(H_r, \overline{F}_r, C_r^d) \tag{5.31}$$

where B stands for regional monetary base, H_r for liabilities of the monetary authority (open market operation), F_r is the exogenous component of regional balance of payment and C_r^d is the regional demand for credit. This point was clearly aimed at introducing the endogenous character of the money supply. The second factor she distinguished was the recognition of the 'speculative component' in the demand for money and, hence, the role played by liquidity preference in the regional credit creation process. The introduction of both the endogeneity of money and the liquidity preference led to the reversal of the causation acknowledged in Moore and Hill's analysis. That is, instead of only considering the possibility that changes in regional income could lead to changes in regional deposits and credits, as Moore and Hill assumed, Dow also opened the possibility for changes in regional liquidity preference (due to greater/lower confidence in regional economy) to lead to endogenous changes in regional credit and, therefore, changes in regional income, instead of the other way round.

A third factor added by Dow's (1987c) paper was the role played by the institutional financial structure. The question addressed was whether the existence of a branch banking system would alter the conclusions reached in her analysis. Indeed, it has been suggested that regions face a mark-up horizontal supply of funds because regional bank branches are able to lend beyond their regional deposit base. This, in turn, means that credit availability is no longer a problem for regions so long as its supply is perfectly elastic at some mark-up over the national interest rate. However, Dow concluded that, even when a branch banking system exists, we cannot assume a regional perfectly elastic supply of funds because, although a low regional deposit base would not necessarily mean less regional credit, it might mean a higher regional liquidity preference on behalf of the national banks and this, in turn, will be the factor which will constrain the regional extension of bank lending. Therefore, and despite the endogenous character of regional money supply, credit availability still remains as a variable that matters for regional analysis.

THE NEW KEYNESIAN REGIONAL LITERATURE ON CREDIT RATIONING

The second distinctive approach noted above consists of the recent attempts to extend the New Keynesian credit-rationing literature to a regional setting (Samolyk 1989, 1991, 1994, Greenwald *et al.* 1993, Faini *et al.* 1993). Unlike the modifications to Neo-Classical models discussed above, which introduce information problems as the regional element, the new Keynesians start with an imperfect information model and apply it to regions. This literature focuses on how asymmetric and imperfect information could lead to low capital mobility and, further, to misallocation of financial resources and regional credit-rationing.[14]

The New Keynesian literature points out that, because of the existence of regional segmentation in credit markets, local banks' wealth, as a determinant factor of banks' ability to extend lending, can become one of the factors which explain regional credit-rationing. Indeed, as local banks are more likely to have superior information on local investment opportunities than outsiders and, therefore, they can monitor them at lower costs, this makes local investors more dependent on local financial institutions because of the unwillingness of national institutions to lend regionally.

Building on this analysis, Samolyk (1991, 1994) developed an empirical model to test for a relationship between banking conditions and economic performance at the state level in the US. The underlying hypothesis was that the existence of information costs may lead to credit constraints in some financially 'distressed regions', but not in financially 'sound regions'. Three models were tested for the period 1983–1990 taking the following form as the more general one:

$$y_{it} = B_0 \, y_{i,t-1} + \sum B_i \, CREDIT_{i,t-1} + \mu \qquad (5.32)$$

where *y* stands for 'growth rate of real gross state product minus growth rate of real gross national product' and *CREDIT* includes variables for regional credit conditions such as: (i) real growth rate of loan loss reserves; (ii) non-performing loan share; (iii) per capita volume of failed business liabilities; (iv) real growth rate of domestic loans; and (v) bank ROA. The second specification tested for differences in this relationship for 'poor' and 'good credit health' states in order to see whether this general relationship changed, depending on whether states had a non-performing loans ratio which was high or low with respect to the national share. The third model was aimed at studying the relationship between low and high income growth states.

Samolyk's conclusions were that 'local-banking sector conditions explain more of real income growth in states where bank loan quality has been poor than in those whose banking conditions are relatively healthy' (Samolyk 1994: 259) thus confirming the power of local banks to affect the local economy when regional segmentation exists.

Faini *et al.* (1993) also tried to build up some relationships between, on the one hand, local banks' monopoly power and banking inefficiencies and, on the other hand, low economic performance for Southern Italy. Particularly, their analysis suggests that the low productivity shown by Southern Italy could be explained by inefficiencies of the financial sector, and that this latter aspect is related to informational problems in Southern Italian credit markets.

The New Keynesian literature, as summarized in Figure 5.3, suggests that asymmetric information explains credit rationing since it inhibits the provision of credit by national (outsider) institutions in regional markets when local ones fail to do it. This conclusion poses the further question of how far branching of national banks in credit-constrained regions would get around the problem of asymmetric information. Porteous (1995) concludes that the optimal banking structure to address the problem of monitoring costs for firms in peripheral regions is a mixed one, with small local banks providing credit to small local firms.

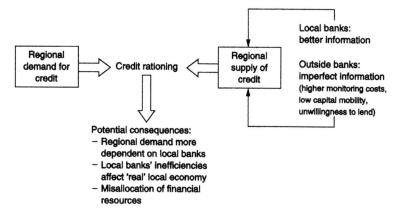

Figure 5.3 New Keynesian theory on regional credit.

THE POST KEYNESIAN REGIONAL VIEW ON THE CREDIT CREATION PROCESS

Rather than focusing on why a perfect flow of financial resources among regions does not exist, the Post Keynesian literature on regional money and credit takes market imperfection as the norm and focuses on the study of regional patterns of credit creation, and how these may vary from one region to another. In so doing Post Keynesian theory makes use of both Chick's stages of banking development and the Keynesian principle of liquidity preference.[15]

Although there are some parallels between the New Keynesian and the Post Keynesian theories, a closer look reveals significant differences. A particular feature of the Post Keynesian theory is that its analysis addresses both the supply side and the demand side of the regional credit market. New Keynesian literature is mainly concerned with the supply side issue of how imperfect information segments regional markets. Regional credit rationing could arise then as a result of the unwillingness of non-local financial institutions to lend within the region (because of their lack of information to assess local project riskiness and profitability). However, post Keynesians point out that credit rationing could also be explained by demand factors to the extent that the amount of regional credit is the result of the interaction between supply and demand, and because both functions are interdependent, being affected by changes in liquidity preference. This point was already raised in Dow's (1987c) modification of Moore and Hill's (1982) analysis. As a consequence, Post Keynesian theory suggests that the understanding of the regional credit creation process implies the analysis both of the supply and demand side of the market. Hence, regional credit rationing is not seen as a unicausal situation explained by regional-discriminatory behaviour on the part of the financial system (mainly banks) which, in turn, leads to an uneven regional distribution of credit, but as a multi-causal situation in which all sectors in the region are involved (Figure 5.4). This is what Dow (1992d) has labelled 'defensive financial

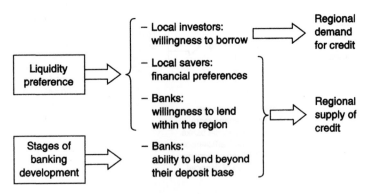

Figure 5.4 Post Keynesian theory on regional credit.

behaviour', which we now explore in more detail in terms of the regional supply of and demand for credit.

Regarding the supply side, Post Keynesian theory considers that regional credit supply is affected both by regional liquidity preference and the stage of bank development. The stage of banking development determines banks' ability to extend credit regardless of their deposit base, either regional or national, i.e. the degree of endogeneity of money supply. The lower the stage of bank development, the more applicable the money multiplier model is. This would imply that regions having banking systems in lower stages of development would be more constrained by, say, lower saving or deposit ratios than others. Thus, local banks at an earlier stage of development than national or international banks will find themselves at a competitive disadvantage, including a lesser capacity to create credit. However, once the banking system reaches higher stages, the foregoing no longer applies. The former analysis also implies that, depending on the own stage of banking development, the constraints on credit expansion are able to change and so the relevant monetary theory also should change.

Post Keynesian theory allows liquidity preference to affect regional suppliers of credit and regional demand for credit. From the banks' point of view, liquidity preference influences the willingness to lend within the region when regional perceived risk is higher or its assessment is more difficult.[16] The New Keynesian approach refers to risk assessment as an objective process, where in principle full information would allow the generation of a risk measure. The Post Keynesian approach rather sees all credit-risk assessment as being subject to uncertainty of varying degrees (Dow 1995, 1998, 2004); that uncertainty is perceived to be greater the more remote the borrower from the lender (where remoteness may be spatial, cultural, etc.: see Porteous 1995). Banks' liquidity preference may hence be influenced by both regional expectations regarding regional income growth, regional instability, etc., and by the expected effects of 'monetary conditions' created by the central bank.

Liquidity preference not only affects lenders' behaviour but also exerts its effect on savers' behaviour. For example, higher liquidity preference encourages savers to adopt more liquid portfolios and that liquidity is more likely to be supplied by extra-regional assets. An increase in liquidity preference by regional agents in peripheral regions could then lead to an outflow of financial resources to central regions which may reduce local availability of funds. Whether or not this outflow affects regional credit availability depends on: (i) the ability of the banking sector to expand credit regardless of its regional deposit base; and (ii) the effect that such regional outflows have on banks' own regional liquidity preference. However, what is worth noting is that this effect has its origins in non-financial sectors.

The demand side has to take into account the effect that liquidity preference could have on the regional demand for credit. For example, lower expectations regarding the regional economy (higher liquidity preference) could lower the regional demand for funds to the extent that investors are less willing to run into debt. Higher regional expectations could drive up regional demand for credit and, to the extent that the banking system shares the optimism and is able to extend credit beyond its deposit-base (a factor which depends on its stage of development), could also increase the regional supply of credit. It is this interdependence between supply of and demand for credit which makes it difficult to identify whether any regional 'credit gap' exists. Some authors have tried to assess the matter in terms of declining long run credit shares by peripheral regions and have found no clear evidence of such a trend. Porteous (1995), for example, presents some empirical evidence from Australia (1950–84) and Canada (1975–90), suggesting that, overall, 'there is little strong evidence of systematic discrimination by national banks as seen in long-run credit shares or in the extent of rationing' (Porteous 1995: 193). Porteous further concluded that: (i) wealthier regions have higher shares of bank credit; (ii) there is no evidence of declining shares of credit in peripheral regions; (iii) monetary policy does not discriminate against peripheral regions; and (iv) some evidence suggests the existence of credit rationing in peripheral regions, but this evidence is not conclusive.

However, Post Keynesian theory does not claim long run decreases in regional credit shares by peripheral regions. It rather claims unstable patterns in regional credit creation in the sense that credit creation can fuel expansions and enhance recessions, generating greater instability.[17] Some empirical evidence for the Spanish regions can be found in the papers by Rodríguez-Fuentes (1998) and Rodríguez-Fuentes and Dow (2003). Since money is credit-driven, rather than the other way around, the issue is no longer limited to looking at whether banks lend more than they borrow regionally, as is often suggested. The matter is no longer how a fixed amount of credit is divided up among regions, but how credit is created (or not) regionally. The focus then is on the interdependent relationships between credit, deposits, money supply and income over business cycles. For example, credit is expected to increase during economic upturns because of higher banks' and borrowers' willingness to lend and borrow, respectively. The deposit total depends on whether most of this credit flows outside the region in terms of imports and capital outflows. Therefore, a high credit/deposit ratio is expected during expansions in peripheral regions. However, what happens in recessions is more difficult to predict. Credit demand and supply are expected to be low during downturns because of higher liquidity preference on behalf of both investors and lenders. Nevertheless, a regional credit gap could still exist to the extent that there is a need to finance working capital. At the same time, higher liquidity preference could lead to financial outflows if safer and more liquid financial assets are not provided within the region. Whether the credit/deposit ratio remains high or low with regard to the expansion phase will depend on the significance of each of the above mentioned factors (credit demand, credit supply and financial outflows). However, no deterministic relationships are to be expected because some of the factors affecting them cannot be deterministically measured or foreseen (such as changes in liquidity preference), or can be modified by others (such as the institutional setting).

5.4 The 'new' orthodox literature on the regional impact of monetary policy

The debate over the economic consequences of the EMU has mainly been developed on two fronts. The first one started with the analysis of the efforts needed in order for members to meet the official criteria to take part in this process (the nominal convergence criteria established in the Maastricht Treaty), the likely uneven spatial distribution of benefits and costs among members of the EMU and its potential consequences for economic growth and employment (higher economic policy coordination and the loss of monetary and exchange rate national policies). However, once the European Union entered the third and final stage of EMU, in January 1999, the discussion moved on to another front: the transmission of the single monetary policy to different member economies.[18] In particular, there is an increasing concern for the implications that differences in financial structure across countries in the euro area[19] may have for the transmission mechanism of the monetary policy in EMU since, for some authors, those differences may produce a differential impact of the ECB's monetary policy (see for example Kashyap and Stein 1997b, Cecchetti 1999, Bondt 2000).

In this section we briefly review this later literature, although some comments will also be made for the first strand of the above-mentioned literature. According to our exposition, the orthodox literature on the regional impact of European monetary policy will be classified into three broad categories (Table 5.3).

First, there is a group of studies which are based on the Optimum Currency Areas approach. Most of these papers are concerned with the asymmetric shocks or asymmetric responses to shocks of member economies of a currency union. The Optimum Currency Area literature has also paid close attention to the mechanisms that would lead economies to recover from an asymmetric shock (wage–price flexibility and labour mobility), or the consequences of a common monetary policy when the currency union member economies show a low business cycle correlation. The second body of literature only assesses differences in responses to monetary policy shocks without giving any formal explanation for the diverse responses. Finally, there is the literature that tries to offer some potential explanations for the differences in responses to monetary policy shocks. The differential effect of monetary policy is usually explained by the asymmetric impact of national monetary shocks on regions having structural differences with respect to the national average (these differences increase the sensitivity of some regions to exogenous changes in national interest rates or business cycles). Sometimes,

Table 5.3 Classification of the new orthodox literature on the regional impact of European monetary policy

Theoretical framework	Assumptions	Explanatory variables
Optimum Currency Area (OCA) framework	• Asymmetric shocks • Asymmetric responses to shocks • Adjustment mechanisms to shocks • Business cycles synchronization	• Sectoral composition • Lack of nominal flexibility (wage and price flexibility and labour mobility) • Lack of business cycle synchronization
Orthodox Monetary Theory (small reduced form models and alike)	• Regional differences in responses to monetary policy shocks	• No explicit or quantitative explanation is provided (but qualitative arguments point to economic and financial structure)
Orthodox Monetary Theory (large macroeconomic models) and New Keynesian Monetary Theory (credit view)	• Regional differences in responses to monetary policy shocks due to heterogeneous economic and financial structures	• Sectoral and demand composition (interest-sensitive industries and expenditure) • Openness (exchange rate effect on net exports) • Firms' size (bank dependence firms) • Banking market structure (concentration, external dependence, ownership, legal framework, . . .) • Banks' size and health • Balance sheet effects • Availability of non-bank sources of finance

Source: Adapted from Rodríguez-Fuentes and Dow (2003: 971).

the differential impact of monetary policy is explained by the central role played by the banking system in some regions, both in the transmission of monetary policy and in the provision of credit. This view thus presumes some segmentation in financial markets, due to market failure and/or asymmetric information, to the extent that borrowers in some regions might not have access to a full, substitutable, range of sources of finance. This literature draws on New Keynesian monetary theory. In other cases the differences in responses to monetary policy shocks are also related to differences in economic structure as well as financial factors.

5.4.1   The economic consequences of currency unions: the case of the EMU

The analysis of the economic consequences of the euro has been primarily developed within the Optimum Currency Areas (OCA) literature. This approach was applied early in the history of European monetary unification by Magnifico (1973), building on the pioneering work of Mundell (1961), McKinnon (1963) and Kenen (1969). A comprehensive treatment of this literature in the context of the European monetary integration can be found in De Grauwe (1997).

This approach assumes that the single monetary policy would have asymmetric effects in the presence of structural differences among euro countries; the single monetary policy would be more suitable for some economies than others. As devaluation is no longer available, any asymmetric shock can only be offset by greater economic flexibility, defined as wage and price flexibility and mobility of factors of production (the emphasis in Europe being on labour mobility, since capital mobility is already high).

This approach has resulted in a large amount of empirical literature that is concerned with the asymmetric shocks or asymmetric responses to shocks of member economies of a currency union. For example, Krugman (1993) has suggested that the EMU would cause a higher vulnerability[20] of some regions to asymmetric shocks, since economic integration leads to higher specialization. Bayoumi and Eichengreen (1993: 222–223) used structural vector auto-regression to identify supply and demand shocks and found important differences in responses to supply shocks between the 'core' and 'periphery' countries, the shocks to the core being both smaller and more correlated across neighbouring countries. The same results were found for the demand shocks, although the differences between core and periphery countries were now less dramatic. The same argument is put forward in the studies by Karras (1996) and Kouparitsas (1999). Karras concludes that Europe is not an optimum currency area since 'country-specific shocks are both large and asymmetric', whereas Kouparitsas points out that the EMU will not be a viable currency area for all European countries.

The OCA literature has also paid close attention to the adjustment mechanisms that would lead economies to recover from an asymmetric shock (wage–price flexibility and labour mobility). Empirical evidence points to a lower degree of labour mobility in Europe (De Grauwe and Vanhaverbeke 1991, Emerson *et al.* 1992, Eichengreen 1993), and so has usually concluded that the EMU is not an optimum currency union since its adjustment mechanisms rely more on public transfers than on price flexibility and factor mobility (Obstfeld and Peri 1998).

The consequences of a common monetary policy when the currency union member economies present a low business cycle correlation has also been a matter of concern within the OCA literature. Employing Optimum Currency Area theory, Carlino and DeFina (1996, 1999) identify the regional impact of monetary policy with the effect of national monetary policy on regional business cycles. Carlino and DeFina's aim is to identify the factors that make some regions more sensitive to national business cycles than others, which (following a monetarist approach) they consider to be caused by monetary shocks. To this end Carlino and DeFina (1996) estimated a VAR model to analyze regional responses to business cycles in the US during 1958–1992. They concluded that regional sensitivity to business cycles was stronger in regions with larger shares of interest-sensitive industries and smaller firms. These conclusions were also confirmed for the state level in Carlino and DeFina (1999).

Ramos *et al.* (1999a) studied the regional impact of single monetary policy by looking at the output correlation among some EMU countries, since a lower correlation may indicate that a single monetary policy may not fit to all. The authors found higher output correlation in the 1980s and this evidence was interpreted as indicative of a lower probability for the single monetary policy to produce asymmetric shocks (demand shocks). However, they also found evidence of higher probability for EMU countries to suffer supply shocks in the 1990s. Angeloni and Dedola (1999) have also found evidence of a higher cross-country correlation among EMU countries in terms of real cycles and inflation. They concluded that these results and the convergence in terms of monetary policy rules followed by the main Eurosystem central banks would reduce the harmful effects of the Single European Monetary Policy. Mihov (2001) has also recently suggested that policy-coordination among EMU countries has contributed to a higher correlation among business cycles during the 1990s.

Overall the pre-EMU empirical literature did not deliver a definitive answer to the question of whether the EMU would be viable for all European countries. In any case, the third and final stage of the EMU started in January 1999 and since then there have not been many shocking aspects which could be solely attributed to it. There is considerable evidence suggesting that Europe is not an optimum currency area. But there are also some authors who argue (Suardi 2001) that these differences are much lower among those European countries which are part of the euro area (such as Belgium, Germany, Spain, France, Italy and Holland), than between euro countries and European non-euro countries (such as Sweden and the United Kingdom). In addition, Suardi points out that the introduction of the euro has removed the differential effect that monetary policy had in the past through exchange rate fluctuations, and has also contributed to improved functioning of financial markets, and thus capital mobility. Some authors have also suggested that the differential effect of the single monetary policy would be reduced in the future as the process of economic integration continues and economic policy coordination increases (see, among many others, Dornbusch *et al.* 1998: 52, Ehrmann 1998: 28, Arnold 1999: 22, Arnold and Vries 2000: 213, Clausen 2001: 172). However, since the third and final stage of EMU did take place in January 1999, the most urgent question now seems to be what the regional effects of the common monetary policy could be. This issue is addressed in the next section.

5.4.2 Regional differences in the transmission mechanism of monetary policy: the case of the EMU

In the last decade many empirical papers have attempted to study the differences in the transmission mechanism of the common monetary policy in Europe. In spite of these efforts, the empirical evidence has not provided a clear answer to the issue, so the topic remains controversial. This section reviews some of these papers with the aim of summarizing what empirical work has been able to sort out and to identify the issues which are still far from being resolved. We do not mean to offer an exhaustive and complete list of empirical papers in this section, but to illustrate the key aspects of the issue with our particular selection of literature.[21]

A quick look at the empirical literature reveals, among other things, the following interesting aspects. There are a large number of papers whose only aim is testing differences among euro countries in their responses to monetary policy shocks. The objective of this strand of the literature is to find a definitive answer to the issue of whether (or not) differences in the responses to monetary policy shocks exist. This strand usually overlooks the point that monetary policy might work differently, not only across countries or regions, but also alongside business cycles as well as depending on the 'behavioural responses' of economic agents. Other papers focus on providing explanations for the differences in responses to monetary policy, but these explanations are almost always related to macroeconomic structural differences and very little is said about those (macro and/or microeconomic) factors that influence the responses of economic agents.[22] Consequently, it is difficult to identify which part of the asymmetric effects is due to structural differences and which part is due to the behaviour of the economic agents (Mazzola *et al.* 2002). This is an important issue since structural differences might disappear and this would not necessarily mean that asymmetries in the transmission of monetary policy would auto-matically vanish: there would be still scope for asymmetries arising from differences in the behavioural responses of economic agents to monetary policy.[23] Finally, there is a wide range of econometric methods used in empirical testing, none of them free from criticism, and this makes it difficult to compare results across different studies (Kieler and Saarenheimo 1998, Guiso *et al.* 1999).

The remaining part of this section reviews some contributions aimed at empirically testing for differences in responses to monetary policy shocks in the EMU, including those which explicitly have tried to offer some explanations for the differences in responses. Finally, this section concludes by summarizing some of the most important issues raised in our survey of the literature.

5.4.2.1   Testing for differences in responses to monetary policy shocks

The empirical literature studying differences in the transmission mechanism of monetary policy in Europe could be classified into two different groups: large and small econometric models (Dornbusch *et al.* 1998: 31–36). The group of the small econometric models is by far both larger and more diverse than the first group. In addition, most empirical papers included in the second group employ Vector Autoregression Models (VAR) to study differences in responses to monetary policy shocks[24] even though these models have been subject to some important criticism.[25]

One example of a large-scale model is the work conducted by the Bank for International Settlements (BIS 1995) to study the transmission mechanism of monetary policy in some industrialized countries.[26] The empirical results of this project showed differences among some EMU countries in terms of their responses to monetary policy shocks, with the larger countries having stronger responses (Guiso *et al.* 1999: 58–59).

The group of small-scale models is more numerous and diverse (from an econometric point of view). Most contributions in this group are based on reduced-form models and the Vector Autoregresion Models (VAR) is the most preferred econometric tool. The countries' responses to monetary policy shocks are studied by means of a VAR model, sometimes with a common structure for every single country, and sometimes with a different structure depending on idiosyncratic aspects which differ from one economy to another. This is the case, for example, in Mojon and Peersman (2001) and Ehrmann (1998), which allow for different VAR specifications in the countries considered. In other cases the countries' response is studied by estimating a VAR model for the EMU area as whole, as if the current EMU member countries had also been engaged in a currency union before it really started in January 1999. The papers by Peersman and Smets (2001), Clements *et al.* (2001) and Peersman (2003) belong to this category.

Table 5.4 Some VAR literature on differences in responses to monetary policy shocks in EMU

	No (or little) cross-country differences	Cross-country differences
VAR with same structure for every country	Gerlach and Smets (1995) Barran *et al.* (1996) Kieler and Saarenheimo (1998)	Ramaswamy and Sloek (1998) Cecchetti (1999) Dedola and Lippi (2000, 2005) McCoy and McMahon (2000) Altavilla (2000) Lo Cascio (2001)
VAR with different structure for every country	Mojon and Peersman (2001)	Ehrmann (1998)
VAR for the whole EMU area	Clements *et al.* (2001) Peersman (2003)	Peersman and Smets (2001)

It is worth mentioning that none of the three alternatives is free from criticisms.[27] Table 5.4 contains some of the contributions made from the VAR literature. The papers considered have been classified according to the following two criteria. We first consider the structure of the VAR model. Then, we look at their conclusions on whether significant cross-country differences were found in terms of responses to monetary policy shocks. A quick look at the table reveals that the results obtained from VAR models are ambiguous and may be 'of only limited relevance for the issue at hand' (Guiso *et al.* 1999: 59).

5.4.2.2 Explaining differences: financial and economic structure heterogeneity

This section considers some of the studies which see the differential regional impact of monetary policy as being caused by differences in economic and/or financial structure among EMU countries. This is the case of Carlino and DeFina's (1998) paper, which provides a ranking of the EMU countries according to their likely sensitivity to a monetary policy shock. Using the empirical evidence found in earlier US studies (Carlino and DeFina 1996), they construct an index to measure the regional effect of ECB monetary policy. They use a VAR model to study the long run response of US states to changes in interest rates. These responses are then regressed on a set of variables (industry mix, firms' size and some banking variables) to explain regional differences. Finally, the estimated coefficients are used to weight some variables included in the index for the EMU countries. The index only takes into account the differences in terms of industry-mix and banks' size, since firms' size was not found significant for the US case. According to their results, three different groups of EMU countries could be distinguished. First, the group of countries most sensitive to monetary policy shocks: Finland, Ireland and Spain; secondly, the group of less-sensitive countries: France, Italy and Netherlands; thirdly, a group with a response close to the EU average: Austria, Belgium, Portugal, Germany and Luxembourg.

For both Arnold (1999) and Guiso *et al.* (1999), the regional effect of the single European monetary policy is again ascribed to differences in economic structure. In particular Arnold (1999) suggests that it is the differential share of industrial employment that explains the differential effect of ECB monetary policy in 68 EU regions. Guiso *et al.* (1999) pay more attention to microeconomic factors, such as business size, propensity to export and location for a survey of business in Italy.

Following the work by Carlino and Defina (1998), Ramos *et al.* (1999b) focused on the regional incidence of Spanish monetary policy by means of the construction of an index that included some of the key variables to explain regional sensitivity to changes in interest rates: sector-mix and firm size. The results showed a high spatial variability in the index values, and therefore seemed to confirm the differential regional incidence of monetary policy in Spain during 1985–1992.

Mihov (2001) also follows the Carlino and Defina (1998) paper to explain heterogeneity in responses to monetary policy shocks. They found that the effects of monetary policy shocks on output are smoother in Anglo-Saxon countries and stronger in Germany. The paper also provides empirical evidence on the heterogeneity in responses within (across regions) Germany, Italy and France.

The paper by Kashyap and Stein (1997b) suggests that regional differences in financial structure in Europe might become a source of (regional) concern for the transmission of the single monetary policy. Kashyap and Stein base their analysis on the assumption that banks play a key role in the transmission of monetary policy, an assumption which clearly contrasts with the 'money view' which is usually assumed in conventional monetary theory. Their arguments rely on empirical evidence about the discriminatory effects of monetary policy changes on large and small business financing, thus they adopt a 'bank-centric view' in order to take into account the importance of bank size in the transmission of monetary policy.[28] They argue that larger banks are more likely to overcome periods of tight money, so that small banks lending is more sensitive to monetary policy changes. Their theoretical conclusions are that the effects of monetary policy are not uniform if there are regional differences in the following variables: (a) the incidence of bank-dependent firms; and (b) bank size and soundness (strong vs weak banking system). After analyzing differences among EMU countries in terms of firm size and the availability of non-bank sources of finance (as proxies for bank-dependence), and the size distribution of banks (as a proxy for bank soundness), they conclude that a single monetary policy will affect more strongly those countries with weaker banks, smaller firms and banks, and less availability of non-bank sources of finance.

Cecchetti (1999) comes to the same conclusion as Kashyap and Stein, namely that differences in financial structure, such as size, concentration, banks' health, and the availability of non-bank sources of finance, may produce asymmetries in the transmission of monetary policy in Europe. Contrary to the official view of the European Commission, he argues that further steps in the process of monetary integration will not necessarily lead to the removal of such differences in financial structure in Europe unless there is an equalization in terms of legal structures protecting shareholders' and creditors' rights in all EU countries. He concluded that differences in financial structure in Europe will make some national economies more sensitive than others to changes in interest rates.[29]

Dornbusch *et al.* (1998) also find that financial structure plays a relevant role in the explanation of the differences in the responses to monetary policy shocks, since the effects of monetary policy are systematically weaker in countries with market-centre financial systems (Dornbusch *et al.* 1998: 43). However, the authors also conclude that 'differences are not dramatic' (Dornbusch *et al.* 1998: 40) and that 'this process is sure to evolve in part as a result of the financial industry restructuring that is already under way and that is accentuated by the common money' (Dornbusch *et al.* 1998: 52).

Finally, Bondt (2000) provides evidence of the existence of cross-country variations in financial structure in six European countries (Germany, France, Italy, the United Kingdom, Belgium and the Netherlands). In particular, by using a variety of econometric techniques, he found evidence on the existence of both a bank lending and balance sheet channel for Germany and Italy and, to a lesser extent, in France, Belgium and the Netherlands (Bondt 2000: 135). He finally concludes that differences in financial structure 'may hamper the implementation of a common European monetary policy' since they might modify the transmission channel of monetary policy in every euro country (Bondt 2000: 129).

5.4.2.3 *Some concluding remarks on available empirical evidence*

Most available surveys of the empirical literature dealing with asymmetries in the transmission mechanism of the monetary policy in Europe conclude that the empirical evidence is not conclusive at all: the results vary not only across countries but also across studies. Few conclusions, robust or not, can therefore be extracted from the available empirical literature (Guiso *et al.* 1998: 61, Kieler and Saarenheimo 1998: 12, Elbourne and Haan 2004: 12–15), and some authors even suggest that, given the complexity of the task, the econometric analysis 'will never be able to resolve this issue' (Kieler and Saarenheimo 1998: 32).

However, there does seem to be a consensus on the following statements. Firstly, country-specific models tend to produce substantial differences in the responses to monetary policy shocks, but it is unclear whether such differences are due to the country-specific nature of the models themselves or to other factors. Secondly, using the same empirical methodology for all countries (for example, a common structure in a VAR model) produces much less cross-country variation in the results. Thirdly, many authors suggest that pre-EMU empirical results are not useful at all for extrapolating post-EMU results since this has implied a change in the model of the economy (the so-called 'Lucas critique'). And finally, the usual explanation for the differences in responses to monetary shocks relies on macroeconomic differences (economic and financial structure), and very little attention has been paid to the determinants of economic agent responses, which for sure influence the macroeconomic outcomes but are always open to change in a non-deterministic way. Since it is expected that further economic and monetary integration, as well as economic policy coordination will reduce structural differences among EMU countries, many authors expect the different responses to common monetary policy shocks to be narrow in the near future (Dornbusch *et al.* 1998: 52, Ehrmann 1998: 28, Arnold 1999: 22, Guiso *et al.* 1999, Arnold and Vries 2000: 213, Clausen 2001: 172, Peersman 2003: 12).

5.5 Conclusions

This chapter has surveyed the literature dealing with the regional impact of monetary policy from an empirical point of view. In so doing we have tried to show that most empirical approaches have been, to a large extent, simple 'regional extensions' of the discussion regarding how monetary policy affects economic activity.

Most of the analysis regarding the potential regional effect of monetary policy has been developed within the standard open version of the IS-LM model since this framework is supposed to suit regions: they are very small open economies which do not dispose of monetary tools. Consequently, most empirical work has focused on identifying regional structural differences in terms of IS and LM slopes, or the factors which may lead to some segmentation in regional credit markets. In fact, these two approaches along with the other contributions which have considered money as being the cause of regional business cycles have attracted most empirical effort.

The 'old' literature on the regional impact of monetary policy has been recently complemented with some contributions which have flourished because of the third stage of EMU. These new contributions are mainly concerned with the consequences which might stem from the existence of significant differences in the transmission mechanism of the European Central Bank monetary policy to the member economies of the euro area.

One of the conclusions to be drawn from the survey literature is that most empirical work assumes the real vs monetary duality, so monetary policy is seen as neutral for real purposes. Therefore, monetary policy can only cause regional effects either when some market failure (lack of information, segmentation, money illusion, etc.) or structural differences make the transmission mechanism differ from one region to another. Nevertheless, this duality is not acknowledged in those contributions made from a Post Keynesian perspective, which were surveyed in the section dealing with regional credit markets.

6 Some empirical evidence*

6.1 Introduction

This chapter gathers some diverse empirical evidence which we think might be useful to illustrate the regional dimension of national monetary policies. However, the evidence provided in this chapter should be interpreted with caution because our empirical approach only addresses some of the theoretical issues raised in the previous chapters of the book. Consequently, our suggestion would be to interpret the empirical evidence within the theoretical framework put forward in Chapters 3 and 4.

The chapter will primarily pay attention to the European Monetary Union, since it has obviously created an increasing concern over the potential regional consequences of the single monetary policy. The chapter also offers some empirical evidence for Spain which we think helps to understand the prospects of the euro area.

The analysis of the regional economic consequences of monetary policies is addressed from two different perspectives. The first one tries to assess whether the European Central Bank (ECB) has effectively succeeded in achieving its primary goal of price stability since it started to control monetary policy for the euro area in year 1999. The second perspective is concerned with the issue of regional monetary asymmetries within currency unions. Instead of looking at the euro area, the chapter concentrates on studying regional monetary policy asymmetries in Spain for two reasons. First, because the empirical literature which addresses this topic at the euro area level is extensive and has already been surveyed in Chapter 5 (Section 5.4). Secondly, because we think the Spanish experience might provide useful insights for understanding the regional consequences of the single monetary policy (actually the Spanish regions already belonged to a currency union before the third stage of the European Monetary Union started in year 1999).

The structure of the chapter is as follows. Section 6.2 first outlines the ECB's monetary framework with the aim of identifying the key role that inflation plays in the ECB's monetary strategy and then studies the theoretical factors that might explain regional inflation differentials and inflation persistence within a currency union. It finally analyzes regional inflation differentials in two long-established currency unions (Spain and the United States) and compares these results with the EMU experience. The purpose of this section is to show that price stability does not always result from the centralization of monetary policy. Section 6.3 approaches the regional effects of national monetary policies by studying regional asymmetries in monetary policy shocks. To some extent this section reproduces some of the empirical approaches surveyed in Chapter 5 (Section 5.4) for the Spanish regions but emphasizes the role of financial structure in monetary transmission from a regional point of view. The empirical evidence provided in this section suggests that Spanish monetary policy has had a differential effect among Spanish regions and, secondly, that regional differences in both financial and economic structure are responsible for such a differential effect. Section 6.4 provides some empirical evidence for the cyclical pattern of regional credit availability in Spain. The aim of this section is to illustrate the influence that monetary policy might have played in the regional patterns of credit availability in Spain. Finally, the chapter offers some conclusions.

6.2 Inflation and monetary policy in currency unions

It is well known that the primary goal of the ECB's monetary policy is to achieve price stability. Empirical evidence shows that during the 1980s and 1990s there was a rapid and strong convergence in terms of price differential among the euro countries, particularly in those countries with higher inflation rates in the past. Nevertheless, convergence in inflation rates has stopped since the mid 1990s and this fact has raised fears that the single monetary policy is not adequate for a number of countries (Björksten and Syrjänen 2000). This latter possibility was not a major concern during the early years of the single monetary policy since the average rate of inflation was low and its dispersion among the EMU countries was expected to be quickly removed by the introduction of the single currency.[1] However, this does not seem to be the case anymore, and even the ECB now acknowledges that inflation differentials across regions are a natural feature of the monetary union and that monetary policy cannot influence them (ECB 2004: 53). In fact, the persistence in inflation differentials within the EMU area was one of the arguments considered by the ECB to explain why it has officially refused to bring inflation below its 2 percent objective and finally adopted the new target of an 'inflation rate below, but close to, 2% over the medium term' in the year 2003 (ECB 2003a).[2]

The perpetuation of the inflation differentials within the euro area raises some interesting issues. Firstly, the persistence of inflation differentials within the euro area might mean that inflation is not *always* and *everywhere* a monetary phenomenon, so the single monetary policy would not be efficient in fighting inflation within the euro area.[3] Secondly, since the

ECB sets the official interest rate according to the average inflation rate of the euro area, the persistence of such price differentials would mean that 'one size does not fit all', and this might have important economic consequences, particularly for the euro countries with structurally lower inflation rates (ECB 2004: 54). For this reason the ECB has pointed out that 'it is necessary for monetary policy to consider the size, persistence and determinants of inflation differentials in assessing area-wide inflation dynamics' (ECB 2003b: 6).

This section is concerned with the existence of persistent inflation differentials within a currency union. Firstly, it reviews the monetary strategy of the ECB in order to identify the key role assigned to the inflation target in it. Secondly, it offers some explanations for inflation differentials across regions of a currency union to arise and persist over time. Thirdly, it studies empirically regional inflation differentials in two long-stablished currency unions (Spain and the United States) and confronts these results with the EMU experience.

6.2.1   The ECB monetary strategy and the role of inflation

The ECB's monetary strategy was formally defined by its Governing Council in October, 1998, and consists of a 'framework and the procedures that the central bank uses to translate relevant information into monetary policy decisions' (Issing *et al.* 2001: 2). Contrary to simple monetary policy rules, such as the so-called Taylor's rule (Taylor 1993), 'the ECB's monetary strategy is presented as an information-processing framework', and as such, 'it cannot be expressed in a simple mathematical function' (Issing *et al.* 2001: 4–5).

It has been pointed out that the ECB cannot follow a fixed (or known) rule because of the uncertainties that surround the European Monetary Union experiment. At the time when the ECB's monetary policy 'architecture' was designed, in 1998, there was uncertainty about the institutional change that the introduction of the single currency would mean.[4] But even after the launching of the euro and the introduction of the single monetary policy uncertainty still remains. Uncertainty about the response given by economic agents (parameter uncertainty) and the nature of the 'true' economic model (model uncertainty) of the euro area (Issing *et al.* 2001: 100) are considered to be crucial for the implementation of the monetary policy.

Even though 'model uncertainty' is claimed, the ECB does have an implicit economic model in its monetary framework.[5] This model takes into account the existence of a high correlation between money and inflation and assumes that money causes inflation in the long run. However, the ECB also acknowledges that the correlation between money and prices vanishes in the short run. Monetary policy has real effects because of the existence of imperfect information, competition or economic rigidities, either real or financial (see Issing *et al.* 2001, particularly Chapter 1). These assumptions are present in the 'two pillars' of the ECB's monetary policy.[6] According to the principle that money causes inflation in the long run, the first pillar monitors monetary aggregates and the ECB has a specific reference value for the rate of growth of the M3 in the long run.[7] On the contrary, the second pillar focuses on short term price developments. The ECB monitors a wide range of economic and financial indicators to carry out this task.

The prominent role assigned to monetary aggregates in the first pillar has led some authors to question the ECB's monetary strategy (see Begg *et al.* 1999, Svensson 1999, Gross *et al.* 2000). These critics point out that the existence of two pillars does not provide a clear explanation of the ECB's strategy and that financial innovation reduces the reliability of the first pillar. However, there are some authors who defend the strategy by pointing out that 'the two pillars symbolize the still insufficient knowledge concerning the functions of the macro-economy and the characteristics of the transmission process' (Issing *et al.* 2001: 108) and that the use of a simple rule would not allow the central bank to take into account 'all potential sources of information' which is relevant for monetary policy decisions (Issing *et al.* 2001).

Although most central banks deny following a deterministic monetary policy rule, there exists a large and growing collection of empirical studies[8] showing that simple monetary rules, such as the one proposed by Taylor (1993), are capable of reproducing central banks' monetary policy decisions on interest rates. Regarding the euro area, Taylor (1999) recently concluded that 'the simple benchmark rule, such as the one I proposed in 1992, with some adjustment in the response coefficients, would be worth considering as a guideline for the ECB'. Gerlach and Schnabel (1999) also found that 'average interest rates for the EMU countries in 1990–98, with the exception of the exchange market turmoil in 1992–93, moved very closely with the average output gap and inflation as suggested by the Taylor rule'. More evidence in this regard can be also found in the papers by Alesina *et al.* (2001), von Hagen and Brückner (2002), Breuss (2002) and Galí (2003), among many others.

These empirical results are not surprising since the Taylor rule assumes that central banks set the official interest rate according to the deviation of both inflation and output from their targets (Taylor 1993). Analytically, the rule can be expressed as follows:

$$i_t = \hat{r} + \hat{\pi} + \phi_\pi(\pi_t - \hat{\pi}) + \phi_x x_t \tag{6.1}$$

where i_t is a money market interest rate under the control of the monetary authority, $\hat{r}$ is the equilibrium or natural real interest rate, $\hat{\pi}$ is the inflation target, π_t is the current rate of inflation and $x_t \equiv y_t - y_t^n$ is the output gap, being y_t and y^n, the current and potential output, respectively. The parameters ϕ_π and ϕ_x indicate the response of monetary authority against deviations of the inflation rate from its target and variations in the output gap.

In this regard, it is worth remembering that 'the primary objective of the ESCB is to maintain price stability'.[9] But the EU treaty also points out that 'without prejudice of the objective of price stability the ESCB shall support the general economic policies in the Community with a view to contributing to the achievement of the objectives of the Community as laid down in Article 2'.[10] It is not surprising, therefore, that the ECB takes into account not only the inflation rate, but also a variable reflecting the economic pulse of the area, such as the output gap, when setting the official interest rates for the euro area. Figure 6.1 confirms this fact by showing a high correlation between the market interest rate and the inflation rate for the euro area as well as the interest rate and the output gap.[11] The second correlation is much higher (0.77) than the first one (0.44).

The same information is shown in Figure 6.2, where the money market interest rate and the benchmark interest rate performed by the Taylor rule are depicted.[12] Figure 6.2 shows that the Taylor rule matches reasonably well with the money market interest rate, particularly up to 2001. It is evident, therefore, that both inflation and output gap play an important role in the determination of the interest rates in the euro area. However, whereas the interest rate is equal for all countries, inflation rates

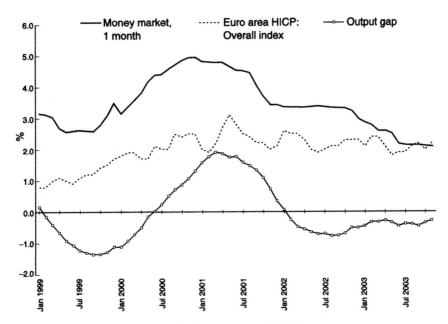

Figure 6.1 Interest rates, inflation and output gap in the euro area.

Source: International Monetary Fund and own calculations.

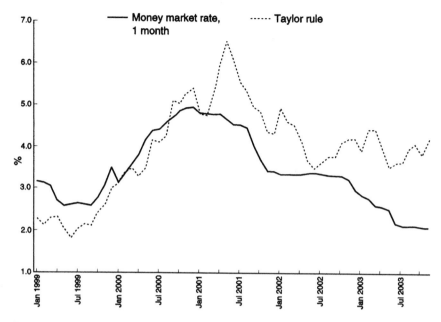

Figure 6.2 Taylor's rule and the market interest rate.

Source: International Monetary Fund and own calculations.

may vary from one country to another. Temporal or small variations would not be a concern. However, if the regional variations in inflation rates were both sizeable and permanent, then the ECB would not really be implementing a one size interest rate policy for the euro area. How important are the inflation differentials within the euro area? Are they also persistent? To what extent is the EMU different to other established currency areas? These issues will be addressed in the remaining part of this section.

6.2.2 *Inflation differentials and persistence in currency unions: some theoretical explanations*

The identification of the factors explaining the evolution of regional inflation differentials in Europe has been a topic of major concern in recent years. In fact, the existence of inflation differentials within the EMU area was considered to be a crucial element in the recent evaluation of the performance of the single monetary policy (see ECB 2003a).

Factors explaining regional inflation differentials in a currency union may be better understood if they were grouped according to their temporal dimension. According to this categorization, we will distinguish, on the one hand, those factors influencing inflation differentials in the short run and, on the other hand, those acting in the medium to long term. Three arguments are usually provided in order to explain inflation differentials within a currency union in the short run. The first one concerns the different impact that the single monetary policy may have on inflation when regional differences in terms of the monetary transmission mechanism exist.[13] The second one assumes that regional divergences in terms of output gaps might cause higher inflationary pressures in those economies with advanced business cycles.[14] The third argument sustains that inflation differentials within a currency union arise because of the regional differences in terms of openness. For example, differences in national oil dependency might spur inflation differential when oil prices go up. Another example is that the inflation rate in the most open economies will be more dependent on the evolution of nominal exchanges rates, therefore the depreciation of nominal exchange rates could increase inflation differentials among the members of a currency union.

There are also factors which explain regional inflation differentials in the medium to long run. One factor is the price level differences which might exist between the regions of a currency union. If price levels differ across countries in the currency union, the expected convergence of prices to a common level could give rise to differences in inflation rates in the transition period, since the countries with lower price levels would experience higher inflation rates than those with higher price levels at the initial stage. The convergence in price levels in the euro countries has been studied, among others, by Hendrikx and Chapple (2002), Honohan and Lane (2003), Rogers (2002), Rogers et al. (2002), ECB (2003b) and Kent (2003). Their empirical results tend to confirm the relevance of price level convergence on the path of inflation differentials among European countries in the last years. However, as argued in Rogers et al. (2002), other forces explain most of the current cross-country differences in the euro area inflation.

Another potential explanation for the inflation differentials within a currency union can be found in the Balassa-Samuelson hypothesis,[15] whereby countries with lower productivity in the traded sector experience more rapid productivity growth on the path of convergence. The adjustment process leads to a higher rate of wage inflation in the economy as a whole, and hence a positive inflation differential.[16] The relevance of the Balassa-Samuelson effect has also been confirmed by Alberola and Tyrväinen (1998), Canzoneri et al. (1999), De Grauwe and Skuldeny (2000), although the empirical evidence provided in these papers does not rule out the possibility for other factors to affect inflation differentials within the euro area.[17]

Whereas the determinants of inflation differentials in currency unions have been a common topic for research in recent years, inflation persistence has received far less attention. This might be explained by the fact that persistence in inflation rates was expected to be removed in the medium term, either by the implementation of the single monetary policy or by cross-border arbitrage among different markets. A single monetary policy avoids the existence of several national monetary policies that target different inflation objectives. At the same time, a single currency enhances price transparency, reducing the scope for persistent differences in the pricing policy followed by firms.

Two reasons have been suggested to explain why inflation differentials persistence may be more important within a currency union than among independent countries. One possibility is that the setting of a single nominal interest rate for the euro area would mean different real interest rates for those member countries with higher inflation rates. If the inflation rates increase during upturns because of higher demand pressure, the resulting lower real interest rate might amplify the business cycle and, therefore, inflation. The second explanation is partly derived from the first one: a higher inflation rate and a lower real interest rate in a booming region may increase both nominal and real housing prices which, in turn, may stimulate consumption through balance sheet effects.[18]

A controversial question with regard to the persistence of inflation differentials within a currency union is the role that the real exchange rate might play in the adjustment process. It is commonly assumed that a booming regional economy is expected to experience a real appreciation in its exchange rate because of the changes in relative prices between the domestic market and the rest of the union. If firms cannot segment markets, the reduction in the external demand (derived from the real appreciation) will mitigate the economic boom, and therefore contributes to the adjustment process (Arnold and Kool 2002). However, recent contributions in the field of international economics suggest that international price discrimination (pricing-to-market policies) reduce the scope for the expenditure-switching effect to work (see Obstfeld 2002). Bergin (2003) proposes a pricing-to-market model for a monetary union[19] and concludes that inflation differentials can appear in a monetary union and persist a long time, even in tradeable products, due to the market power of firms that engage in price discrimination among different markets.

Although we have focused on differences in the degree of persistence of inflation differentials within the regions of a monetary union and across independent countries, there are also several reasons why the persistence of inflation differentials can vary across currency unions. A first argument points to the existence of different degrees of economic policy centralization. For example, a higher degree of budgetary centralization can ameliorate demand pressures in different regions of the monetary union. Another argument highlights the role of nominal rigidities in the goods and labour markets. Let us assume two currency unions. In one currency union we observe a better coordination between firms and workers, thus nominal price and wage rigidities are similar across its regions. In the other currency union the coordination is lower. Less-persistent inflation differentials are expected to be observed in this scenario as the coordination between firms and workers increases.

So far we have surveyed some of the arguments put forward to explain the existence of inflation differentials within a currency union, along with those suggested to explain their degree of persistence. The next section explores these questions from an empirical point of view in order to answer a set of questions. We employ a dataset of EMU countries, before and after forming the currency union and among different regions of two long-established currency unions: the United States and Spain.

6.2.3　*Inflation differentials and persistence in currency unions: some empirical evidence*

This section studies the regional inflation differentials and their persistence between the euro countries, the Spanish regions and some regions in the United States. Since some analysts have suggested that it is still too soon to evaluate whether the ECB has succeeded in achieving the price stability goal (the single European monetary policy started in year 1999), the comparison with the results achieved in some other longer-established currency unions, such as Spain or the United States, might offer some clues in this regard.

Inflation data for the European Union was collected from the International Monetary Fund (IMF) database 'Internacional Financial Statistics'. Spanish regional data for the 17 Autonomous Communities were extracted from the Instituto Nacional de Estadística (INE), while the data for the 14 USA Metropolitan Statistical Areas (MSA) was taken from the Bureau of Labor Statistics (BLS). All data are monthly, except for 11 MSA where bimonthly data are available, and extend from January 1980 to December 2002.

The trend of inflation rates among the EMU countries shows a convergence pattern since the beginning of the 1980s. The high-inflation economies have achieved outstanding results in terms of the reduction in inflation rates, particularly from the mid 1990s. This success is to a large extent explained by the political determination of some countries to meet the Maastricht criteria. Figure 6.3 shows the maximum and minimum inflation rates among the EMU countries, and also the standard deviation for the whole area. The observed reduction both in the maximum rate and in the standard deviation reveals the underlying convergence process in terms of inflation rates in the euro area.

The trend shown in Figure 6.3 could lead some authors to expect that inflation differentials would definitively disappear with the establishment of the single currency. However, a closer look at the inflation trends in some countries does not seem to support this assumption. In particular, there is a group of countries, such as Portugal or Spain, where the inflation rate has persistently remained well above the euro area rate (see Figure 6.4).

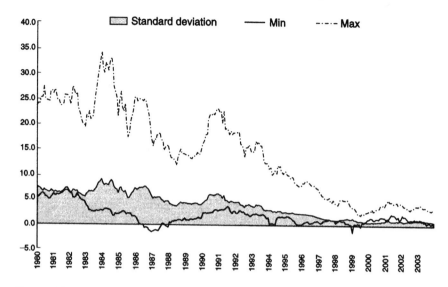

Figure 6.3 Evolution of inflation rates in EMU countries.

Source: International Monetary Fund and own calculations.

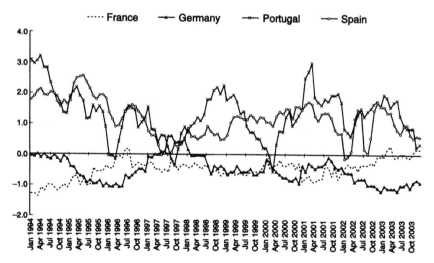

Figure 6.4 Differentials in inflation rates in some European countries (with respect to EU-15).

Source: International Monetary Fund and own calculations.

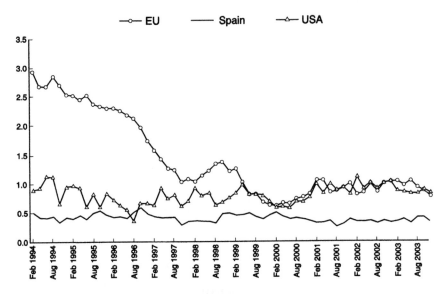

Figure 6.5 Standard deviation (unweighted) of inflation rates in EMU countries, the Spanish regions and some US regions.

Source: International Monetary Fund and own calculations.

Conversely, there is another group of countries (France or Germany) which has persistently experienced lower inflation rates. It is interesting to note that inflation rates were quite close among these countries in 1997 and 1998, coinciding with the evaluation of the Maastricht criteria, but they started to diverge when the third stage of the EMU took place.

The above-mentioned trends in inflation rates have raised some concerns for European policymakers. Some authors have pointed out that the differences observed for the euro area can also be found in other long-established monetary unions, such as the United States, Germany or Spain. Figures 6.5 and 6.6 are included to study this possibility, and present standard deviation and the absolute spread in inflation rates for the euro area countries, the Spanish regions and some regions in the United States. The time period considered extends from 1994 to 2003, thus we focus on a recent period where nominal stability has been a political priority.

There are three features worth mentioning in both cases. A first trend confirms the existence of convergence in inflation rates among the euro economies which stops at the beginning of 2000 and rises slightly afterwards. This result is consistent with the important role played by the fulfilment of the Maastricht criteria and the monetary unification in the reduction of inflation differentials. However, differences in inflation rates have not totally disappeared with the implementation of the single European monetary policy. As can be seen in Figures 6.5 and 6.6, significant inflation

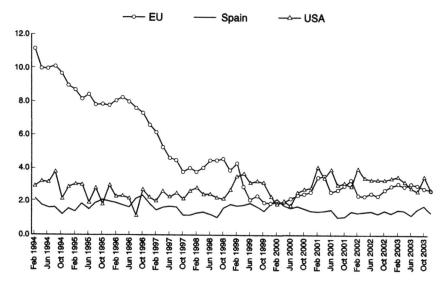

Figure 6.6 Absolute spread in inflation rates in EMU countries, the Spanish regions and some US regions.

Source: International Monetary Fund and own calculations.

dispersion is present in all the currency unions considered in our analysis. However, some relevant differences exist when comparing the three currency unions. In particular, the inflation dispersion for the euro area and the United States is almost twice as much as the value for the Spanish regions. The higher dispersion for the inflation rates in the EMU area and the United States could be explained by the lower degree of economic policy centralization achieved in terms of fiscal, labour and product market policies and also by the higher geographical distance in comparison to the Spanish regional case (see ECB 2003b). The close similarity between the euro area and the United States after the introduction of the euro put into question the relevance of some exclusive explanation to the observed inflation differentials within the euro area, among them the differences in terms of price and productivity levels. The most interesting conclusion, which can be derived from Figures 6.5 and 6.6, is that inflation differentials are not a specific problem of euro area members, since the size of inflation differentials observed at present in the euro area is not so different from the ones observed in the United States.

The empirical evidence reveals that inflation differentials are not an exclusive feature of the euro area, since they also exist in the other two case studies. However, this description does not necessarily apply for the persistence in inflation. It would thus be interesting to determine whether (and why) persistence in inflation among the euro countries is higher than in the other two currency unions, as well as to study its potential consequences for the implementation of the single monetary policy. In order to study inflation persistence, we will proceed as follows. First, the degree of persistence of inflation differentials will be compared among the regions belonging to a monetary union and the euro area countries before the beginning of stage three of EMU. Second, we will test for the existence of different degrees of persistence across currency unions. Data for the euro area countries, the Spanish regions and some regions of the United States during the period 1999–2003 will be used.[20]

In order to address the first issue, we have employed a set of unit root and stationary tests. To understand the mechanics of these tests, consider the following simple autoregressive process of order one AR(1) for the inflation rates differentials:

$$\left(\pi^i - \pi^{area}\right)_t = \alpha + \rho\left(\pi^i - \pi^{area}\right)_{t-1} + \varepsilon_t \tag{6.2}$$

where $(\pi^i - \pi^{area})$ is the inflation differential for country i with respect to the reference area considered, α and ρ are the parameters to be estimated and ε_t is assumed to be white noise. If $|\rho| \geq 1$, the inflation differential is a non-stationary process and therefore no convergence is expected to take place. On the contrary, if $|\rho| < 1$, the inflation differential is a stationary series and convergence is expected to take place. The value of ρ also determines the speed of the convergence process.

The unit root test studies the null hypothesis H_0: $\rho = 1$ against the one-sided alternative H_1: $\rho < 1$. We employ different unit root tests proposed in the literature, such as the Augmented Dickey–Fuller test (Dickey and Fuller 1979), the Phillips–Perron test (Phillips and Perron 1988), the Dickey–Fuller test with GLS detrending (Elliot *et al.* 1996) and the Elliot, Rothemberg and Stock optimal point test (Elliot *et al.* 1996).

Stationary tests are used to test the alternative null hypothesis H_0: $\rho < 1$. We have also applied the KPSS test proposed by Kwiatkowski *et al.* (1992). This combination of different tests allows us to obtain a more robust conclusion about the convergence (or lack of convergence) of inflation differentials in the long run.

We compare the stationary properties of inflation differentials among some European countries, the Spanish regions and some regions of the United States before the start of the EMU. Data availability limits the time period considered from January 1980 to December 1998. The aim of this comparison is to find some clues to answer the question of whether inflation differentials are more persistent among countries with independent monetary policies than among regions within a currency union.

Tables 6.1 and 6.2 sum up the results of applying the stationary and unit root tests to the inflation differential series for the euro area countries and the regions in Spain and some regions in the United States. With regard

Table 6.1 Unit root and stationary tests of inflation differentials in euro area countries (1980:01–1998:12)

	Unit root tests				Stationary test	Conclusion
	ADF	PP	DF-GLS	ERS	KPSS	
Austria	NO	NO	NO	NO	**	Non-stationary
Belgium	*	*	NO	NO	**	Inconclusive
Finland	*	**	NO	NO	NO	Inconclusive
France	NO	NO	NO	NO	**	Non-stationary
Germany	NO	NO	NO	NO	**	Non-stationary
Greece	NO	NO	NO	NO	**	Non-stationary
Italy	NO	NO	NO	NO	**	Non-stationary
Luxembourg	*	*	NO	NO	*	Inconclusive
Netherlands	NO	NO	NO	NO	**	Non-stationary
Portugal	NO	NO	NO	NO	**	Non-stationary
Spain	NO	NO	NO	NO	**	Non-stationary

Notes: One and two asterisks represent statistical significance at a 5 and 1 percent level, respectively.

Table 6.2 Unit root and stationary tests of inflation differentials in the Spanish and the United States regions (1980:01–1998:12)

	Unit root tests				Stationary test	Conclusion
	ADF	PP	DF-GLS	ERS	KPSS	
Spanish regions						
Andalucia	**	**	NO	**	*	Inconclusive
Aragon	**	**	NO	*	NO	Stationary
Asturias	*	**	**	NO	NO	Stationary
Baleares	*	**	NO	**	NO	Stationary
Canarias	*	*	**	**	NO	Stationary
Cantabria	**	**	NO	**	NO	Stationary
Castilla y León	*	**	*	**	NO	Stationary
Castilla La Mancha	NO	**	NO	NO	NO	Inconclusive
Cataluña	NO	**	*	*	NO	Stationary
Com. Valenciana	**	**	NO	NO	NO	Inconclusive
Extremadura	**	**	*	**	NO	Stationary
Galicia	*	**	NO	**	NO	Stationary
Madrid	**	**	**	NO	NO	Stationary
Murcia	NO	**	NO	**	NO	Inconclusive
Navarra	**	**	**	**	**	Inconclusive
País Vasco	NO	*	NO	NO	NO	Inconclusive
La Rioja	**	**	NO	NO	NO	Inconclusive
United States regions						
New York	*	**	NO	NO	NO	Inconclusive
Chicago	**	**	NO	*	NO	Stationary
Los Angeles	NO	**	NO	NO	*	Inconclusive

Notes: One and two asterisks represent statistical significance at a 5 and 1 percent level, respectively.

to persistence in inflation, the results confirm the existence of a higher persistence in inflation differentials among the current euro area countries. Table 6.1 suggests that the non-stationary behaviour of inflation differentials cannot be rejected in most cases (in eight countries out of the 11 considered). In the remainder of cases, the evidence is mixed; that is, we cannot clearly determine the nature of the data.

The degree of persistence of the different series was also calculated from the ADF test obtained, using for this purpose the half-life of the adjustment process for each country. The half-life statistic depends on the value of ρ and its analytical expression is as follows: $HL = (\ln 0.5 / \ln \rho)$. The expression gives us a measure of the time that a series needs to return to its equilibrium once it is affected by a shock. As we have a different estimated ρ value for each of the series, we will take its pooled value as representative for the whole group so we can obtain ρ values for each of the two groups considered: the European countries and the regions in Spain and in the United States. The differences between the estimated values are very important. Hence, whereas for the European countries the half-life is approximately 22 months, for the Spanish and the United States regions it is only 4.5 months.

Although these results are interesting, the study of persistent inflation differentials across currency unions may provide more useful insights in this issue. Accordingly, Table 6.3 summarizes some measures within the euro area countries, the Spanish regions and some regions of the United States for the period 1999–2003. Although monthly data are available, the limited sampling of the data does not recommend applying unit root tests in order to determine the stationary properties of inflation differentials, so alternative statistics were used to assess the degree of persistence. On the one hand, we calculate the autoregressive coefficient of different orders (first, second and forth) for the inflation differentials among the regions and the currency area as a whole. On the other hand, and following Batini (2002), Kozicki and Tinsley (2002) and Kieler (2003), the persistence of inflation differentials was measured as the sum of coefficients from an estimated autoregressive model of inflation differential, considering two alternative autoregressive orders (sixth and twelfth).

The European inflation rates seem to diverge more persistently than in Spain and in the United States for all the measures calculated.[21] Consequently, persistence in inflation differentials seems to be an intrinsic feature of the euro area economies.

A possible explanation for the higher persistence in inflation differentials in the European Monetary Union is that nominal rigidities might be more similar among the Spanish and the United States regions than among the euro countries. This argument could be supported by the evidence in other works. For example, Benigno and López-Salido (2002) suggest that there are important differences in the degree of price stickiness in the five major countries of the euro area. In particular, they point out that

Table 6.3 Persistence in inflation differentials among the EMU countries, the Spanish regions and some regions in the United States: 1999–2003

		AR(1)	AR(2)	AR(4)
EMU	Average	0.812	0.725	0.543
	Maximum	0.941	0.919	0.946
	Minimum	0.712	0.561	0.309
United States	Average	0.756	0.552	0.416
	Maximum	0.911	0.807	0.647
	Minimum	0.549	0.149	0.050
Spain	Average	0.763	0.607	0.380
	Maximum	0.937	0.890	0.781
	Minimum	0.570	0.250	−0.333

		Sum of coefficients from AR of order	
		Sixth	Twelfth
EMU	Average	0.856	0.717
	Maximum	0.974	0.951
	Minimum	0.738	0.497
United States	Average	0.752	0.297
	Maximum	0.974	0.926
	Minimum	0.405	−0.754
Spain	Average	0.734	0.523
	Maximum	0.935	0.956
	Minimum	0.359	−0.106

for Germany, the Netherlands and France, the degree of price stickiness seems to be lower than that observed in both Italy and Spain. Along the same line, Nickell (2003) suggests that labour market institutions diverge across the European economies, which could produce differentiated patterns in the rigidities of the labour markets.

6.3   The regional effects of monetary policy shocks in Spain

An increasing concern exists over the implications that the differences in financial structure among the euro countries might have for the ECB monetary policy. These concerns are based on empirical evidence revealing current substantial differences among the financial structures of the European Monetary Union countries (see Danthine *et al.* 1999, De Bandt and Davis 1999, Schmidt 1999, Bondt 2000, Maclennan *et al.* 2000, Padoa-Schioppa 2000, Kleimeier and Sander 2001, Cabral *et al.* 2002), even though they have shared a common monetary policy since 1999. Consequently, it is crucial to determine whether those differences in financial structure may affect the way the single European monetary policy works; and in the affirmative case, to understand how these differences affect the member countries of the euro area.

Even though some authors suggest that differences in financial structure may produce asymmetries in the transmission mechanism of the single monetary policy (Kashyap and Stein 1997b, Cecchetti 1999, Bondt 2000), many others expect these asymmetries to disappear in the long run since the process of increased economic integration and economic policy coordination will end by eroding such differences in financial structure (Dornbusch *et al.* 1998: 52, Ehrmann 1998: 28, Arnold 1999: 22, Arnold and Vries 2000: 213, Clausen 2001: 172).

This section aims at contributing to this current debate by studying the regional effects of Spanish monetary policy during the 1990s. It specifically concentrates on determining whether regional differences in financial structure in Spain help explain the differential effects of national monetary shocks during 1988–1998.

The empirical approach followed in this section is carried out in three different steps. The first step aims at identifying the exogenous monetary shocks[22] by means of the estimation of a Vector Autoregression model (VAR) and a reaction function of the central bank (the Bank of Spain). We are aware that this is a very controversial question, both from a theoretical[23] and an empirical point of view.[24] Nevertheless, we have chosen to follow this orthodox approach to produce empirical results which are comparable with the current empirical literature on the real effects of monetary policy (Christiano *et al.* 1999). A second aim is to offer some alternative explanations for the results obtained. Once the 'exogenous monetary shock' is identified, the second step consists of regressing the exogenous shock against the industrial production index growth for every region in Spain. This step allows us to identify differences in the regional responses to monetary shocks. Finally, in the third step the regional responses to monetary shocks are explained according to the explanatory variables included in a cross-section regression. The empirical results presented in this section point out that the Spanish regions responded differently to the national monetary policy shocks during the period 1988–1998 and, secondly, that some regional financial variables seemed to have played a crucial role in the explanation of these differences in regional responses. Consequently, one potential implication that could be drawn from our results is that if differences in financial structure among the Spanish regions existed under a single monetary policy and a uniform regulatory framework for a long time, it is not unreasonable to assert that current differences among financial structures of the euro countries will not easily vanish in the near future and could contribute to a non-homogenous impact of the single monetary policy of the ECB.

6.3.1 The identification of the exogenous monetary shocks

Following the recent orthodox empirical literature on monetary policy (Christiano *et al.* 1999), the identification of the exogenous monetary shocks is estimated both from a VAR model and a reaction function of the central bank.

The VAR model was estimated for a period which extends from January 1988 to December 1998 and its structure is shown below:

$$\begin{bmatrix} X_t \\ Y_t \end{bmatrix} = \begin{bmatrix} A(L) & 0 \\ C(L) & D(L) \end{bmatrix} \begin{bmatrix} X_{t-1} \\ Y_{t-1} \end{bmatrix} + \begin{bmatrix} a & 0 \\ c & d \end{bmatrix} \begin{bmatrix} e_t^X \\ e_t^Y \end{bmatrix} \tag{6.3}$$

where Y_t is a vector of endogenous variables for the Spanish economy which includes the Industrial Production Index, the Consumer Price Index, a short-term interest rate in Germany, the monetary aggregate M3, the long-term return for public debt, the 3-month interest rate for the non-transferable deposits and the Peseta–Deutsche Mark exchange rate. X_t is a vector of exogenous variables which includes a constant term, a trend and a world commodity price index. All variables are monthly, expressed in levels (except for the interest rates) and in logarithmic form. The data were extracted from the Bank of Spain. The monetary policy shocks were identified through a recursive Choleski decomposition with the variables ordered as above and with a 2-month lag structure. The identifying assumptions are that unanticipated monetary policy shocks do not have a contemporaneous impact on output (proxied by the Industrial Production Index) and prices.

The monetary policy shocks were also estimated through the estimation of a reaction function, following the contributions made by Clarida *et al.* (1998, 2000), Taylor (1999), Batini and Haldane (1999), Angeloni and Dedola (1999), Gerlach and Schnabel (2000) and Nelson (2000). We assumed that the Bank of Spain sets the official interest rates according to the deviation of both inflation and output from their targets. In particular, the reaction function proposed is shown below:

$$i_i = \rho i_{t-1} + (1-\rho)\left[\alpha + \beta\pi_{t+k} + \gamma x_{t+p} + \lambda X_t\right] + \varepsilon_t \tag{6.4}$$

The proposed reaction function can be interpreted as a linear Taylor rule with interest rate smoothing, represented by the parameter ρ, X represents a vector of variables which influence the central bank's decisions on interest rates, such as the exchange rate or the foreign interest rate, x is the output gap, π is the deviation of inflation from its target and i is the money market interest rate under the control of the monetary authority. The parameters β and γ indicate, respectively, the response of monetary authority to deviations in inflation from its target and variations in the output gap. This expression was estimated by the Generalized Method of Moments (GMM) method.[25]

Figure 6.7 shows the effects of the cumulated shock estimated both from the VAR model (shock-VAR) and the reaction function (shock-FR), as well as the evolution of a short-term interest rate. An interesting obser-

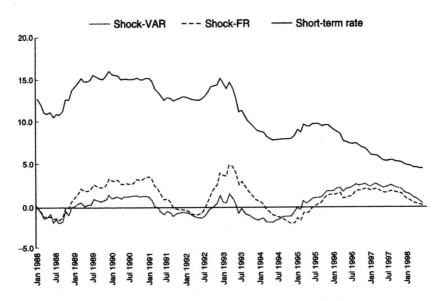

Figure 6.7 Monetary shocks and short-term interest rates in Spain.

Source: Own estimates.

vation is that the estimated shocks show a close correlation with the short-term interest rates, at least until the mid 1990s.

6.3.2   *Differences in regional responses to monetary policy shocks*

The next step in our empirical exercise was to identify differences in the regional responses to national exogenous monetary shocks. To this end the following expression was estimated for the Spanish regions:

$$ipi_{i,t} = \alpha_i + \sum_{j=1}^{12} \beta_i \cdot ipi_{i,t-j} + \gamma_i \cdot shock_{t-1} + \eta_{i,t} \tag{6.5}$$

where *ipi* is the Industrial Production Index growth for every Spanish region and *shock* is the national monetary shock estimated in the previous section. The estimates for the regional responses to monetary shock (γ) are shown in Table 6.4, where the 17 Spanish regions are classified according to their responsiveness to national monetary shocks.

It is worth noting that in all cases the response to national monetary shocks is negative, and that the classification (ranking) of the different regions does not change depending on the shock which is used (shock-VAR or shock-FR). Three groups seem to emerge from Table 6.4. The first group includes regions which seem to be less sensitive to monetary shocks (Castilla-La Mancha, Baleares, Extremadura, Andalucía and Murcia).

Table 6.4 Regional responses to monetary shocks

Shock-FR			Shock-VAR		
Castilla la Mancha	−0.0240		Murcia	−0.0007	
Baleares	−0.0523		Baleares	−0.0040	
Extremadura	−0.0748		Extremadura	−0.0172	
Andalucía	−0.0941		Andalucía	−0.0285	
Murcia	−0.1135		Castilla La Mancha	−0.0390	
Canarias	−0.1231		Galicia	−0.0763	
Madrid	−0.1671		Aragón	−0.0813	
Galicia	−0.2074	**	Asturias	−0.0953	
Asturias	−0.2281	**	Valencia	−0.1015	
Cantabria	−0.2434	**	Madrid	−0.1131	
Aragón	−0.2601	**	Navarra	−0.1251	
Cataluña	−0.2609	**	Castilla y León	−0.1293	
Valencia	−0.2623	**	Cataluña	−0.1308	
Navarra	−0.2968	**	Cantabria	−0.1428	
Castilla y León	−0.3332	*	Canarias	−0.1553	
País Vasco	−0.3345	**	País Vasco	−0.1691	
La Rioja	−0.4347	**	La Rioja	−0.3956	**
Wald test = 24.7941 (0.0735)			Wald test = 17.2552 = (0.3693)		

* and ** denote 1 and 5% significance, respectively.

A second group is most sensitive to monetary shocks (La Rioja and País Vasco). Finally, the third group (Castilla-León, Navarra, Valencia and Cataluña) is less sensitive to monetary shocks than the second one. Overall, the results seem to confirm the existence of important differences across the Spanish regions in terms of their responses to national monetary shocks. This result is also confirmed by the Wald test on the shock-FR. The value of the test for the shock-VAR does not allow us to reject the null hypothesis of parameter equality. However, when the test is carried out for the groups the null hypothesis is also rejected for the shock-VAR.

6.3.3 Some potential explanations for the regional differences in responses to monetary policy shocks

Several cross-section regressions were carried out in order to explain differences in regional responses to national monetary shocks. In particular, five different models were estimated (Table 6.5), both for the VAR (shock-VAR) and the reaction function (shock-FR) shocks.

The five equations share a common structure: a constant term (CTE), the ratio 'investment/regional Gross Domestic Product' (INVEST), the ratio '(exports + imports)/regional Gross Domestic Product' (OPEN) and the percentage of small businesses, which was proxied by the share of business branches with up to six employees (SME). The estimates show the expected signs. The regional 'investment' variable (INVEST) shows a positive

Table 6.5 Cross section regressions to explain regional responses to monetary policy shocks

	Model no. 1		Model no. 2		Model no. 3		Model no. 4		Model no. 5	
	FR	VAR	FR	VAR	FR	VAR	FR	VAR	FR	VAR
CTE	6.1648	2.5678	6.1784	2.646	4.7714	0.294	6.6511	2.9267	5.1753	0.6346
	(3.98)	(1.32)	(3.69)	(1.26)	(3.06)	(0.18)	(4.47)	(1.46)	(3.82)	(0.39)
INVEST	0.7823	−0.0953	0.7874	−0.0659	1.1178	0.4522	0.9515	0.0297	1.3494	0.6475
	(1.42)	(−0.14)	(1.32)	(−0.09)	(2.13)	(0.79)	(1.8)	(0.04)	(2.92)	(1.17)
OPEN	−0.3842	−0.1986	−0.3845	−0.2002	−0.3259	−0.1035	−0.483	−0.2715	−0.433	−0.1938
	(−4.05)	(−1.67)	(−3.86)	(−1.60)	(−3.61)	(−1.05)	(−4.44)	(−1.85)	(−4.74)	(−1.77)
SME	−7.065	−2.7219	−7.0867	−2.8467	−5.504	−0.1745	−6.9853	−2.6631	−5.2394	0.0486
	(−3.91)	(−1.20)	(−3.53)	(−1.13)	(−3.04)	(−0.09)	(−4.11)	(−1.16)	(−3.37)	(0.03)
DEPR3	−0.2384	−0.2702	−0.2359	−0.2561	−0.1611	−0.1442	−0.272	−0.295	−0.1912	−0.1696
	(−1.68)	(−1.52)	(−1.41)	(−1.22)	(−1.21)	(−1.00)	(−2.01)	(−1.62)	(−1.66)	(−1.22)
REG-BANKS	–	–	0.0057	0.0329	–	–	–	–	–	–
			(0.03)	(0.16)						
PUB-ASSETS	–	–	–	–	−1.7626	−2.8764	–	–	−1.9581	−3.0412
					(−1.96)	(−2.93)			(−2.53)	(−3.23)
INEFF	–	–	–	–	–	–	−1.2427	−0.9171	−1.427	−1.2034
							(−1.59)	(−0.87)	(−2.22)	(−1.56)
R^2	0.735	0.3546	0.735	0.3559	0.8038	0.6371	0.7847	0.3964	0.8685	0.7081
R^2 Adjusted	0.6466	0.1395	0.6145	0.0631	0.7146	0.4722	0.6869	0.1221	0.7896	0.5329
Log likelihood	24.6	20.72	24.6	20.73	26.63	21.68	26.37	21.29	30.92	27.47
Durbin-Watson	2.48	2.32	2.48	2.31	2.71	2.56	2.75	2.53	2.62	2.07

correlation with the regional response to monetary shocks. Since estimated monetary shocks were both negative (Table 6.5), the positive sign for INVEST means that, the larger the regional investment effort, the lower the contraction in the regional production index after a monetary shock. The use of the variable OPEN is to reflect the region's exposure to exchange rate fluctuations: the more open a region is to trade, the larger the effect of the exchange rate appreciation on economic activity after a monetary contraction. Consequently, the expected sign for OPEN is negative, which is confirmed by our results. The variable SME also shows a negative correlation with the regional response. The sign for SME is compatible with the conventional credit channel literature explanation, which maintains that small-sized businesses face higher credit constraints because of their higher dependence on bank-credit financing. Consequently, those regions with larger shares of small businesses must experience a higher reduction in credit availability after a monetary shock. The reduction in credit might have important consequences for regional economic activity (particularly for bank-dependent firms).

A fourth variable is included in Model 1: market share in the regional market for deposits of the top three banking institutions (DEPR3). This variable was included as a proxy for 'concentration' in the regional market. The estimates show a negative sign for DEPR3: the higher the concentration in the market for deposits, the larger the regional response (in terms of a contraction in the industrial production) to national monetary shocks. One potential explanation for such a link could be that, in a context of higher market concentration, financial institutions might pass on any increase in costs to their customers (borrowers). Consequently, a rise in national interest rates (due to a monetary shock) might have a higher effect on the credit market (in terms of raising the cost or reducing the availability) in those regions with a higher banking concentration (higher market power).

Model 2 also includes the variable REG-BANKS, which is a proxy for the relevance of regional-based financial institutions in the region. The estimates show a positive sign for this variable. This result could be interpreted as if the regional-based financial institution tends to diminish or absorb the negative impact of monetary policy on regional activity. However, it should also be noted that the estimated value for this variable is not significant from a statistical point of view. Since 'regional banks' tend to concentrate their lending within the region boundaries, and lending is usually by far their most important business, they might have incentives to avoid excessive short term cyclical turns in their customers' solvency and profitability (by pushing up interest rates in a period of tight monetary policy), and focus instead on long term (not cyclical) profitability and lending relationships. This potential explanation can be reinforced by the fact that, as some authors maintain, 'local banks usually exploit better the soft information which is generated in lending relationships' (Williams 2003). This interpretation is in line with those authors who suggest that 'the segmentation of the European banking system could realize higher growth rates in European regions through information asymmetries', particularly because there is also evidence suggesting that such banks are highly cost efficient (Williams and Gardener 2003: 327).

Model 3 includes the variable PUB-ASSETS, which is defined as the share of public sector debt investments in total assets. To some extent this variable reflects the investment behaviour of the financial institutions and the estimates show a negative and significant sign. We interpret this result as follows: the 'conservative' portfolio decisions of financial institutions during episodes of tight monetary policy might reinforce the restrictive effect on economic activity since banks might protect themselves from risk by buying more public debt.

Model 4 includes the inefficient ratio (INEFF), which is measured as the proportion of 'Gross income' absorbed by 'Operating expenses'. Our empirical results reveal a negative sign for this variable, meaning that the higher the bank inefficiency, the larger the contraction in the regional industrial production. Finally, Model 5 only includes the variables which were significant in previous models, and the results seem to confirm the ones obtained before.

6.4   Regional credit availability and the role of monetary policy: some empirical evidence for Spain

The aim of this section is to provide some empirical evidence for the cyclical pattern of regional credit availability in Spain. Following the analysis developed by Dow (1998) and the theoretical framework put forward in Chapter 4, Section 6.4.1 will first review some of the theoretical arguments to explain why some regions may exhibit higher instability in credit availability along business cycles, namely the regional differences in terms of stages of banking development and liquidity preference of financial agents (including the banks). It will also pay attention to the influence that monetary policy might have on financial agents' behaviour (liquidity preference) and, consequently, on the regional patterns of credit availability (see Rodríguez-Fuentes and Dow 2003, Dow 2004b). Section 6.4.2 then provides some empirical evidence of credit market instability for the Spanish regions.

6.4.1   Sources of instability in the regional credit expansion process

The Post Keynesian explanation for credit expansion instability derives from theory concerning changes in liquidity preference over the business cycle. This framework has been explicitly applied to a regional setting by Dow (1998) and some empirical evidence for the Spanish regions can be found in Rodríguez-Fuentes (1998) and Rodríguez-Fuentes and Dow (2003).

From a regional perspective, the hypothesis is that changes in banks' liquidity preference lead to 'excessive' optimism with respect to credit

Table 6.6 Summary of empirical results for non-financial variables

Variable	INVEST	OPEN	SME
Definition	Investment/regional GDP	(exports + imports)/regional GDP	% of business branches with up to six employees
Sign	Positive	Negative	Negative
Statistical meaning	The larger the investment, the smaller the contraction in the regional industrial production index after a monetary shock	The more open a region is to trade, the larger the contraction in the regional industrial production index after a monetary shock	The larger the share of small business, the larger the contraction in the regional industrial production index after a monetary shock
Possible theoretical explanation		Exchange rate channel: The monetary shock produces an exchange rate appreciation that reduces regional competitiveness	Credit channel: The monetary shock reduces credit availability for small-sized business

Table 6.7 Summary of empirical results for financial variables

Variable	DEPR3	REG-BANKS	PUB-ASSETS	INEFF
Definition	Market share of top-three banking institutions in the regional market for deposits	'Proxy' for the relevance of region-based financial institution	Share of public sector debt investments in total assets of banks	Gross income/operating expenses
Sign	Negative	Positive (but not significant)	Negative	Negative
Statistical meaning	The higher the concentration in the market for deposits, the larger the contraction in the regional industrial production after a monetary shock	The higher the share of the region-based financial institutions, the lower the negative impact of monetary policy on regional activity	The larger the share of public sector debt investments in total assets, the larger the negative impact of monetary policy on regional activity	The larger the inefficiency ratio, the larger the negative impact of monetary policy
Potential theoretical explanation	In a context of higher market concentration (market power), financial institution can pass on to demand any worsening of monetary conditions	Local financial institution may counterbalance the negative impact for their own interests and because they 'exploit better the soft information which is generated in lending relationships' (Williams 2003)	The 'conservative' portfolio decisions of financial institution during episodes of tight monetary policy might reinforce the restrictive effect on economic activity since banks might protect from risk by buying more public debt (defensive financial behaviour, Dow 1992d)	

creation in peripheral economies in upturns, and 'excessive' pessimism in downturns. In upturns, competing banks are prepared to hold less liquid portfolios as they strive to extend their market share in peripheral economies. Their expectations regarding risk and return are influenced by the general state of optimism, but are based on more limited knowledge than their expectations with respect to the more developed economies. At the same time, lower liquidity preference among borrowers in peripheral economies in upturns creates additional demand for credit to finance expenditure; however peripheral economies are characterized by a relatively high liquidity preference over the entire cycle, because of past experience of what tends to happen in downturns. When confidence in peripheral economies falters there is scope for sharp retractions of credit availability, particularly given the weak knowledge base of banks with respect to the periphery. The banks' liquidity preference rises in general as the national economy declines, but it is the credit to peripheral economies which tends to be at the margin where credit contraction bites hardest. The end result is greater instability in credit growth in peripheral economies.

Credit instability then is not only explained by structural differences but by changes in financial behaviour which might well be influenced by monetary policy. This alternative explanation (which gives room also to liquidity preference) is what leads us to suggest that a comprehensive understanding of the regional effects of a single monetary policy should take into account the behavioural effects mentioned in Chapter 4 (Section 4.3), and not just structural differences among regions.

6.4.2 Empirical evidence on regional credit instability in Spain

The following expression was estimated for the 17 Spanish regions with the aim of testing credit instability alongside business cycles:

$$cred_{i,t} = \alpha_i + \beta y_{i,t} + \theta D_t y_{i,t} + v_{i,t} \tag{6.6}$$

where $cred_{i,t}$ is the rate of growth of credit for the region i in year t, α is an individual fixed effect, y is the regional real Gross Domestic Product and D is a dummy variable which takes on value 1 for the recession period (1991–1993) and 0 for the rest. The 17 regions were classified into two groups according to their relative levels of per capita income. The first sample includes the wealthier regions[26] in the year 1986, whereas the second group is made up of those with lower levels.[27] We used annual data for the period 1986–2001 and panel data techniques for the estimates.

Tables 6.8 and 6.9 show the estimated results for different specifications of equation (6.6) for both samples using the Seemingly Unrelated Regressions (SURE) method.[28] It is worth noting that the inclusion of the dummy variable for the recession period increases the sensitivity of credit to regional income for the poorer regions. Two regions (Extremadura

Table 6.8 Estimates for the low-income regions

	Coefficient	t-statistic	P value	R^2-co
SURE method				
α	10,241	9,533	0.000	
β	1,011	6,691	0.000	0,147
SURE Fixed effects				
β	0,933	5,885	0.000	0,118
SURE Fixed effects with dummy				
β	0,912	4,676	0.000	0,110
θ	−0,050	−0,155	0.877	
SURE Fixed effects with dummy and excluding Extremadura and Castilla - La Mancha				
β	1,188	4,479	0.000	0,189
θ	−0,762	−1,889	0.062	

Source: Dow and Rodríguez-Fuentes (2003: 976).

Table 6.9 Estimates for the wealthier regions

	Coefficient	t-statistic	P value	R^2-co
SURE Fixed effects				
α	9,641	13,960	0.000	
β	0,867	5,807	0.000	0,193
SURE Fixed effects				
β	0,792	5,453	0.000	0,227
SURE Fixed effects with dummy				
β	0,709	3,961	0.000	
θ	0,229	0,671	0.530	0,224
SURE Fixed effects with dummy and excluding Baleares				
β	0,702	3,714	0.000	0,273
θ	0,818	2,082	0.049	

Source: Dow and Rodríguez-Fuentes (2003: 977).

and Castilla La Mancha) were excluded during the recession period due to their anomalous behaviour.[29] The results in this case seem to reinforce our hypothesis of higher instability of credit in lower-income regions than in higher-income regions.

The results show that for every 1% of growth in regional GDP (y) the rate of growth of credit for the poorer regions is 1.188%, much higher than for the wealthier regions (0.702%). It is significant that for the period of slower growth (1991–1993), the responsiveness of credit to income change during recessions is less for the lower-income regions, at 0.426%, compared to 1.520% for the more advanced regions. The results show that during expansionary periods the rate of growth of credit for the low-income regions is 1.69 times the rate for the wealthier, whereas for the period of slower growth it is only 0.28. We believe that these results support the Post Keynesian theory that claims a more unstable pattern for credit expansion alongside business cycles in low-income regions, and are also consistent with those obtained in earlier studies of Spanish regions (Rodríguez-Fuentes 1998).

6.5 Conclusions

This chapter has offered some empirical evidence which we think illustrates how monetary policy might produce different effects across regions or countries. The evidence provided in the chapter mainly refers to Europe, since the third stage of the EMU has raised fears that the single monetary policy will have asymmetric effects across the euro area countries. The chapter also presented some evidence for Spain in this regard, because we consider that the Spanish experience might provide useful insights for understanding the regional consequences of the single monetary policy.

The empirical results reported in Section 6.2 suggest that the single monetary policy has been quite inefficient in reducing inflation differentials among the euro member economies. In fact, our empirical evidence shows that from year 2000 on inflation has remained above its 2 percent objective and that inflation differentials among the euro area countries have not been removed despite monetary unification. In addition, persistence in inflation differentials in Europe seems to be much stronger than that observed in other long-established currency unions (Spain and the United States). The persistence of inflation differentials among the euro area countries not only questions the assumption that inflation in Europe is exclusively a monetary phenomenon, but also that the European Central Bank is implementing a 'one size' interest rate policy for the euro area. These two aspects might have important consequences for the macroeconomic performance of some regions/countries in the euro area.

The empirical evidence included in Section 6.3 showed that the Spanish regions responded differently to the monetary shocks during 1988–1998. Our empirical evidence also suggested that regional differences both in financial and economic structure were responsible for such differences in responses. Consequently, if differences in financial structure among the Spanish regions were not fully abolished, even under a unique monetary policy and regulatory framework for a long time, we concluded that current differences in financial structure of the euro area might well last much longer than expected and so contribute to a non-homogeneous impact of the single monetary policy.

Finally, Section 6.4 provided evidence on the existence of a more unstable pattern for credit availability in some regions in Spain. In particular, the results showed a much higher instability for the credit growth in the lower-income regions in Spain along business cycles, this result being compatible with the Post Keynesian theory that emphasizes the role of uncertainty, liquidity preference and financial structure in the determination of the regional credit markets, as well as the influence that monetary policy decisions might have on all these variables.

7   Conclusions

This book has presented a theoretical framework to study the regional effects of monetary policy. With this framework we aim to make a useful contribution to the current debate over the regional implications of the European Central Bank monetary policy.

The analysis of the real effects of monetary policy has usually been conducted from the transmission mechanism perspective. Our review of this literature in Chapter 2 showed that many discrepancies exist between different schools of economic thought with regard to the specification of the transmission mechanism. In addition, our review also suggested that most of these differences were more of degree than of kind as the idea of a mechanism that links real and monetary forces is commonly shared by all the participants in the debate. In fact, all the contributions reviewed in this chapter share the assumption that monetary policy is neutral unless there are some distortions in the economy (that of course are always removed in the long run). These distortions usually take the form of temporary nominal rigidities (wage and price stickiness) or imperfect (or asymmetric) information. But, without such distortions, monetary policy is always neutral since money is only the oil which lubricates the machine by acting as a medium of exchange. However, the oil is not considered to be an integral part of the machine itself.

In contrast, our analysis in Chapters 3 and 4 focused on the elaboration of a theoretical framework which explored the ways through which money and monetary policy may affect regions. Our framework emphasizes the role that the banking system and the liquidity preference of economic agents (including banks) play in the transmission of central banks' monetary policy decisions to regions within a country, or countries within a currency union.

As shown in Chapter 3, our theoretical framework is based on the assumption that, as the financial system develops (stage of banking development), the increase in liquidity depends more on banks' and borrowers' liquidity preference than on the central bank's direct interventions. Thus money supply becomes increasingly endogenous to the economic system. However, the concept of endogenous money in Chapter 3 does not imply that monetary policy does not influence the liquidity of the economic system, nor that the money supply is always horizontal. Instead, we suggested that central banks can always influence the liquidity of the system, but it is only influence, since monetary policy is only one of many factors which are involved in the process of liquidity creation. Our analysis also showed that, under certain conditions, money supply may become inelastic even though money is endogenous; for example, in an environment of high liquidity preference among borrowers and lenders. Furthermore, it was suggested that the money supply is likely to be more elastic during expansions rather than during downturns. That is, the pattern of credit expansion follows a cyclical pattern, as do changes in liquidity preference. Consequently, the notion of endogenous money in Chapter 3 does not mean that money is not important, as some orthodox and non-orthodox economists could argue. Instead, the endogenous money approach only removes the causal role attributed to money by orthodox economists, but not necessarily its power to affect real variables nor to affect the whole process of credit creation (Dow 1993a: 26).

As far as the analysis of the effects of monetary policy on economic activity is concerned, we pointed out that the debate over whether 'money matters vs doesn't matter' only makes sense when (i) there is a sharp distinction between the real and monetary sides of the economy and (ii) money is perfectly exogenous to the system. It is only when these two conditions are met that it is possible to analyze what happens to the real side when we introduce an exogenous change in the money supply. Only by assuming that economic activity depends on real factors such as labour, physical capital, etc. and monetary flows simply mirror real ones, can it be assured that money and monetary policy are neutral with respect to output and employment. Otherwise, the issue regarding whether money is neutral would not make any sense, just as it would not make sense to consider whether labour or physical capital were neutral. If such a clear distinction between real and monetary sides of the economy are not drawn, then efforts should be put into studying *when* and *how* rather than *whether* monetary policy is neutral or not. Whether monetary policy is neutral or not could only be addressed from a theoretical standpoint which, by assuming money to be exogenous to the economic process, tries to determine the long run effect of an exogenous increase in the money supply. However, if money were not exogenous then this matter would not be relevant, and the issue to analyze would rather be how exogenous monetary interventions in financial markets affect the liquidity of the system and thereby economic activity.

Our framework also suggested that, when money is endogenous, the analysis of the effects of monetary policy must be context-dependent since the final effect of any monetary change will depend on the final use given to the new money which is supplied. This is what Chick (1973: 132) has labelled as the second half of the monetary transaction. In this sense, an endogenous money supply perspective would mean that the time and location where 'the helicopter' throws the money is of crucial importance when analyzing its effects. This led us to distinguish two dimensions when analyzing the effects of monetary policy on economic activity: a structural dimension and a behavioural dimension. The first is concerned with the effects of exogenous monetary changes on different economic variables (the *structural effect*). The second dimension is related to the effect that such changes may have on agents' behaviour (the *behavioural effect*). The more developed the financial system is, the more relevant this second factor will be.

Chapter 4 presented a theoretical framework to explore the ways through which monetary policy can affect regions. One of the peculiarities of the analysis presented in this chapter is that it explicitly considers the regional differences in terms of banking structures and liquidity preference of financial agents (including banks). These two variables allowed us to consider a new way through which monetary policy can affect regions differently: the *behavioural effect*. In particular, our analysis suggested that monetary policy can affect regional credit availability through its influence on banks' and borrowers' liquidity preference and that regional differences in banking development and liquidity preference may produce higher instability in credit availability in the less-developed regions. This argument clearly contrasts with the belief that peripheral regions face a long run decrease in their credit shares because banks tend to lend in these markets less than they borrow, whereas the contrary applies to more-developed regions. On the contrary, our analysis suggested that cyclical changes in the liquidity preference of economic agents, which might be influenced by monetary policy, are likely to produce unstable patterns of credit availability for some particular regions.

This argument has important implications for empirical work. Whereas most empirical work concentrates on studying the structural differences which might cause different regional responses to national monetary policy shocks, our theoretical framework suggests focusing on the factors which determine regional credit availability. Consequently, empirical research cannot be limited to the study of regional differences in response to exogenous monetary shocks, nor how a given amount of credit is distributed among regions by the banking system. These might be the right issues to address when money is exogenous (the banking multiplier applies because of a low level of banking development), but not when the supply of credit increasingly depends on banks' and borrowers' financial decisions (reflecting a high level of banking development). One of the many consequences of the framework presented in this book is that the proper analysis of the regional impact of monetary policy should explicitly take into account the spatial differences in terms of banking development and liquidity preference, as well as the influence that monetary policy may have on such variables (the *behavioural effect*), and not only the structural differences that might produce regional asymmetric responses to exogenous monetary policy shocks (the *structural effect*).

Nevertheless, our survey of regional finance literature (Chapter 5) revealed that most contributions attribute the regional effects of monetary policy to either the existence of a market failure (lack of information, segmentation, money illusion, etc.) or to structural differences which make the transmission mechanism differ from one region to another. This is true both for the early contributions in this field (Beare 1976) and for the more recent contributions concerned with the implications that the cross-country differences in financial and economic structure in EMU may have for the transmission mechanism of the ECB monetary policy (see Kashyap and Stein 1997b, Cecchetti 1999, Bondt 2000). Consequently, most empirical works have focused on studying what we have called the *structural effect* of monetary policy, where the asymmetric impact of monetary policy is usually explained by differences in economic and/or financial structure that increase the sensitivity of some regions to exogenous monetary shocks.

It should be noted that the literature concerning monetary transmission in EMU omits an important point: that the real effects of monetary policy also depend on the 'behavioural responses' of economic agents, and not only on the existence of temporary nominal rigidities or asymmetric information. The analysis developed in this book was aimed to highlight this point: that monetary policy can have real regional effects both for the differences in economic structure and for the differences in responses of economic agents. We think this argument is important because the current structural differences in Europe might disappear sometime in the future, but this would not necessarily mean that asymmetries in the transmission of monetary policy would automatically vanish: there would still be scope for asymmetries arising from differences in the behavioural responses of economic agents to monetary policy.

Chapter 6 presented some partial empirical evidence which we think illustrates why monetary policy matters for regions. Three different (but related) results were reported in this chapter. First, for the EMU area, our results suggest that the single monetary policy has been quite inefficient in reducing inflation differentials among the euro member economies. In fact, our evidence shows that from the year 2000 on inflation has stayed above its 2 percent objective and that inflation differentials among the euro area countries have not been removed despite monetary unification. In addition, persistence in inflation differentials in Europe seems to be much stronger than that observed in other long-established currency unions (Spain and the United States). The persistence of inflation differentials among the euro area countries not only questions the assumption that inflation in Europe is exclusively a monetary phenomenon, but also that the European Central Bank is implementing a 'one-size' interest rate policy for the euro area. These two aspects might have important consequences for the macroeconomic performance of some regions/countries in the euro area.

The second result regards the Spanish experience. The empirical evidence included in Chapter 6 showed that the Spanish regions responded differently to the monetary shocks during 1988–1998. Our empirical evidence also suggested that regional differences both in financial and economic structure were responsible for such differences in responses. Consequently, if differences in financial structure among the Spanish regions were not fully abolished, despite having had a unique monetary policy and regulatory framework for a long time, we concluded that current differences in financial structure of the euro area might well last for longer than expected and so contribute to a non-homogeneous impact of the single monetary policy.

Finally, Chapter 6 also reported evidence of a more unstable pattern for credit availability in some regions in Spain. In particular, the results showed a much higher instability for credit growth in the lower-income regions in Spain along business cycles. This result is compatible with the Post Keynesian theory that emphasizes the role of uncertainty, liquidity preference and financial structure in the determination of the regional credit markets, as well as the influence that monetary policy decisions might have on all these variables.

Notes

1 Introduction

1 See the book by Angeloni *et al.* (2003), which gathers the results of a multi-year collaborative project conducted by the ECB and other Eurosystem central banks.

2 See the empirical evidence provided in Chapter 6 and in other published works (Rodríguez-Fuentes 1998, Rodríguez-Fuentes and Dow 2003).

3 Richardson (1973) has also offered some interesting clues as to why regional scientists have usually neglected any role for money and financial variables. One reason is that they have borrowed too freely from neoclassical growth theory the assumptions of free and costless movement of labour and capital among regions, full and costless availability of information, etc. These assumptions leave no role for money at the regional level. He also mentions that both the open character of regional economies and the absence of regional monetary tools leave regional economies without any monetary identity (Richardson 1973: 9–14).

4 Global monetarism points out the low effectiveness of monetary and exchange rate policies in small open economies. The underlying argument is that exogenous and expansive monetary shocks will lead to imbalances in the external sector due to the highly open character of these economies (see, for example, Ally 1975, Khatkhate and Short 1980, Corbo and Ossa 1982, Caram 1985, 1993, Worrel 1991). However, some authors have also recognized some effectiveness for certain policies such as selective credit controls (Khatkhate and Villanueva 1978, Crusol 1986, Blejer 1988). Rodríguez-Fuentes (2004) offers a survey of this literature and explores the possibilities for monetary policy in small island economies.

5 In these kinds of models national monetary policy affects regions through its incidence on national business cycles, which determine regional exports growth.

6 This is evident for example in the paper by Beare (1976), which can be regarded as a regional application of Andersen and Jordan's (1968) paper. The same could be said for Mathur and Stein (1980) and Garrison and Kort (1983).

7 One exception in this regard seems to be the paper by Chatelain *et al.* (2002).

2 A dichotomized view of the economic process: the transmission channels of monetary policy

1 Leeuw and Gramlich (1969), Spencer (1974), Tobin (1978), Laidler (1978), Romer and Romer (1990), Blanchard (1990), Miles and Wilcox (1991), Bernanke and Blinder (1992), Gertler and Gilchrist (1993b), Cecchetti (1995), Mishkin (1995, 1996 and 2001) and Handa (2000) deal specifically with

this issue. However, either intentionally or not, most literature on the effects of monetary policy on economy also includes references to such a concept.

2 The long list of contributions in this regard should start with the influential paper by Friedman and Meiselman (1963), where the authors tested the relationship between money and aggregate expenditure for the US economy, and could go on with, among others, the contributions by Andersen and Jordan (1968), Meiselman and Simpson (1971), Keran (1970a, 1970b, 1970c), Sims (1972), Carlson (1978), Dewald and Marchon (1978), Hafer (1982), Batten and Hafer (1983), Batten and Thornton (1983), Chowdhurry *et al.* (1986), Kretzmer (1992), Becketti and Morris (1992) and Rasche (1993). However, these 'monetarist' results have also been questioned and challenged by many others: Poole and Kornblith (1973), Waud (1974), Lombra and Torto (1974), Williams *et al.* (1976), Friedman (1977), Vrooman (1979), Feige and Pearce (1979), Seaks and Allen (1980), Cooley and Leroy (1985), Darrat (1986), Spencer (1989), Chowdhurry (1986a, 1986b) and Friedman and Kuttner (1992).

3 It is said that money may affect output within the short term when price increases precede cost increases. The former is likely to happen when some costs are fixed, at least within the short term (for example, wages). In turn, this 'price–cost gap' would allow some producers to make profits by increasing their production and so employment. However, this situation cannot last for long since cost, both financial – interest rates and labour – wage indexation will finally rise.

4 Johnson has considered these two points, i.e. the fact that inflation is an important question and that monetarism has provided both its explanation and a policy to deal with it, among the factors which would help to explain the relative success of the monetarist counter-revolution. He put it as follows: 'New ideas win a public and a professional hearing, not on their scientific merits, but on whether or not they promise a solution to important problems...the monetarist counter-revolution has ultimately been successful because it has encountered a policy problem – inflation...for which...[it] has both a theory and a policy solution.' (Johnson 1971: 12).

5 Friedman symbolized the theoretical demand function for money for an individual wealth holder in the way shown in equation 2.6, and considered that, with some minor adjustments in some variables, the business demand for money could be obtained and therefore, by aggregation, the total demand for money (Friedman 1970: 202–206).

6 Although Friedman has given a specific rate of monetary growth to follow (4 or 5 per cent according to his empirical estimates), he has also pointed out many times that 'a *steady* and known rate of increase in the quantity of money is more important than the precise numerical value of the rate of increase.' (Friedman 1970: 48). See also Friedman, opus cit., pp. 108–109 and 184–187.

7 For a formal exposition on how to arrive at such expressions see, for example, Branson (1985), Chapter 5.

8 This is the transmission in the closed version, i.e. the model which neglects the existence of the external sector for the economy. The open version of the mechanism will be considered later on.

9 See, among others, Tobin (1947, 1956, 1958), Latané (1954), Friedman (1959), Bronfenbrenner and Mayer (1960), Meltzer (1963), Brunner and Meltzer (1964), Courchene and Shapiro (1964), Laidler (1966, 1977), Laidler and Parkin (1970), Goldfeld (1973) and Judd and Scadding (1982).

10 See, for example, Akthar and Harris (1987), Chouraqui *et al.* (1988, 1989), Mauskopf (1990) and Mosser (1992).

11 The existence of such a difference could only be explained by transaction costs, differential risks and low substitutability among national and international financial assets.

12 Unless some effective sterilization policy is being run by the national monetary authorities.

13 This does not necessarily mean that national rates are equal to international ones since some mark-up may allow for differential country risks, imperfect asset substitution, transaction costs or whatever. This would imply that international differences in interest rates would move in the same direction.

14 This would happen when there is a lack of information (imperfect information) which misleads agents in their expectation formation process.

15 See among others Mishkin (1982), Boschen and Grossman (1982), Fitzgerald and Pollio (1983) and Driscoll *et al.* (1983).

16 They also agree in their belief that 'macroeconomics should be grounded in microeconomic principles, and that understanding macroeconomic behavior requires the construction of a (simple) general equilibrium model' (Greenwald and Stiglitz 1993b: 23–24). This is also claimed by the proponents of the New Neoclassical Synthesis, as it will be shown in the next section.

17 See, among others, Stiglitz and Weiss (1981), Bernanke (1983, 1993), Gertler (1988), Bernanke and Blinder (1988, 1992), Bernanke and Gertler (1995), Romer and Romer (1990), Greenwald and Stiglitz (1993a), Gertler and Gilchrist (1993b), Kashyap *et al.* (1993) and Kashyap and Stein (1997a).

18 Bernanke and Blinder (1988) take into account this assumption and introduce both money and credit into the standard IS-LM model with the aim to give a role to the bank-lending channel.

19 See, for example, Bernanke and Blinder (1992), Gertler and Gilchrist (1993b) and Kashyap *et al.* (1993).

20 Meyer has suggested that even though 'money plays no explicit role in today's consensus model', the influence of monetarism is beneath its surface, particularly regarding the issues of what monetary policy can and cannot do, and the key role played by central banks to achieve price stability (Meyer 2001: 3).

21 According to Meyer (2001: 2), the consensus macro model is represented by the three following dynamic equations:

$$Y_t^g = aY_{t-1}^g + bE_t\left(Y_{t+1}^g\right) - c[R_t - E_t(p_{t+1})] + x_t \tag{a}$$

$$p_t = d\left(Y_t^g\right) + w_1 p_{t-1} + w_2 E_t(p_{t+1}) + z_t \tag{b}$$

$$R_t = r^* + E_t(p_{t+1}) + f Y_t^g + g\left(p_{t-1} - p^t\right) \tag{c}$$

where Y^g is the output gap, R is the nominal interest rate, r^* is the equilibrium interest rate, p is inflation, p^t is the inflation target, x and z are stochastic shocks, and $w_1 + w_2 = 1$.

22 See Romer (2000) for further details in this respect.

23 For example, the monetary policy rule employed in the Clarida *et al.* (1999: 1696) paper is a forward-looking version of the simple Taylor rule (Taylor 1993) with interest rate smoothing.

24 Further details can be found in Clarida *et al.* (1999: 1665–1667) and Meyer (2001: 3).

25 The average mark-up is defined as the ratio of the average firm's price to marginal cost of production (Goodfriend and King 1998: 26).

3 Beyond transmission mechanisms

1 One exception to this exogenous money view is the Real Business Cycle theory (Kydland and Prescott 1982, 1990, Long and Plosser 1983), which considers

that money mirrors real output changes and that these changes are caused by real shocks (mainly technological ones) that have nothing to do with monetary policy (King and Plossser 1984).

2 On this point, see Davidson (1978a, 1992, 1994), Chick (1984), Kregel (1984–85) and Arestis (1992).

3 For example, Moore sees the money supply as horizontal in interest rate because banks will always meet any demand for credit. He argues his position saying that 'banks are price setters and quantity takers in both their retail loan and their deposit markets' (Moore 1988b: 381). However, this position, which has been labelled as horizontalist, is not universally shared by all post Keynesians. See, for example, Wray (1990), Dow (1993a, 1996b) and Chick and Dow (2002).

4 Dow (1995) offers a review and a categorization of the concept of uncertainty whereas Dow (1998, 2004a) explores its consequences for credit availability and monetary policy, respectively.

5 See Shackle (1955), particularly Chapters I–IX.

6 The papers by Wray (1992a) and Desai (1998) deal with the distinction between endogenous and exogenous. See also Dow (1993a), Chapter 3, for the implications of an endogenous money approach.

7 For an account on Keynes' own view on endogeneity and further developments of this concept made by post Keynesian, see Dow (1996a). See also Foster (1986) for Keynes' view on endogenous and exogenous money.

8 Chick (2005) offers an interesting analysis of the 'story of the struggle for, and loss of, the concept of endogenous money'. Her analysis suggests that the concept of endogenous money was one time widely accepted but 'was lost in favour of the money-base theory through very subtle changes of emphasis and language. Partly through excessive formalization of the multiplier and partly through reinterpreting cash reserves from a limitation on banks to an instrument of control, the multiplier came to support the monetarist project' (Chick 2005: 63).

9 This price rigidity is also explained by the existence of long term contracts in the labour market. See, for example, Fischer (1977).

10 Feige and McGee (1977) and Feige and Pearce (1979) have studied the causal relationship between reserves and money supply, and money and income. respectively. Neither found clear evidence suggesting that the FED can control reserves nor money causes income. Some further evidence on the 'reverse causation argument' can be found in Lombra and Torto (1973) and Wray (1990: Chapter 7). The general argument is that it is impossible to clearly distinguish between the influence of the money stock on economic activity from the influence of economic activity on the money stock. It is impossible then to clearly 'identify' money demand and supply ('identification problem').

11 Although this point will be taken again below, we must point out here the matter regarding whether the supply of money is fully determined by the demand for credit remains controversial.

12 Wray provides some empirical evidence of the ways through which the banking system frees from reserve constraints (Wray 1990: Chapter 7).

13 Some authors have interpreted Moore's model as an IS-LM model with a horizontal money supply. However, and as Wray has rightly pointed out, 'the primary difference between Moore's position and that of an IS-LM model with and interest rate target [horizontal money supply] lies in the mechanism through which money enters the economy. In the IS-LM models, the central bank supplies more reserves and ... banks find they can make more loans ... In Moore's model, money demand rises because economic agents desire to

increase spending [and] ... banks passively respond by issuing more money and then try to obtain reserves to meet legal requirements' (Wray 1992a: 1155).

14 Goodhart (1989c).

15 An example of this implicit separation is seen in the design of the European Monetary Union.

16 See Duca (1993) and Clair and Tucker (1993) for an account of these arguments.

17 Interbank lending, discount window and lender of last resort facilities, access to external financial markets, increased banking competition, financial innovation, etc., would be among the factors which would explain this process.

18 Chick and Dow (2002) also mention that the 'central bank's influence is not simply a matter of determining *the interest rate*. Rather, monetary policy generally consists of a combination of quantity effects and price effects, none of which is deterministic. The scope for the central bank to get these effects to *bite* is limited by the state of expectations, by the institutional arrangements through which interest rate effects are transmitted, and by the capacity of the banks to rearrange portfolios in order to avoid quantity effects' (Chick and Dow 2002: 605).

19 Reference removed.

20 Credit demand for speculative activities (speculative demand) is likely to be less interest elastic as these activities may have attached higher returns, because of their risky nature, within shorter periods of time. As regards personal demand, this could also show low interest elasticity since personal borrowing decisions are likely to be determined by personal income expectations (wages, employment, etc.) rather than by its cost (interest rates). The former is reinforced by the fact that personal borrowing is sometimes aimed to provide households with goods of first need (low price elasticity, such as housing, etc.).

21 This factor may depend on borrower's size since larger firms usually have access to other financial sources than bank credit.

22 Moore (1988a) being the leading author.

23 See Cottrell (1994) for a survey.

24 J.C.R. Dow and Saville (1990: 23–27) have also made a similar point to this. They have distinguished two points in bank intermediation. The first one is a 'potential equilibrium point' whereas the second one would be the 'operative equilibrium point', both of which would move forward in a growing economy. The potential equilibrium point is defined as the 'desired lending' by final lenders and borrowers, being the operative equilibrium point that banks themselves find profitable.

25 See Minsky (1982), especially Chapters 5–7.

26 J.C.R. Dow and Saville (1990: 55) argue that 'although banks are many and separate, collectively the banking system behaves in some respects as a block. ... The conformity in behaviour probably reflects not oligopoly but other reasons, ... Banks are in the business of maturity transformation ... Short-term funding will become harder to obtain if doubt develops about the quality of bank loans; ... Thus, it is essential to each bank to maintain market confidence in its management, and this in general will require following lending policies similar to those other banks'.

27 The papers by Moore (1989a), Niggle (1989b), Ash and Bell (1991) and Arestis and Howells (1994) have dealt with some of the redistributional effects of high levels of interest rates.

28 However, one wonders how money could possibly matter within a model which explicitly assumes real variables (real income) to depend only on real factors (physical capital and labour). If by definition we take money away

from the real sector, how could it matter for real purposes? How could labour force matter if we consider that output does not depend on labour?

29 This is what Chick has labelled as the other half of monetary change (Chick 1992: 159–160).

30 By monetary conditions we do not only mean interest rates, but also expectations on future interest rates, economic growth and any other variable (information) which may affect borrowers' and lenders' behaviour.

4 The regional effects of monetary policy: a theoretical framework

1 See, for example, the contributions by Mathur and Stein (1980, 1982, 1983) and Garrison and Kort (1983). The papers by Mathur and Stein suggest that the use of reduced-form models was rather misleading since their results were biased. Garrison and Kort (1983) tried instead to support empirically the view that a strong and reliable relationship between regional income and fiscal variables also existed at the regional level.

2 For a review on the differential effects of monetary policy on different components of aggregate demand see, among others, Friedman (1989, 1990a), Fisher and Sheppard (1972, 1974), Meiselman and Simpsom (1971), Chouraqui *et al.* (1988, 1989), Akthar and Harris (1987), Mauskopf (1990) and Mosser (1992).

3 On this particular point see Jones (1985), and Carlino, Cody and Voith (1990). Some remarks on the Spanish case have been made by Martinez and Pedreño (1990), Pedreño and Pardo (1990), Pedreño (1992), and Martínez (1994). See also Hung (1992–93) for a study of the impact of the exchange rate appreciation on aggregate profits of exporting and import-competing firms in the US.

4 This is precisely the New Keynesian argument of credit rationing applied to a regional credit market.

5 For example, Doyle (1992) has made this the case for the regional impact of the EMU in Europe. See also Doyle (1988, 1991).

6 As we have seen, this is almost the same argument that current followers of the Optimum Currency Area theory now employ to explain the asymmetries that a one-size interest rate policy may have in Europe.

7 See, for example, Marelli (1985) and Folmer and Nijkamp (1985).

8 It is generally agreed that higher long term interest rates have a stronger effect on some economic sectors and some types of expenditure, particularly investment, than others, and that it is unlikely that those sectors and investments are to be evenly distributed within a national economic space. It is also generally agreed that a strong appreciation of the exchange rate will affect open regions more than closed ones. Furthermore, even among the 'open regions group', exchange rate changes would have different regional effects as long as there were differences in the price elasticity of demand for exports.

9 For instance, it is argued that if no intervention exists and information is made available to all agents, financial markets would allocate funds in the 'best place'.

10 See Chick (2000) for a discussion of the distinctions between these approaches.

11 On this point, see Chapter 3, particularly Section 3.4 and also Chapter 5, particularly Section 5.3, where the Post Keynesian theory of regional finance is reviewed.

12 See Chapter 3, particularly Section 3.2.

13 This was found to be the case for Scotland in Dow (1992d).

14 Rodríguez-Fuentes (1998) and Rodríguez-Fuentes and Dow (2003) have provided some empirical evidence for the Spanish regions in this regard.

15 See Section 3.1 in Chapter 5.

16 It is known that small firms are more bank dependent than larger ones. This bank dependence has been explained by factors such as: (i) the existence of higher administrative costs, which could make it unprofitable to borrow small amounts in capital markets, (ii) the existence of thinner markets for financial assets supplied by small firms (low marketability); (iii) lack of (standard) information from small business; (iv) owner-managers unwilling to open 'family businesses' to outsiders (investors in capital markets); (v) lower collateral to be offered by small business, and (vi) greater difficulties attached to the credit risk assessment process (due to lack of information). All these factors would explain why small businesses are highly vulnerable to credit rationing.

17 One point to consider here would be the effect that financial regulation may have on different regional banks, or, alternatively, the existence of regional differences in financial regulation. Evanoff and Israilevich (1991) studied this latter effect for a sample of large US banks, and found evidence of 'adverse effect' of regulation by banks of one particular region in comparison to the rest. However, they also concluded that these banks seemed to be in a better position to bear the burden of regulation, this being explained by 'apparent adjustments' in their production technology (Evanoff and Israilevich 1991: 51–52).

18 At a higher price of course, but it would always supply the quantity needed.

19 Rousseas (1986), especially Chapters 4 and 5.

20 See Dow and Saville (1990), and particularly Chapters 3, 4, 8 and 9 as they offer an account of a central banks' power to influence both market interest rates and commercial banks' behaviour, respectively.

21 See the stages of banking development by Chick (1986, 1988).

22 Amado also mentions this particular problem when interpreting the ratio loans to deposits to study the role of the financial system in regional economic development in Brazil (Amado 1997: 141–147).

23 By means of offering information on sources of finance available to them, costs, etc.

24 This is the traditional new Keynesian 'adverse selection' effect.

25 The papers by Moore (1989a), Niggle (1989b), Ash and Bell (1991) and Arestis and Howells (1994) have addressed the consequences of monetary policy for personal income.

26 However, and even in the case that a regional monetary policy could be put in practice, most researchers also acknowledge that this would not be desirable because, after considering the advantages and disadvantages attached to this, it would be of little help. In fact, the running of a regional monetary policy would mean either the introduction of exchange controls or a regional currency. These, in turn, may entail some disadvantages. For example, exchange controls (higher transaction costs) could affect regional trade relationships. A regional currency would open the possibility for exchange rate management and, hence, some kind of balance of payment management. However, it is also acknowledged that the effectiveness of such policy would be of minor importance due to the adverse effects it could have on trade relations and because of the small and very open character of such economies. The papers by Tait (1977) and Robertson (1985) offer an analysis of these possibilities for the Scottish case. An analysis of the relative ineffectiveness of exchange rate policy in small open (island) economies can be found in Ally (1975), Khatkhate and Short (1980), Corbo and Ossa (1982), Crusol (1986), Worrell (1991) and Rodríguez-Fuentes (2004).

27 By looking at interest rates? The higher the interest rates the tighter the monetary policy is? By looking at the growth of monetary aggregates? The lower the growth the tighter the monetary policy? Clearly all these criteria only fit in

a world of perfect exogenous money, i.e. in a world where central banks can unilaterally decide whether to reduce monetary growth or not, for example. However, once we assume monetary growth to depend also on banks' behaviour the former argument is not so clear. Therefore, a low monetary growth could be also explained by either high banks' or borrowers' liquidity preference, since monetary growth now depends on whether borrowers decide to borrow and banks decide to meet all these demands as well, and not only on the central bank's (unilateral) decision of supplying more liquidity. Could central banks force banks to lend? Could commercial banks force borrowers to borrow? Couldn't banks first decide to lend if it is profitable to them and, afterwards, look for the reserves needed, either in national or international financial markets, or claiming them in the discount window? And, finally, could central banks really neglect such liquidity when banks really need it? Aren't central banks responsible for looking after the stability of the financial system?

28 Whether banks partially or totally meet this increase in demand for credit will depend on (i) their ability to satisfy such increase in credit demand and (ii) their willingness to supply such credit. The former factor depends on their capacity to extend credit beyond their deposit-base and on central bank interventions since they can make it more difficult, or not. The second factor will depend on whether banks share the same optimism, which leads borrowers to increase their demand, i.e. their regional liquidity preference.

5 Monetary policy, financial flows and credit markets: a survey of the regional literature

1 The 'experimentation' pointed out by Beare was prompted by some multi-collinearity problems (Beare 1976: 60, footnote 5).

2 Early models developed by, among others, Czamanski (1969) and Glickman (1977) would be included in this group, and clearly contrast with those other Neo-Classical models of regional growth which explicitly have denied any role for monetary variables to play in the explanation of regional economic growth. An example of the latter can be found in Borts (1968).

3 However, there are also some papers which explicitly do not fall in either of the categories as they do not explicitly show the implicit model followed. This is the case of Chase Econometric Associates (1981).

4 The indicator of the degree of 'monetary tightness' was M2 (money stock plus net time deposits) rate of growth.

5 Although YMFG, YAGR and YMIN are considered as the export regional sector (the basic sector), the authors chose YMFG as the only one which was directly affected by national monetary and fiscal variables. They assume both YAGR and YMIN were expected to respond to other external stimulus, such as movements in world food prices in the case of YAGR.

6 Miller defines these variables as 'the differences between cash items in process of collection and deferred availability cash items on the individual Reserve Bank balance sheets'. Since Federal Reserve Banks credit members banks for checks not collected yet, this may mean that 'regions having larger volume of checks flowing in from other areas will be the regions that have larger proportional increases in their net source base due to any increase in the national float item' (R.J. Miller 1978: 12–13).

7 However, there have also been contributions which have arrived at the conclusion that such lags do not exist. See, for example, Bryan (1967). Some

others have also argued that even if they existed, lags would be reduced by improvements introduced in the workings of the monetary markets during the 1960s and 1970s. However, McPheters (1976) found no significant change between the periods 1946–1960 and 1961–1969.

 8 We are referring here to the Chick's model of stages of banking development (Chick 1986). See also Chick and Dow (1988), and Chick (1993a) for two applications to a regional setting.

 9 Rockoff (1977) attributed the high interest rates existing in some US regions during 1870–1914 to their higher rates of bank failures.

10 Another difference with Schaaf's findings was that 'distance' was not significant any more.

11 As reported in Faini *et al.* (1993: 209).

12 The empirical evidence provided by Ebner (1976) showed that some regional differences existed in terms of the sensitivity of savings to changes in national interest rates. The model to test the hypothesis was (as reported in Roberts and Fishkind 1979: 22–24):

$$SLA = \beta_0 + \beta_1\,SA2L + \beta_2\,RTBL + \beta_3\,TIME$$

where *SLA* is deposits/state personal income, *SA2L* is *SLA* lagged one period, *RTBL* is the 3 month treasury bill rate and *TIME* a time trend variable.

13 This was estimated as:

$$M_i = \frac{national\ money\ supply}{national\ demand\ deposits} \times state\ demand\ deposits$$

14 On this point see, among others, the papers by Stiglitz and Weiss (1981), Gertler (1988), Bernanke and Blinder (1988, 1992), Bernanke and Gertler (1989), Bernanke (1993), Greenwald and Stiglitz (1993a) and Gertler and Gilchrist (1993b). A survey of this literature can be found in Cosci (1993) and Mattesini (1993).

15 See Chick and Dow (1988) and Dow (1987a, 1988) for a theoretical account. Dow (1987b) applies that theory to an open economy whereas Dow (1990, 1992d) and Chick (1993a) offer a case study for Canada, Scotland and the European Union, respectively. More recent contributions have applied that framework to study the regional patterns of credit availability in Spain (Rodríguez-Fuentes 1998, Rodríguez-Fuentes and Dow 2003).

16 This is the New Keynesian imperfect-information argument.

17 See Dow (1993a), Chapter 3, especially pp. 38–40. Minsky's (1982) Chapter 5 offers a comprehensive account of the relationship between lending expansion (contraction) and business cycles.

18 See the collection of papers included in Angeloni *et al.* (2003).

19 These differences are documented in De Bandt and Davis (1999), Danthine *et al.* (1999), Schmidt (1999), Bondt (2000), Maclennan *et al.* (2000), Padoa-Schioppa (2000), Kleimeier and Sander (2001) and Cabral *et al.* (2002).

20 To some extent this pessimistic view was challenged in Emerson *et al.* (1992: 212–234), where an optimistic evaluation of the effects of the European Monetary Union for the less-favoured regions in the EU is provided.

21 Several surveys of this literature can be found in Britton and Whitley (1997), Dornbusch *et al.* (1998), Kieler and Saarenheimo (1998), Guiso *et al.* (1999) and Mojon and Peersman (2001). Angeloni *et al.* (2003) gathers a collection of papers on this issue.

22 One exception in this regard seems to be the paper by Chatelain *et al.* (2002).

23 The relevance of the behavioural responses will be emphasized in the next chapter.

24 Christiano *et al.* (1999) offer a survey of the literature that employs VAR to study the transmission of monetary policy shocks.
25 See Rudebusch (1998). Kieler and Saarenheimo (1998) and Guiso *et al.* (1999: 58–61) expand further on how this criticism may affect the results and conclusions obtained in the empirical literature for the EMU.
26 Kieler and Saarenheimo (1998: 8–9) report other examples of large-scale macroeconomic multi-country models, such as the US Federal Reserve's MCM model, the IMF's Multimod standard simulations.
27 Apart from the above mentioned works by Kieler and Saarenheimo (1998) and Guiso *et al.* (1999), see Peersman and Smets (2001), van Els *et al.* (2002) and Peersman (2003).
28 See Bernanke (1993) for an account of the bank lending view, and Greenwald *et al.* (1993) for its regional implications. Gertler and Gilchrist (1991) and Kashyap *et al.* (1993) analyze the implications for firms' financing.
29 However, Elbourne and Haan (2004: 21) provide some empirical evidence that shows that 'the result and conclusion of Cecchetti (1999) is not robust across model specifications'.

6 Some empirical evidence

* The empirical evidence provided in this chapter is the result of my joint research with other colleagues. In particular, Sections 6.2 and 6.3 are co-authored with David Padrón and Antonio Olivera, while section 6.4 is co-authored with Sheila Dow.

1 The single currency was expected to remove market segmentation, enhance market competition and therefore make the law of one price work in the medium term.
2 The purpose of this change is 'to maintain a sufficient safety margin to guard against the risks of deflation' (ECB 2003a: 79). However, if inflation is a monetary phenomenon, as the ECB seems to believe when justifying the first pillar of its monetary policy scheme, there should not be room for deflation because the central bank could always produce inflation by increasing the money supply. If the central bank has the tools to avoid excess money, it should also be able to avoid the reverse situation. If this is not the case, then what's the point in keeping an eye on the rate of growth of the M3 in the long run (the first pillar)?
3 Of course, the ECB could always reply that inflation is a monetary phenomenon only in the long run, so it is still too soon to say anything about monetary policy effectiveness in Europe (actually, the single monetary policy has been working only since 1999). However, there is empirical evidence showing that the correlation between money and inflation is weak for the low inflation countries, and that 'country specific factors have a significant influence on the strength of such relationship' (De Grauwe and Polan 2001). King (2002) provides evidence on the strong correlation between monetary growth and inflation in the long run, although in the short run this correlation is less evident. In addition, he points out that 'correlation, of course, is not causation'.
4 That institutional change had straightforward and substantial implications for the continuity and availability of reliable statistical information which would be crucial for the decision-making process at the ECB, for example.
5 A comprehensive analysis of the implications of model uncertainty for monetary policy transmission can be found in Dow (2004a).

6 For a fuller description see Issing *et al.* (2001), Chapter 7.
7 The reference value was set in terms of an annual rate of growth of 4.5 percent for the entire euro area. Interestingly, this value was worked out by using the quantity theory of money, assuming a 2 percent rate of growth for prices, a 2–2.5 percent rate of growth for GDP and a declining trend in the income-money velocity of circulation (ECB 1999).
8 See, for example, Gerlach and Schnabel (2000), Taylor (1999), Clarida *et al.* (1998, 2000), Nelson (2000), Batini and Haldane (1999) and Angeloni and Dedola (1999).
9 Article 105 of the EU Treaty.
10 Article 2 states that: 'The Community shall have as its task ... to promote throughout the Community a harmonious and balanced development of economic activities, sustainable and non-inflationary growth respecting the environment, a high degree of convergence of economic performance, a high level of employment and social protection, the raising of the standard of living and quality of life, and economic social cohesion and solidarity among Member States'.
11 We employed the industrial production index as an output variable and the Hodrick-Prescott filter as the method to extract the potential output. Output gap is measured as the 12 month average, intending to provide a smooth indicator of this variable.
12 In relation to expression (6.9), Taylor (1993) assumed the following values for the different parameters in the rule: $\hat{r} = \hat{\pi} = 2$, $\varphi_\pi = 1.5$ and $\varphi_\pi = 0.5$.
13 These factors can be of a real or financial nature. For a recent survey of this issue in the European Monetary Union, see Angeloni *et al.* (2002).
14 An explanation of the inflationary Spanish experience based on these factors can be found in Ledo *et al.* (2002).
15 See Balassa (1964) and Samuelson (1964).
16 Wage inflation is proportional to productivity growth in the traded sector. However, in the non-traded sector prices have to rise because productivity is assumed to grow slower than wage inflation.
17 Olivera (2003) provides evidence for Spain.
18 The recent developments of the housing markets both in Spain and Ireland could support this explanation.
19 An aspect that must be mentioned is the relevance of the analytical approach employed to introduce the pricing-to-market behaviour in the model. As Bergin (2003) states, the models that generate pricing to market by assuming that goods prices are sticky in the currency of the importer are unable to explain pricing to market in the context of a monetary union. However, models that use translog preferences (as the one proposed by Bergin, 2003) rely neither on multiple currencies nor sticky prices. For this reason, they can generate pricing to market in currency unions. These models have the advantage of remaining closer to the initial development of pricing to market in the microeconomic literature.
20 We employed the Harmonised Consumer Price Index (HCPI) data from Eurostat for the euro area countries, which is available from 1990 on.
21 We used three MSA for the United States; that is, the three MSA for which monthly data were available.
22 For drawing comparison, we stick here to the 'common practice' in current empirical work where the term monetary policy is understood as unanticipated (or non-systematic) monetary policy shocks (Christiano *et al.* 1999). However, it is important to take into account that this approach does not consider the systematic part of the monetary policy (Romer and Romer 1989 and Taylor

1995), which in reality can be at least as important as the 'monetary surprises'. McCallum has pointed out that 'the systematic component of monetary policy actions is at least as important as the study of the unsystematic component, also known as policy shocks' (McCallum 2001: 12). He concludes that, in studying the monetary policy transmission process, 'more emphasis should be given to the systematic portion of the policy behaviour and correspondingly less to random shocks – basically because shocks account for a very small fraction of policy instrument variability' (McCallum 2001: 38).

23 Although necessary for the empirical purposes of this section, we are aware that the very idea of identifying (or isolating) the so-called exogenous monetary shocks is misleading because it implicitly draws a sometimes arbitrary distinction between endogenous (real variables that respond to exogenous monetary interventions) and exogenous variables (monetary shocks which are aimed to affect real variables) which might impose hidden assumptions on the way monetary policy works in reality.

24 It should be noted that the use of VAR models to identify exogenous monetary shocks is not free from criticism (see Rudebusch 1998).

25 For further details on the estimation procedure see Rodríguez-Fuentes *et al.* (2004b).

26 Aragón, Baleares, Cataluña, Comunidad Valenciana, Madrid, Navarra, País Vasco and La Rioja.

27 Andalucía, Asturias, Canarias, Cantabria, Castilla La Mancha, Castilla León, Extremadura, Galicia y Murcia.

28 We use SURE instead of OLS (Ordinary Least Squares) due to the existence of high correlation in the variable *cred*. However, the estimates using OLS method offer similar results.

29 We follow here the results reported by Raymond (1990, 1993).

References

Akhtar, M.A. and Harris, E.S. (1987) 'Monetary policy influence on the economy: an empirical analysis', *Federal Reserve Bank of New York, Quarterly Review*, Winter, 19–31.

Alberola, E. and Tyrväinen, T. (1998) 'Is there scope for inflation differentials in EMU?', Working Paper no. 9823, Bank of Spain, Madrid.

Alberts, W. and Jung, A.F. (1970) 'Some evidence of the intra-regional structure of interest rates on residential mortgage loans', *Land Economics*, 46: 208–213.

Alesina, A., Blanchard, O., Galí, J., Giavazzi, F. and Uhlig, H. (2001) *Defining a macroeconomic framework for the euro area: Monitoring the European Central Bank, 3*, London: Centre for Economic Policy Research.

Ali, M.M. and Greenbaum, S.I. (1977) 'A spatial model of the banking industry', *Journal of Finance*, 32(4): 1283–1303.

Allen, L. and Price, D. (1984) 'Variations on the flow of credit from regional financial institutions as a source of instability in the regional economy: an application of causal analysis', *Regional Science Perspectives*, 14(2): 3–14.

Ally, A. (1975) 'The potential for autonomous monetary policy in small developing countries', in P. Selwyn (ed.) *Development Policy in Small Countries*, Croom Helm, Beckenham.

Altavilla, C. (2000) 'Measuring monetary policy asymmetries across EMU countries', CES Discussion Paper no. 00-22, Katholieke Universiteit Leuven, Belgium.

Amado, A. (1997) *Disparate Regional Development in Brazil*, Aldershot: Ashgate.

Amos, O.M. (1992) 'The regional distribution of bank closings in the United States from 1982 to 1988', *Southern Economic Journal*, 58(3): 805–815.

Amos, O.M. and Wingender, J.R. (1993) 'A model of the interaction between regional financial markets and regional growth', *Regional Science and Urban Economics*, 23(1): 85–110.

Andersen, L.C. and Jordan, J.L. (1968) 'Monetary and fiscal actions: a test of their relative importance in economic stabilization', *Federal Reserve Bank of St. Louis Review*, 50: 11–21.

Angeloni, I. and Dedola, L. (1999) 'From the ERM to the euro: new evidence on economic and policy convergence among EU countries', Working Paper no. 4, European Central Bank, Frankfurt.

Angeloni, I., Kashyap, A., Mojon, B. and Terlizzese, D. (2002) 'Monetary transmission in the Euro area', Working Paper no. 114, European Central Bank, Frankfurt.

Angeloni, I., Kashyap, A.K. and Mojon, B. (eds) (2003) *Monetary Policy Transmission in the Euro Area: A study by the Eurosystem Monetary Transmission Network*, Cambridge: Cambridge University Press.

Arestis, P. (1992) *The Post-Keynesian Approach to Economics: an Alternative Analysis of Economic Theory and Policy*, Aldershot: Edward Elgar.

Arestis, P. (ed.) (1988) *Post Keynesian Monetary Economics: New approaches to financial modelling*, Aldershot: Edward Elgar.

Arestis, P. and Howells, P. (1992) 'Institutional developments and the effectiveness of monetary policy', *Journal of Economic Issues*, 26(1): 135–157.

Arestis, P. and Howells, P. (1994) 'Monetary policy and income distribution in the UK', *Review of Radical Political Economics*, 26(3): 56–65.

Arestis, P. and Howells, P. (1996) 'Theoretical reflections on endogenous money: the problem with 'convenience lending' ', *Cambridge Journal of Economics*, 20: 539–551.

Arnold, I.J.M. (1999) 'The regional effects of monetary policy in Europe', unpublished manuscript, Universiteit Nyenrode, The Netherlands.

Arnold, I.J.M. (2001) 'The regional effects of monetary policy in Europe', *Journal of Economic Integration*, 16(3): 399–420.

Arnold, I.J.M. and Kool, C.J.M. (2002) 'The role of inflation differentials in regional adjustment: evidence from the United States', Department of Economics, University of Nyenrode, The Netherlands.

Arnold, I.J.M. and Vries, C.G. de (2000) 'Endogenous financial structure and the transmission of ECB policy', in J. von Hagen and C.J. Waller (eds) *Regional Aspects of Monetary Policy in Europe*, pp. 193–218, Boston: Kluwer Academic Publishers.

Arnold, I.J.M. and Vrugt, E.B. (2002) 'Regional effects of monetary policy in The Netherlands', *International Journal of Business and Economics*, 1(2): 123–134.

Ash, C. and Bell, D.N.F. (1991) 'The regional impact of changes in interest rates', Economics Department, Working Paper Series no. 91/5, University of Stirling, Scotland.

Aspinwall, R.C. (1979) 'Market structure and commercial bank mortgage interest rates', *Southern Economic Journal*, 36: 376–384.

Baghestani, H. and Mott, T. (1988) 'The money supply process under alternative federal reserve operating procedures: an empirical examination', *Southern Economic Journal*, 55(2): 485–493.

Bain, K. (1994) *Monetary Economics. Theory, Policy and Institutions*. Aldershot: Edward Elgar.

Balassa, B. (1964) 'The purchasing power parity doctrine: a reappraisal', *Journal of Political Economy*, 72: 584–592.

Balbach, A.B. (1981) 'How controllable is money growth?', *Federal Reserve Bank of St. Louis Review*, 63(4): 3–12.

Banco de Bilbao (1980) 'Flujos monetarios regionales y balanza de pagos', *Situación*, 7: 18–49.

Barran, F., Coudert, V. and Mojon, B. (1996) 'The transmission of monetary policy in European countries', Working Paper no. 96-03, CEPII (Centre d'Etudes Prospectives et d'Informations Internationales), Paris.

Barro, R.J. (1976) 'Rational expectations and the role of monetary policy', *Journal of Monetary Economics*, 2(1): 1–32.

Barro, R.J. (1977a) 'Long-term contracting, sticky prices, and monetary policy', *Journal of Monetary Economics*, 3: 305–316.

Barro, R.J. (1977b) 'Unanticipated money growth and unemployment in the United States', *American Economic Review*, 67(2): 101–115.

Barro, R.J. (1978) 'Unanticipated money, output, and the price level in the United States', *Journal of Political Economy*, 86(4): 549–580.

Barth, J., Phaup, M. and Pierce, D.M. (1975) 'Regional impact of open market operations on member bank reserves', *Journal of Economics and Business*, 28(1): 36–40.

Batini, N. (2002) 'Euro area inflation persistence', European Central Bank, Working Paper no. 201.

Batini, N. and Haldane, A.G. (1999) 'Forward-looking rules for monetary policy', in J.B. Taylor (ed.) *Monetary Policy Rules*, NBER Studies in Business Cycles, Volume 31, Chicago: University of Chicago Press and NBER.

Batten, D.S. and Hafer, R.W. (1983) 'The relative impact of monetary and fiscal actions on economic activity: a cross-country comparison', *Federal Reserve Bank of St. Louis Review*, 65(1): 5–12.

Batten, D.S. and Thornton, D.L. (1983) 'Polynomial distributed lags and the estimation of the St. Louis Equation', *Federal Reserve Bank of St. Louis Review*, 65(1): 12–25.

Batten, D.S. and Thornton, D.L. (1986) 'The monetarist-fiscal policy debate and the Andersen-Jordan Equation', *Federal Reserve Bank of St. Louis Review*, 68(8): 9–17.

Bayoumi, T. and Eichengreen, B. (1993) 'Shocking aspects of European Monetary Integration', in F. Torres and F. Giavazi (eds) *Adjustment and Growth in the European Monetary Union*, Cambridge: Cambridge University Press.

Bean, C., Larsen, J. and Nikolov, K. (2001) 'Financial frictions and the monetary transmission mechanism: theory, evidence and policy implications', Working Paper no. 113, European Central Bank, Frankfurt.

Beare, J.B. (1976) 'A monetarist model of regional business cycles', *Journal of Regional Science*, 16(1): 57–63.

Becketti, S. and Morris, C. (1992) 'Does money matter anymore? a comment on Friedman and Kuttner', Research Working Paper 92-07, Federal Reserve Bank of Kansas City, Kansas City.

Begg, D., Canova, F., Grauwe, P. de, Fatas, A. and Lane, P.R. (2002) *Surviving the Slowdown: Monitoring the European Central Bank, 4*, London: Centre for Economic Policy Research.

Begg, D., Wyplosz, C., Grauwe, P. de, Giavazzi, F. and Uhlig, H. (1999) *Monitoring the European Central Bank*, London: Centre for Economic Policy Research.

Benigno, P. and López-Salido, D. (2002) 'Inflation persistence and optimal monetary policy in the euro area', Working Paper no. 215, Bank of Spain, Madrid.

Beretta, S. and Iannini, G. (1982) 'Flows of bank credit and interregional financial disparities. The case of Italy, general aspects and hypotheses of research', *Giornalle degli Economisti e Annali di Economia*, 41(9–10): 639–650.

Bergin, P.R. (2003) 'One money one price? Pricing to market in a monetary union', *European Economic Review*, 47: 569–586.

Bernanke, B.S. (1983) 'Nonmonetary effects of the financial crisis in the propagation of the Great Depression', *American Economic Review*, 73(3): 257–276.

Bernanke, B.S. (1993) 'Credit in the macroeconomy', *Federal Reserve Bank of New York, Quarterly Review*, 18(1): 50–70.

Bernanke, B.S. and Blinder, A.S. (1988) 'Is it money or credit, or both, or neither?', *American Economic Review*, 78(2): 435–439.

Bernanke, B.S. and Blinder, A.S. (1992) 'The Federal Funds Rate and the channels of monetary transmission', *American Economic Review*, 82(4): 901–921.

Bernanke, B.S. and Gertler, M. (1989) 'Agency costs, net worth, and business fluctuations', *American Economic Review*, 79(1): 14–31.

Bernanke, B.S. and Gertler, M. (1995) 'Inside the black box: the credit channel of monetary policy transmission', *Journal of Economic Perspectives*, 9(4): 27–48.

Bias, P.V. (1992) 'Regional financial segmentation in the United States', *Journal of Regional Science*, 32(3): 321–334.

BIS (1995) *Financial Structure and the Monetary Policy Transmission Mechanism*, Basle: Bank for International Settlements.

Björksten, N. and Syrjänen, M. (2000) 'How problematic are internal euro area differences?', Working Paper 2000/14, European Institute, Robert Schuman Centre.

Blackburn, K. and Christensen, M. (1989) 'Monetary policy and policy credibility: theories and evidence', *Journal of Economic Literature*, 27: 1–45.

Blanchard, O. (1990) 'Why does money affect output? A survey', in B.M. Friedman and F.H. Hahn (eds) *Handbook of Monetary Economics*, Vol. II, Amsterdam: North Holland.

Blanchard, O. (2000) 'What do we know about macroeconomics that Fisher and Wicksell did not?', Working Paper 7550, National Bureau of Economic Research.

Blejer, M.I. (1988) 'Growth, investment, and the specific role of fiscal policies in very small developing economies', in A. Jorge and J. Salazar-Carrillo (eds) *Foreign Investment, Debt and Economic Growth in Latin America*, London: Macmillan Press.

Blinder, A.S. and Stiglitz, J.E. (1983) 'Money, credit constraints, and economic activity', *American Economic Review*, 73(2): 297–302.

Bober, S. (1988) 'Alternative views of the monetary sector in the macroeconomics course', *Eastern Economic Journal*, 14(4): 381–388.

Bondt, G.J. (2000) *Financial Structure and Monetary Transmission in Europe. A Cross-country Study*, Cheltenham: Edward Elgar.

Borts, G.H. (1968) 'Regional economic models. Growth and capital movements among US Regions in the Post-war period', *American Economic Review*, 58(2): 155–161.

Boschen, J.F. and Grossman, H.I. (1982) 'Tests of equilibrium macroeconomics using contemporaneous monetary data', *Journal of Monetary Economics*, 10: 309–333.

Bowsher, N.N., Daane, J.D. and Einzig, R. (1957) 'The flow of funds between regions of the United States', *Papers of the Regional Science Association*, 3: 139–159.

Boyd, W.E. (1970) 'Regional response to monetary policy 1960–1969', Ph.D. Dissertation, Florida State University.

Brainard, W.C. and Cooper, R.N. (1975) 'Empirical monetary macroeconomics: what have we learned in the last 25 years?', *American Economic Review*, 65(2): 167–175.

Brancati, R. (1988) 'Macro-economic and monetary control', in W. Molle and R. Cappellin (eds) *Regional Impact of Community Policies in Europe*, Aldershot: Avebury.

Branson, W. (1990) 'Financial market integration, macro-economic policy and the EMS', in C. Bliss and J. Braga et al. (eds) *Unity with Diversity*, Cambridge: Cambridge University Press.

Branson, W.H. (1985) *Teoría y política macroeconómica*, sixth edition, Madrid: Fondo de Cultura Económica.

Breuss, F. (2002) 'Is ECB's monetary policy optimal?', Working Paper no. 173, WIFO (Austrian Institute of Economic Research).

Britton, E. and Whitley, J. (1997) 'Comparing the monetary transmission in France, Germany and the United Kingdom: some issues and results', *Bank of England Quarterly Bulletin*, May, 37(2): 152–162.

Bronfenbrenner, M. and Mayer, T. (1960) 'Liquidity functions in the American economy', *Econometrica*, 28(4): 810–834.

Brunner, K. (1998) Money supply, in J. Eatwell, M. Milgate and P. Newman (eds) *The New Palgrave: a Dictionary of Economics*, Vol. 3, New York: Palgrave Publishers Ltd.

Brunner, K. (1989) 'The role of money and monetary policy', *Federal Reserve Bank of St. Louis Review*, 71(5): 4–22.

Brunner, K. and Meltzer, A.H. (1964) 'Some further evidence on the supply and demand functions for money', *Journal of Finance*, 19: 240–83.

Brunner, K. and Meltzer, A.H. (1988) 'Money and credit in the monetary transmission', *American Economic Review*, 78(2): 446–451.

Bryan, W.R. (1967) 'Bank adjustment to monetary policy: alternative estimates of the lag', *American Economic Journal*, 57(4): 855–864.

Cabral, I., Dierick, F. and Vesala, J. (2002) 'Banking integration in the Euro area', Occasional Paper Series, no. 6, European Central Bank, Frankfurt.

Cagan, P. (1990) 'A review of horizontalists and verticalists: the macroeconomics of credit money', *Journal of Economic Literature*, 28: 696–697.

Cagan, P. (1998) 'Monetarism', in J. Eatwell, M. Milgate and P. Newman (eds) *The New Palgrave: a Dictionary of Economics*, Vol. 3, pp. 492–497, New York: Palgrave Publishers Ltd.

Canzoneri, M., Cumby, R. and Diba, B. (1999) 'Relative labour productivity and the real exchange rate in the long run: evidence for a panel of OECD countries', *Journal of International Economics*, 47: 245–266.

Caram, A.R. (1985) 'Guidelines for monetary policy in small developing countries', in Kamiramides *et al.* (eds) *The Economic Development of Small Countries: Problems Strategies and Policies*, International Conference on Small Countries, 22–24 May, Malta.

Caram, A.R. (1993) 'The repercusions of financial imbalances in Suriname', *World Development*, 21(2): 291–299.

Carbó Valverde, S., Humphrey, D. and Rodríguez Fernández, F. (2003) 'Deregulation, banking competition and regional growth', *Regional Studies*, 37(4): 321–330.

Carbó Valverde, S., López del Paso, R. and Rodríguez Fernández, F. (2003) 'Medición de la competencia en mercados bancarios regionales', *Revista de Economía Aplicada*, 32: 5–33.

Carlino, G. and Lang, R. (1989) 'Interregional flows of funds as a measure of economic integration in the United States', *Journal of Urban Economics*, 26(1): 20–29.

Carlino, G., Cody, B. and Voigh, R. (1990) 'Regional impacts of exchange rates movements', *Regional Science Perspectives*, 20(1): 89–102.

Carlino, G.A. and Defina, R.H. (1996) 'Does monetary policy have differentials effects?', *Business Review*, Federal Reserve Bank of Philadelphia, March, 17–27.

Carlino, G.A. and Defina, R.H. (1998) 'Monetary policy and the U.S. states and regions: some implications for the European Monetary Union', Working Paper no. 98-17, Federal Reserve Bank of Philadelphia.

Carlino, G.A. and Defina, R.H. (1999) 'Do states respond differently to changes in monetary policy?', *Federal Reserve Bank of Philadelphia Business Review*, July-August, 17–27.

Carlson, K.M. (1978) 'Does the St. Louis Equation now believe in fiscal policy?', *Federal Reserve Bank of St. Louis Review*, 60(2): 13–19.

Carlson, K.M. (1986) 'A monetarist model for economic stabilization: review and update', *Federal Reserve Bank of St Louis Review*, 68(8): 18–28.

Carlson, K.M. and Hein, S.E. (1973) 'Four econometric models and monetary policy: the longer-run view', *Federal Reserve Bank of St. Louis Review*, 65(1): 13–23.

Carr, H.C. (1960) 'A note on regional differences in discount rates', *Journal of Finance*, 15: 62–68.

Caskey, J. and Fazzari, S. (1986) 'Macroeconomics and credit markets', *Journal of Economic Issues*, 20(2): 421–429.

Castells, A. and Sicart, F. (1980) 'Flujos financieros interregionales: una aproximación', *Hacienda Pública Española*, 63: 43–96.

Castelnuovo, E. (2003) 'Describing the Fed's conduct with Taylor rules: is interest rate smoothing important?', Working Paper no. 232, European Central Bank.

Cebula, R.J. and Zaharoff, M. (1974) 'Interregional capital transfers and interest rate differentials: an empirical note', *The Annals of Regional Science*, 8(1): 87–94.

Cecchetti, S.G. (1995) 'Distinguishing theories of the monetary transmission mechanism', *Federal Reserve Bank of St. Louis Economic Review*, 77: 83–97.

Cecchetti, S.G. (1999) 'Legal structure, financial structure, and the monetary policy transmission mechanism', NBER Working Paper no. 7151, National Bureau of Economic Research, Cambridge, Massachusetts, USA.

Cetorelli, N. and Gambera, M. (2001) 'Banking market structure, financial dependence and growth: international evidence from industry data', *Journal of Finance*, 56(2): 617–648.

Chase Econometric Associates (1981) 'Rural impacts of monetary policy', *Agricultural Economics Research*, 33(4): 1–11.

Chatelain, J.B., Ehrman, M., Generale, A., Martinez-Pages, J., Vermeulen, P. and Worms, A. (2002) 'Monetary transmission in the euro area: evidence from micro data on firms and banks', *Journal of the European Economic Association*, 1(2–3): 731–742.

Chick, V. (1973) *The Theory of Monetary Policy*, London: Gray-Mills Publishing.

Chick, V. (1983) *Macroeconomics After Keynes: A Reconsideration of the General Theory*, Oxford: Philip Allan.

Chick, V. (1984) 'Monetary increases and their consequences: streams, backwaters and floods', in A. Ingham and A.M. Ulph (eds) *Demand Equilibrium and Trade*, New York: St. Martin's Press.

Chick, V. (1985) 'Keynesians, Monetarists and Keynes: the end of the debate or a beginning?', in P. Arestis and T. Skouran (eds) *Post Keynesian Economic Theory. A Challenge to Neo Classical Economics*, Wheatsheaf Books, M.E. Sharpe.

Chick, V. (1986) 'The evolution of the banking system and the theory of saving, investment and interest', *Economies et Sociétés 20, Monnaie et Production*, 3: 111–126.

Chick, V. (1988) 'The evolution of the banking system and the theory of monetary policy', paper presented at the Symposium on 'Monetary Theory and Monetary policy: New Tracks for the 1990s', Berlin, 1988.

Chick, V. (1992), *On Money, Method and Keynes: Selected Essays of Victoria Chick* (edited by P. Arestis and S.C. Dow), London: Macmillan.

Chick, V. (1993a) 'Some scenarios for money and banking in the EC and their regional implications', in I.H. Rima (ed.) *The Political Economy of Global Restructuring, Volume II. Trade and Finance*, Aldershot: Edward Elgar.

Chick, V. (1993b) 'The evolution of the banking system and the theory of monetary policy', in S.F. Frowen (ed.) *Monetary Theory and Monetary Policy: New tracks for the 1990s*, London: Macmillan.

Chick, V. (2000) 'Money and effective demand', in J. Smithin (ed.) *What is Money?*, London: Routledge.

Chick, V. (2005) 'Lost and found: some history of endogenous money in the twentieth century', in G. Fontana and R. Realfonzo (eds) *The Monetary Theory of Production: Essays in Honour of Augusto Graziani*, London: Palgrave Macmillan.

Chick, V. and Dow, S.C. (1988) 'A Post Keynesian perspective on the relation between banking and regional development', in P. Arestis (ed.) *Post Keynesian Monetary Economics: New approaches to financial modelling*, Aldershot: Edward Elgar.

Chick, V. and Dow, S.C. (1996) 'Regulation and differences in financial institutions', *Journal of Economic Issues*, 30(2): 517–523.

Chick, V. and Dow, S.C. (2002) 'Monetary policy with endogenous money and liquidity preference: a nondualistic treatment', *Journal of Post Keynesian Economics*, 24(4): 587–607.

Chouraqui, J.C., Driscoll, M. and Strauss-Kahn, M. (1988) 'The effects of monetary policy on the real sector: an overview of empirical evidence for selected OECD economies', Working Paper no. 51, OECD (Organization for Economic Cooperation and Development), Paris.

Chouraqui, J.C., Driscoll, M.J. and Strauss-Kahn, M. (1989) 'The effects of monetary policy on the real sector: what do we know?', *Banca Nazionale del Lavoro Quarterly Review*, 168: 3–46.

Chowdhury, A.R. (1986a) 'A note on the relative impact of monetary and fiscal actions in India', *Indian Economic Journal*, 34(1): 89–93.

Chowdhury, A.R. (1986b) 'Monetary and fiscal impact on economic activities in Bangladesh: a note', *Bangladesh Development Studies*, 14(1): 101–106.

Chowdhury, A.R. (1988) 'Monetary policy, fiscal policy and aggregate economic activity: some further evidence', *Applied Economics*, 20: 63–71.

Chowdhury, A.R., Fackler, J.S. and Macmillin, W.D. (1986) 'Monetary policy, fiscal policy, and investment spending: an empirical analysis', *Southern Economic Journal*, 52(3): 794–806.

Christiano, L. and Eichenbaum, M. (1992) 'Liquidity effects, the monetary transmission mechanism, and monetary policy', *Federal Reserve Bank of Chicago, Economic Perspectives*, 16(6): 2–14.

Christiano, L., Eichenbaum, M. and Evans, C. (1999) 'Monetary policy shocks: what have we learned and to what end?', in J. Taylor and M. Woodford (eds) *Handbook of Macroeconomics*, Amsterdam: North Holland.

Clair, R.T. and Tucker, P. (1993) 'Six causes of the credit crunch', *Federal Reserve Bank of Dallas, Economic Review*, Third Quarter, 1–20.

Clarida, R., Galí, J. and Gertler, M. (1998) 'Monetary policy rules in practice: some international evidence', *European Economic Review*, 42: 1033–1067.

Clarida, R., Galí, J. and Gertler, M. (1999) 'The science of monetary policy: a new Keynesian perspective', *Journal of Economic Literature*, 37(4): 1661–1707.

Clarida, R., Galí, J. and Gertler, M. (2000) 'Monetary policy rules and economic stability: evidence and some theory', *Quarterly Journal of Economics*, 115(1): 147–180.

Clausen, V. (2001) *Asymmetric monetary transmission in Europe*, Berlin: Springer.

Clements, B., Kartolemis, Z.G. and Levy, J. (2001) 'Monetary policy under EMU: differences in the transmission mechanism?', Working Paper no. 01/102, International Monetary Fund (IMF), Washington, USA.

Cohen, B. and Kaufman, G. (1965) 'Factors determining bank growth by state: an empirical analysis', *Journal of Finance*, 20: 59–70.

Cohen, J. (1972) 'Copeland's money flows after twenty-five years: a survey', *Journal of Economic Literature*, 10(1): 1–25.

Cohen, J. and Maeshiro, A. (1977) 'The significance of money on the state level', *Journal of Money, Credit and Banking*, 9: 672–678.

Commission for the European Communities (1990) 'One market, one money', *European Economy*, October, 44.

Commission on Money and Credit (1971) 'The differential effects of monetary policy', in Prager, J. (ed.) *Monetary economics: Controversies in theory and policy*, New York: Random House.

Congdon, T. (1992) *Reflections on Monetarism*, Aldershot: Edward Elgar.

Cooley, T. and Leroy, S. (1981) 'Identification and estimation of money demand', *American Economic Review*, 71(5): 825–844.

Cooley, T. and Leroy, S. (1985) 'Atheoretical macroeconomics: a critique', *Journal of Monetary Economics*, 16: 283–308.

Corbo, V. and Ossa, F. (1982) 'Economías pequeñas y abiertas: una visión general', Pontificia Universidad Católica de Chile, Working Paper no. 80.

Cosci, S. (1993) *Credit Rationing and Asymmetric Information*, Aldershot: Edward Elgar.

Cottrell, A. (1986) 'The endogeneity of money and money-income causality', *Scottish Journal of Political Economy*, 33(1): 2–27.

Cottrell, A. (1988) 'The endogeneity of money: reply', *Scottish Journal of Political Economy*, 35(3): 295–297.

Cottrell, A. (1994) 'Post-Keynesian monetary economics', *Cambridge Journal of Economics*, 18: 587–605.

Courchene, T.J. and Shapiro, H.T. (1964) 'The demand for money: a note from the time series', *Journal of Political Economy*, 62(5): 498–503.

Cover, J.P. (1992) 'Asymmetric effects of positive and negative money supply shocks', *Quarterly Journal of Economics*, 107(4): 1261–1282.

Crusol, J. (1986) 'La politique monetaire dans les tres petites economies insulaires: l'experience des iles de la Caraibe anglophone: Barbade, Jamaique, Trinidad et Tobago', *Mondes en Developpement*, 14(56): 109–122.

Cutler, H. (1990) 'The accumulated effects of monetary policy', *Journal of Macroeconomics*, 12(4): 587–598.

Czamanski, S. (1969) 'Regional econometric models: a case study of Nova Scotia', in A.J. Scott (ed.) *Studies in Regional Science*, London: Pion Press.

D'Amico, N., Parigi, G. and Trifilidis, M. (1990) 'I tassi d'interesse e la rischiosita degli impieghi bancari', in Banca d'Italia, (ed.) *Il sistema finnaziario nel Mezzogiorno*, Roma: Banca d'Italia.

Danthine, J.P., Giavazzi, F., Vives, X., and von Thadden, E.L. (1999) *The future of European banking: Monitoring European Integration, 9*, London: Centre for Economic and Policy Research (CEPR).

Darrat, A.F. (1986) 'The economic impact of taxes in the US: some test based on the St. Louis Model', *Journal of Economic Studies*, 13(2): 3–13.

Davidson, P. (1978a) *Money and the Real World*, London: Macmillan.

Davidson, P. (1978b) 'Why money matters: lessons from a half-century of monetary theory', *Journal of Post Keynesian Economics*, 1(1): 46–70.

Davidson, P. (1982–83) 'Rational expectations: a fallacious foundation for studying crucial decision-making processes', *Journal of Post Keynesian Economics*, 5(2): 182–198.

Davidson, P. (1986) 'Finance, funding, saving, and investment', *Journal of Post Keynesian Economics*, 9(1): 101–110.

Davidson, P. (1988) 'Endogenous money, the production process, and inflation analysis', *Economie Appliquee*, 41(1): 151–169.

Davidson, P. (1989) 'On the endogeneity of money once more', *Journal of Post Keynesian Economics*, 11: 388–390.

Davidson, P. (1991) *Controversies in Post Keynesian Economics*, Aldershot: Edward Elgar.

Davidson, P. (1992) *International Money and the Real World*, second edition, London: Macmillan.

Davidson, P. (1994) *Post Keynesian macroeconomic theory: A foundation for successful economic policies for the twenty-first century*. Aldershot: Edward Elgar.

Davidson, P. and Weintraub, S. (1973) 'Money as cause and effect', *Economic Journal*, 83: 1117–1132.

Davis, E.P. (1992) *Debt, financial fragility and systemic risk*, Oxford: Clarendon Press.

Davis, R.G. and Banks, L. (1965) 'Interregional interest rate differentials', *Monthly Review, Federal Reserve Bank of New York*, August, 165–174.

De Bandt, O. and Davis, E.P. (1999) 'A cross-country comparison of market structures in European banking', European Central Bank Working Paper Series, no. 7, Frankfurt.

De Bandt, O. and Davis, E.P. (2000) 'Competition, contestability and market structure in European banking sectors on the eve of EMU', *Journal of Banking and Finance*, 24: 1045–1066.

De Grauwe, P. (1997) *The Economics of Monetary Integration*, third revised edition, Oxford: Oxford University Press.

De Grauwe, P. and Polan, M. (2001) 'Is inflation always and everywhere a monetary phenomenon', Discussion Paper no. 2841, London: Centre for Economic and Policy Research (CEPR).

De Grauwe, P. and Skuldeny, F. (2000) 'Inflation and productivity differentials in EMU', CES Discussion Paper no. 00-15, Katholieke Universiteit Leuven, Belgium.

De Grauwe, P. and Vanhaverbeke, W. (1991) 'Is Europe and optimum currency area? Evidence from regional data', Discussion Paper no. 555, Centre for Economic Policy Research, London.

Dedola, L. and Lippi, F. (2000) 'The monetary transmission mechanism: evidence from the industries of five OECD countries', Banca d'Italia Temi di Discussione no. 389.

Dedola, L. and Lippi, F. (2005) 'The monetary transmission mechanism: evidence from the industries of five OECD countries', *European Economic Review*, 49: 1543–1569.

Dehesa, G. and Krugman, P. (1992) 'EMU and the regions', Occasional Paper no. 39, London: Centre for Economic Policy Research.

Deiss, J. (1978) 'The regional adjustment process and regional monetary policy', *Rivista Internazionale di Scienzi Echonomiche e Commerciali*, 25(10): 858–877.

Desai, M. (1981) *Testing Monetarism*, London: Frances Printer.

Desai, M. (1998) 'Endogenous and exogenous money', in J. Eatwell, M. Milgate and P. Newman (eds) *The New Palgrave: A Dictionary of Economics*, Vol. 2, pp. 136–137, New York: Palgrave Publishers Ltd.

Dewald, W.G. and Marchon, M.N. (1978) 'A modified federal reserve of St. Louis spending equation for Canada, France, Germany, Italy, the United Kingdom, and the United States', *Kredit und Kapital*, 11(2): 194–212.

Dickey, D.A. and Fuller, W.A. (1979) 'Distribution of the estimators for autoregressive time series with a unit root', *Journal of the American Statistical Association*, 74: 427–431.

Dimand, R.W. (1986) 'The macroeconomics of the Treatise on Money', *Eastern Economic Journal*, 12(4): 431–442.

Dornbusch, R. and Giovannini, A. (1990) 'Monetary policy in the open economy', in B.M. Friedman and F.H. Hahn (eds) *Handbook of Monetary Economics*, North Holland.

Dornbusch, R., Favero, C. and Giavazzi, F. (1998) 'Immediate challenges for the ECB. Issues in formulating a single monetary policy', in D. Begg, D.J. von Hagen, C. Wyplosz and K. Zimmermann (eds) *EMU: Prospects and Challenges for the Euro*, Oxford: Blackwell Publishers.

Dow, A.C. and Dow, S.C. (1985) 'Animal spirits and rationality', in T. Lawson and H. Pesaran (eds) *Keynes' Economics: Methodological Issues*, London: Croom Helm.

Dow, A.C. and Dow, S.C. (1989) 'Endogenous money creation and idle balances', in J. Pheby (ed.) *New directions in Post Keynesian Economics*, Aldershot: Edward Elgar.

Dow, J.C.R. and Saville, I.D. (1990) *A Critique of Monetary Policy: Theory and British Experience*, Oxford: Clarendon Press.

Dow, S.C. (1982) 'The regional composition of the money multiplier process', *Scottish Journal of Political Economy*, 29(1): 22–44.

Dow, S.C. (1985) *Macroeconomic Thought: a Methodological Approach*, Oxford: Basil Blackwell.

Dow, S.C. (1986) 'The capital account and regional balance of payments problems', *Urban Studies*, 23(3): 173–184.

Dow, S.C. (1987a) 'Money and regional development', *Studies in Political Economy*, 23(2): 73–94.

Dow, S.C. (1987b) 'Post Keynesian Monetary Theory for an open economy', *Journal of Post Keynesian Economics*, 9(2): 237–257.

Dow, S.C. (1987c) 'The treatment of money in Regional Economics', *Journal of Regional Science*, 27(1): 13–24.

Dow, S.C. (1988) 'Incorporating money in regional economic models', in F. Harrigan and P. McGregor (eds) *Recent Advances in Regional Economic Modelling*, London Papers in Regional Science 19, London: Pion Press.

Dow, S.C. (1990) *Financial Markets and Regional Economic Development: the Canadian Experience*, Aldershot: Avebury.

Dow, S.C. (1992a) 'European monetary integration and the distribution of credit availability', in S. Corbridge, R. Martin and N. Thrift (eds) *Money, Power and Space*, Oxford: Blackwell.

Dow, S.C. (1992b) 'Money, finance and the role of the state', *Journal of Economic Surveys*, 6(2): 195–200.

Dow, S.C. (1992c) 'European Monetary Integration and the distribution of credit availability', paper presented at the Twenty Third Conference of the Regional Science Association International: British Section, University of Dundee, Scotland.

Dow, S.C. (1992d) 'The regional financial sector: a Scottish case study', *Regional Studies*, 26(7): 619–631.

Dow, S.C. (1993a) *Money and the Economic Process*, Aldershot: Edward Elgar.

Dow, S.C. (1993b) 'European Monetary Integration, endogenous credit creation and regional economic development', paper presented at the international congress 'The European Periphery Facing the New Century', IDEGA, Santiago de Compostela, Spain, 1993.

Dow, S.C. (1995) 'Uncertainty about uncertainty', in S.C. Dow and J. Hillard (eds) *Keynes, Knowledge and Uncertainty*, Aldershot: Edward Elgar.

Dow, S.C. (1996a) 'Endogenous money', in G.C. Harcourt and P. Riach (eds) *The Second Edition of Keynes's General Theory*, London: Routledge.

Dow, S.C. (1996b) 'Horizontalism: a critique', *Cambridge Journal of Economics*, 20(4): 497–508.

Dow, S.C. (1998) 'Knowledge, information and credit creation', in R.J. Rotheim (ed.) *New Keynesian Economics/Post Keynesian Alternatives*, London: Routledge.

Dow, S.C. (2002) *Economic Methodology: an Inquiry*, Oxford: Oxford University Press.

Dow, S.C. (2004a) 'Uncertainty and monetary policy', *Oxford Economic Papers*, 56: 539–561.

Dow, S.C. (2004b) 'Conocimiento, información y creación de crédito: impacto de la política monetaria', *Papeles de Economía Española*, 101: 99–111.

Dow, S.C. and Earl, P.E. (1982) *Money Matters: a Keynesian Approach to Monetary Economics*, Oxford: Martin Roberson.

Dow, S.C. and Rodríguez-Fuentes, C.J. (1997) 'Regional finance: a survey', *Regional Studies*, 31(9): 903–920.

Dow, S.C. and Rodríguez-Fuentes, C.J. (1998) 'The political economy of monetary policy', in P. Arestis and M. Sawyer (eds) *The Political Economy of Central Banking*, Aldershot: Edward Elgar.

Dow, S.C. and Rodríguez-Fuentes, C.J. (2000) 'Integración monetaria y estructura financiera. Implicaciones para los mercados regionales de crédito', *Información Comercial Española*, 785: 133–145.

Doyle, M.F. (1988) 'Economic and Monetary Union: the regional dimension', *Bank of Ireland, Quarterly Bulletin*, Winter: 44–51.

Doyle, M.F. (1991) 'European Monetary Union: an Irish perspective', *Bank of Ireland, Quarterly Bulletin*, Spring, No. 1.

Doyle, M.F. (1992) 'European Monetary Union: the impact on Ireland', *Bank of Ireland, Quarterly Bulletin*, Autumn, No. 3.

Dreese, G.R. (1974) 'Banks and regional economic development', *Southern Economic Journal*, 40(4): 647–666.

Driscoll, M.J., Ford, J.L., Moullineux, A.W. and Sen, S. (1983) 'Money, output, rational expectations and neutrality: some econometric tests for the UK', *Economica*, 50: 259–268.

Duca, J.V. (1993) 'Regulation, bank competitiveness and episodes of missing money', *Federal Reserve Bank of Dallas, Economic Review*, second quarter: 1–23.

Dwyer, G.P. Jr and Hafer, R.W. (1988) 'Is money irrelevant?', *Federal Reserve Bank of St. Louis Review*, 70(3): 3–17.

Earl, P.E. (1982) *Monetary Scenarios: A Modern Approach to Financial Systems*, Aldershot: Edward Elgar.

Earl, P.E. (1988) 'Bounded rationality, psychology and financial evolution: some behavioural perspectives on Post Keynesian analysis', in J. Pheby (ed.) *New Directions in Post Keynesian Economics*, Aldershot: Edward Elgar.

Eastburn, D.P. (1971) 'Uneven impacts of monetary policy: what to do about them?', in Praeger (ed.) *Monetary Economics: Controversies in Theory and Policy*, New York: Random House.

Ebner, M. (1976) 'Development, estimation and forecasting accuracy of regional financial models: an application within the State of Florida', Ph.D. Dissertation, University of Florida, Gainesville, FL.

ECB (1999) 'The stability oriented monetary policy strategy of the Eurosystem', *Monthly Bulletin, European Central Bank*, January, 39–50.

ECB (2000) 'The two pillars of the ECB's monetary policy strategy', *Monthly Bulletin, European Central Bank*, November, 37–48.

ECB (2003a) 'The outcome of the ECB's evaluation of its monetary policy strategy', *Monthly Bulletin, European Central Bank*, June, 79–92.

ECB (2003b) *Inflation differentials in the euro area: potential causes and policy implications*, European Central Bank: Frankfurt.

ECB (2004) *The monetary policy of the ECB*, European Central Bank: Frankfurt.

Edgar, R. (1978) 'Regional lags in deposit adjustment', Ph.D. Dissertation, Department of Economics, Ohio State University, Columbus, OH.

Edwards, F. (1964) 'Concentration in banking and its effects on business loan rates', *Review of Economics and Statistics*, 46: 294–300.

Ehrmann, M. (1998) 'Will EMU generate asymmetry? Comparing monetary policy transmission across European countries', EUI Working Paper ECO no. 98/28, European University Institute, Italy.

Eichengreen, B. (1993) 'Labor markets and European monetary unification', in P.R. Masson and M.P. Taylor (eds) *Policy Issues in the Operation of Currency Unions*, Cambridge: Cambridge University Press.

Eichner, A.S. and Kregel, J.A. (1975) 'An essay on Post-Keynesian Theory: A new paradigm in Economics', *Journal of Economic Literature*, 13(4): 1293–1314.

Elbourne, A. and Haan, J. (2004) 'Asymmetric monetary transmission in EMU: the robustness of VAR conclusions and Cecchetti's legal family theory', CESifo Working Paper no. 1327, Centre for Economic Studies (CES) and Institute for Economic Research (ifo), Munich.

Elliott, G., Rothenberg, T.R. and Stock, J.H. (1996) 'Efficient tests for an autoregressive unit root', *Econometrica*, 64: 813–836.

Emerson, M., Gros, D., Italianer, A., Pisani-Ferry, J. and Reichenbach, H. (1992) *One Market, One Money: An Evaluation of the Potential Benefits and Cost of Forming an Economic and Monetary Union*, Oxford: Oxford University Press.

Emmer, R.E. (1957) 'Influences on regional credit expansion', *Papers of the Regional Science Association*, 3: 166–179.

Evanoff, D.D. and Israilevich, P.R. (1991) 'Regional differences in bank efficiency and technology', *Annals of Regional Science*, 25(1): 41–54.

Evans, G. (1984a) 'The long run endogenous money supply', *Journal of Economic Issues*, 18: 66–74.

Evans, G.R. (1984b) 'The evolution of financial institutions and the ineffectiveness of modern monetary policy', *Journal of Economic Issues*, 18(2): 439–448.

Faini, R., Galli, G. and Giannini, C. (1993) 'Finance and development: the case of Southern Italy', in A. Giovannini (ed.) *Finance and Development: Issues and Experience*, Cambridge: Cambridge University Press.

Fazzari, S. and Minsky, H.P. (1984) 'Domestic monetary policy: If not monetarism, what?', *Journal of Economic Issues*, 18(1): 101–116.

Fazzari, S., Hubbard, R.G. and Petersen, B.C. (1988) 'Financing constraints and corporate investment', *Brookings Papers on Economic Activity*, 1: 141–195.

Feige, E.L. and McGee, R. (1977) 'Money supply control and lagged reserve accounting', *Journal of Money, Credit and Banking*, 9(4): 536–551.

Feige, E.L. and Pearce, D.K. (1979) 'The causal relationship between money and income: some caveats for time series analysis', *Review of Economics and Statistics*, 61(4): 521–533.

Fernández, F. and Andreu, J.M. (1978) 'Algunas consideraciones sobre los flujos financieros geográficos', *Estudios Regionales*, 2: 119–133.

Fischer, S. (1975) 'Recent developments in monetary theory', *American Economic Review*, 65(2): 157–165.

Fischer, S. (1977) 'Long-term contracts, rational expectations, and the optimal money supply rule', *Journal of Political Economy*, 85(1): 191–205.

Fisher, G.R. and Sheppard, D.K. (1972) *Effects of Monetary Policy on the United States Economy: A Survey of Econometric Evidence*, Occasional Economic Studies Series, OECD (Organization for Economic Cooperation and Development), Paris.

Fisher, G.R. and Sheppard, D.K. (1974) 'Interrelationship between real and monetary variables: some evidence from recent US empirical studies', in Johnson and Nobay (eds) *Issues in Monetary Economics*, Oxford: Oxford University Press.

Fishkind, H.H. (1977) 'The regional impact of monetary policy: an economic simulation study of Indiana 1958–1973', *Journal of Regional Science*, 17(1): 77–88.

Fitzgerald, M.D. and Pollio, G. (1983) 'Money, activity and prices: some inter-country evidence', *European Economic Review*, 23: 279–314.

Flechsig, T.G. (1965) 'The effect of concentration on bank loan rates', *Journal of Finance*, 20: 298–311.

Foley, D. (1998) 'Money in economic activity', in J. Eatwell, M. Milgate and P. Newman (eds) *The New Palgrave: a Dictionary of Economics*, Vol. 3, pp. 519–527, New York: Palgrave Publishers Ltd.

Folmer, H. and Nijkamp, P. (1985) 'Methodological aspects of impacts analysis of regional economic policy', *Papers of the Regional Science Association*, 57: 165–181.

Foster, G.P. (1986) 'The endogeneity of money and Keynes' General Theory', *Journal of Economic Issues*, 20(4): 953–967.

Frenkel, J.A. and Goldstein, M. (1991) 'Monetary policy in an emerging European Economic and Monetary Union. Key issues', *IMF Staff Papers*, 38(2): 356–373.

Friedman, B.M. (1977) 'Even the St. Louis Equation believes in fiscal policy', *Journal of Money, Credit and Banking*, 9: 365–367.

Friedman, B.M. (1988) 'Monetary policy without quantity variables', *American Economic Review*, 78(2): 440–445.

Friedman, B.M. (1989) 'Changing effects of monetary policy on real economic activity', in Federal Reserve Bank of Kansas City (ed.), *Monetary Policy Issues in the 1990s*, Missouri: Federal Reserve Bank of Kansas City.

Friedman, B.M. (1990a) 'Changing effects of monetary policy on real economic activity', NBER ng Working Paper no. 3278, National Bureau of Economic Research, Cambridge, Massachusetts, USA.

Friedman, B.M. (1990b) 'Targets, and instruments of monetary policy', in B.M. Friedman and F.H. Hahn (eds) *Handbook of Monetary Economics*, Amsterdam, North Holland.

Friedman, B.M. and Kuttner, K.N. (1992) 'Money, income, prices and interest rates', *American Economic Review*, 82(3): 472–492.

Friedman, M. (1956) 'The quantity theory of money: A restatement', in M. Friedman (ed.) *Studies in the Quantity Theory of Money*, Chicago-London: The University of Chicago Press.

Friedman, M. (1959) 'The demand for money: some theoretical and empirical results', *Journal of Political Economy*, 67(4): 327–351.

Friedman, M. (1969) *The Optimum Quantity of Money and Other Essays*, London: Macmillan.

Friedman, M. (1970) *A Theoretical Framework for Monetary Analysis*, New York: National Bureau of Economic Research.

Friedman, M. and Meiselman, D. (1963) 'The relative stability of monetary velocity and the investment multiplier in the United States', in Commission of Money and Credit (ed.) *Impacts of Monetary Policy*, Englewood Cliffs: Prentice-Hall.

Friedman, M. and Meiselman, D. (1964) 'Keynes and the Quantity Theory. Reply to Donald Hester', *Review of Economics and Statistics*, 46: 369–376.

Friedman, M. and Schwartz, A.J. (1963) 'Money and business cycles', *Review of Economics and Statistics*, 45(1): 32–64.

Fry, M.J. (1989) 'Financial development: theories and recent experience', *Oxford Review of Economic Policy*, 5(4): 13–28.

Galí, J. (2001) 'New perspectives on monetary policy, inflation and the business cycle', invited lecture at the Congress of the Econometric Society, Seattle, August 11–16, 2000.

Galí, J. (2003) 'Monetary policy in the early years of EMU', in M. Buti and A. Sapir (eds) *EMU and Economic Policy in Europe: The Challenges of the early years*, Cheltenham: Edward Elgar.

Ganley, J. and Salmon, C. (1997) 'The industrial impact of monetary policy shocks: some stylized facts', Working Paper no. 68, Bank of England, London.

Gardener, E.P.M. (1988) 'Innovation and new structural frontiers in banking', in P. Arestis (ed.) *Contemporary Issues in Money and Banking*, London: Macmillan.

Garrison, C.B. and Chang, H.S. (1979) 'The effect of monetary and fiscal policies on regional business cycles', *International Regional Science Review*, 4(2): 167–180.

Garrison, C.B. and Kort, J.R. (1983) 'Regional impact of monetary and fiscal policy: a comment', *Journal of Regional Science*, 23(2): 249–261.

Gentle, C. (1993) *The Financial Service Industry: The Impact of Corporate Reorganisation on Regional Economic Development*, Aldershot: Avebury.

Gentle, C. and Marshall, N. (1992) 'The deregulation of the financial services industry and the polarization of regional economic prosperity', *Regional Studies*, 26(6): 581–585.

Gerlach, S. and Schnabel, G. (1999) 'The Taylor rule and interest rates in the EMU area: a note', Working Paper no. 73, Bank for International Settlements, Basle.

Gerlach, S. and Schnabel, G. (2000) 'The Taylor rule and interest rates in the EMU area', *Economic Letters*, 67: 165–171.

Gerlach, S. and Smets, F. (1995) 'The monetary transmission mechanism: evidence from the G-7 countries', BIS Working Paper no. 26, Bank for International Settlements, Basle.

Gerlach, S. and Smets, F. (1999) 'The monetary transmission: evidence from G-7 countries', in BIS (ed.) *Financial Structure and the Monetary Policy Transmission Mechanism*, Basle: Bank for International Settlements.

Gertler, M. (1988) Financial structure and aggregate economic activity: an overview, *Journal of Money, Credit and Banking*, 20(3): 559–588.

Gertler, M. and Gilchrist, S. (1991) 'Monetary policy, business cycles and the behaviour of small manufacturing firms', NBER Working Paper no. 3892, National Bureau of Economic Research, Cambridge, Massachusetts, USA.

Gertler, M. and Gilchrist, S. (1993a) 'The cyclical behaviour of short-term business lending: Implications for financial propagation mechanisms', *European Economic Review*, 37: 623–631.

Gertler, M. and Gilchrist, S. (1993b) 'The role of credit market imperfections in the monetary transmission mechanism: arguments and evidence', *Scandinavian Journal of Economics*, 95(1): 43–64.

Giammarioli, N. and Valla, N. (2003) 'The natural real rate of interest in the euro area', ECB Working Paper no. 233.

Gibson, H.D. and Tsakalotos, E. (1993) 'European integration and the banking sector in Southern Europe: competition, efficiency and structure', *Banca Nazionale del Lavoro Quarterly Review*, 186: 299–325.

Gilbert, J.C. (1937–1938) 'The mechanism of interregional redistribution of money', *Review of Economic Studies*, 5: 187–194.

Glasner, D. (1985) 'A reinterpretation of classical monetary theory', *Southern Economic Journal*, 52(1): 46–67.

Glasner, D. (1989) 'On some classical monetary controversies', *History of Political Economy*, 21: 201–229.

Glickman, N.J. (1977) *Econometric Analysis of Regional Systems: Explorations in Model Building and Policy Analysis*, New York: Academic Press.

Glickman, N.J. (1980a) *The Urban Impacts of Federal Policies*, Baltimore: Johns Hopkins University Press.

Glickman, N.J. (1980b) 'Impact analysis with regional econometric models', in S. Pleeter (ed.) *Economic Impact Analysis: Methodology and Applications*, pp. 143–155, Studies in Applied Regional Science no. 19, Martinus Nijhoff Publishing.

Goldberg, M.A., Helsley, R.W. and Levi, M.D. (1989) 'The location of interregional financial activity: an interregional analysis', *Regional Studies*, 23(1): 1–7.

Goldfeld, S.M. (1966) *Commercial Banks Behaviour and Economic Activity*, Amsterdam: North Holland.

Goldfeld, S.M. (1973) 'The demand for money revisited', *Brookings Papers on Economic Activity*, 3: 577–638.

Goldfeld, S.M. (1976) 'The case of the missing money', *Brookings Papers on Economic Activity*, 3: 683–739.

Goldfeld, S.M. (1998) 'Demand for money: empirical studies', in J. Eatwell, M. Milgate and P. Newman (eds) *The New Palgrave: A Dictionary of Economics*, Vol. 1, pp. 770–775, New York: Palgrave Publishers Ltd.

Goldsmith, R.W. (1969) *Financial Structure and Development*, New Haven: Yale University Press.

Goodfriend, M. (1988) 'Comment on Financial Structure and aggregate economic activity: an overview', *Journal of Money, Credit and Banking*, 20(3): 589–593.

Goodfriend, M. (2004) 'Monetary policy in the New Neoclassical Synthesis: a primer', *Federal Reserve Bank of Richmond, Economic Quarterly Review*, 90(3): 21–45.

Goodfriend, M. and King, R.G. (1998) 'The New Neoclassical Synthesis and the role of monetary policy', Working Paper 98-5, Federal Reserve Bank of Richmond, Richmond.

Goodhart, C.A.E. (1973) 'Analysis of the determinants of the stock of money', in M. Parking and A.R. Nobay (eds) *Essays in Modern Economics (Proceedings of the Association of University Teachers of Economics)*, London: Longmans.

Goodhart, C.A.E. (1984) *Monetary Theory and Practice: The UK Experience*, London: Macmillan.

Goodhart, C.A.E. (1986) 'Financial innovation and monetary control', *Oxford Review of Economic Policy*, 2(4): 79–102.

Goodhart, C.A.E. (1989a) 'Has Moore become too horizontal?', *Journal of Post Keynesian Economics*, 12(1): 29–34.

Goodhart, C.A.E. (1989b) 'The conduct of monetary policy', *Economic Journal*, 99: 293–346.

Goodhart, C.A.E. (1989c) *Money, Information and Uncertainty*, second edition, London: Macmillan.

Goodhart, C.A.E. (1993) 'Can we improve the structure of financial systems?', *European Economic Review*, 37: 269–291.

Goodhart, C.A.E. (1998) 'Monetary base', in J. Eatwell, M. Milgate and P. Newman (eds) *The New Palgrave: A Dictionary of Economics*, vol. 3, pp. 500–502, New York: Palgrave Publishers.

Goodhart, C.A.E. (2001) 'The endogeneity of money', in P. Arestis, M. Desai and S. Dow (eds) *Money, Macroeconomics and Keynes, Essays in Honour of Victoria Chick, vol. 1*, London: Routledge.

Gordon, R.J. (1990) 'What is New Keynesian Economics', *Journal of Economic Literature*, 28: 1115–1171.

Green, C.J. and Llewellyn, D. (eds) (1991) *Surveys in Monetary Economics*, Oxford: Blackwell.

Green, G.D. (1975) 'Comparison of monetary systems and regional economies: a comment', *Journal of History*, 35(1): 212–215.

Greenwald, B.C. and Stiglitz, J.E. (1993a) 'Financial market imperfections and business cycles', *Quarterly Journal of Economics*, 58(1): 77–114.

Greenwald, B.C. and Stiglitz, J.E. (1993b) New and Old Keynesians, *Journal of Economic Perspectives*, 7(1): 23–44.

Greenwald, B.C., Levinson, A. and Stiglitz, J.E. (1993) 'Capital market imperfections and regional economic development', in A. Giovannini (ed.) *Finance and Development: Issues and Experience*, Cambridge: Cambridge University Press.

Gross, D., Davanne, O., Emerson, M., Mayer, T., Tabellini, G. and Thygesen, N. (2000) *Quo vadis Euro? The Cost of Muddling Through*, Second report of the CEPS Macroeconomic Policy Group, Brussels: CEPS.

Gross, D., Durrer, K., Jimeno, J., Monticelli, C. and Perotti, R. (2002) *Fiscal and Monetary Policy for a Low-speed Europe*, Fourth Annual Report of the Centre for European Policy Studies (CEPS) Macroeconomic Policy Group, Brussels: CEPS.

Guiso, L., Kashyap, A.K., Panetta, F. and Terlizzese, D. (1999) 'Will a common European Monetary Policy have asymmetric effects?', *Federal Reserve Bank of Chicago, Economic Perspectives*, fourth quarter, 56–75.

Guiso, L., Kashyap, A.K., Panetta, F. and Terlizzese, D. (2000) 'Will a common European monetary policy have asymmetric effects?', Banca d'Italia Temi di Discussione, no. 384.

Gurley, J.G. and Shaw, E.S. (1955) 'Financial aspects of the economics development', *American Economic Review*, 45: 515–523.

Gurley, J.G. and Shaw, E.S. (1956) 'Financial intermediaries and the saving-investment process', *Journal of Finance*, 11: 672–700.

Gurley, J.G. and Shaw, E.S. (1960) *Money in a Theory of Finance*, Washington: The Brookings Institution.

Gurley, J.G. and Shaw, E.S. (1967) 'Financial structure and economic development', *Economic Development and Cultural Change*, 15(3): 257–268.

Hafer, R.W. (1982) 'The role of fiscal policy in the St. Louis Equation', *Federal Reserve Bank of St. Louis Review*, 64(1): 17–22.

Hafer, R.W. (1984) 'The money-GNP link: assessing alternative transaction measures', *Federal Reserve Bank of St. Louis Review*, 66(3): 19–27.

Handa, J. (2000) *Monetary Economics*, London: Routledge.

Hansen, B. (1973) 'On the effects of fiscal and monetary policy: a taxonomic discussion', *American Economic Review*, 63: 546–571.

Harrigan, F.J. and McGregor, P.G. (1987) 'Interregional arbitrage and the supply of loanable funds: a model of intermediate financial capital mobility', *Journal of Regional Science*, 27(3): 357–367.

Harrigan, F.J. and McGregor, P.G. (1988) 'Introduction: new directions for regional economic modelling', in F. Harrigan and P.G. McGregor (eds) *Recent Advances in Regional Economic Modelling*, London Papers in Regional Science, 19, London: Pion Press.

Harrigan, F.J. and McGregor, P.G. (1989) 'Neoclassical and Keynesian perspectives on the regional macro-economy: a computable general equilibrium approach', *Journal of Regional Science*, 29(4): 555–573.

Harrigan, F.J. and McGregor, P.G. (eds) (1988) *Recent Advances in Regional Economic Modelling*, London Papers in Regional Science, 19, London: Pion Press.

Harris, D.G. (1974) 'Interest rates, nonprice terms, and the allocation of bank credit', *Southern Economic Journal*, 40(3): 428–433.

Hartland, P.C. (1949) 'Interregional payments compared with international payments', *Quarterly Journal of Economics*, 63(3): 392–407.

Hayo, B. and Uhlenbrock, B. (1999) 'Industry effects of monetary policy in Germany', in J. von Hagen and C. Waller (eds.) *Common Money, Uncommon Regions*, Boston: Kluwer Academic Press.

Hellwig, M.F. (1993) 'The challenge of monetary theory', *European Economic Review*, 37: 215–242.

Hendershott, P. and Kidwell, D. (1978) 'The impact of relative security supplies: a test with data from a regional tax-exempt bond market', *Journal of Money, Credit and Banking*, 20(3): 337–347.

Henderson, J. (1944) 'Regional differentials in interest rates', *Southern Economic Journal*, 11(2): 113–132.

Hendrikx, M. and Chapple, B. (2002) 'Regional inflation divergence in the context of EMU', Monetary and Economic Policy Department Working Paper, Series no. 2002-19, De Nederlandsche Bank, The Netherlands.

Hernando, I. (1997) 'El canal crediticio en la transmisión de la política monetaria', in Servicio de Estudios del Banco de España (ed.) *La política monetaria y la inflación en España*, Madrid: Alianza Editorial.

Hernando, I. and Vallés, J. (1991) 'Inversiones y restricciones financieras: evidencia en las empresas manufactureras españolas', Working Paper no. 9113, Bank of Spain, Madrid.

Hester, D.D. (1964) 'Keynes and the Quantity Theory: a comment on the Friedman-Meiselman CMC paper', *Review of Economics and Statistics*, 46: 364–368.

Hicks, J.R. (1937) 'Mr Keynes and the Classics', *Econometrica*, 5: 147–159.

Hicks, J.R. (1974) *The Crisis in Keynesian Economics*, Oxford: Basil Blackwell.

Hochwald, W. (1957) 'Discussion: the flow of funds between regions of the United States', *Papers of the Regional Science Association*, 3: 160–162.

Holland, A.S. (1985) 'Rational expectations and the effects of monetary policy: a guide for the uninitiated', *Federal Reserve Bank of St. Louis Review*, 67(5): 5–11.

Holland, S. (1976) *Capital Versus the Regions*, London: Macmillan.

Honohan, P. and Lane, P.R. (2003) 'Divergent inflation rates in EMU', Trinity Economic Papers no. 2003/4, The University of Dublin, Trinity College, Dublin.

Hoover, K.D. (2003) 'History of Postwar Monetary and Macroeconomics', in W. Samuels, J. Biddle and J. Davis (eds) *A Companion to the History of Economic Thought*, Oxford: Blackwell.

Hubbard, R.H. (1995) 'Is there a credit channel for monetary policy?', *Federal Reserve Bank of St. Louis Proceedings*, May/June, 63–82.

Hughes, M. (1991) 'General equilibrium of a regional economy with a financial sector – part i: an accounting framework with budget and balance sheet linkages', *Journal of Regional Science*, 31(4): 385–396.

Hughes, M. (1992) 'General equilibrium of a regional economy with a financial sector – part ii: a simple behavioral model', *Journal of Regional Science*, 32(1): 19–37.

Hung, J. (1992–1993) 'Assessing the exchange rate's impact on US manufacturing profits', *Federal Reserve Bank of New York, Quarterly Review*, 17(4): 44–63.

Hutchinson, R.W. and Mckillop, D.G. (1990) 'Regional financial sector models: an application to the Northern Ireland financial sector', *Regional Studies*, 24(5): 421–431.

Hutchinson, R.W. and McKillop, D.G. (1992) 'Banks and small to medium sized business financing in the United Kingdom: some general issues', *National Westminster Bank Quarterly Review*, February, 84–95.

Ingram, J.C. (1959) 'State and regional payments mechanisms', *Quarterly Journal of Economics*, 73: 619–632.

Issing, O., Gaspar, V., Angeloni, I. and Oreste, T. (2001) *Monetary Policy in the Euro Area: Strategy a Decision Making at the European Central Bank*, Cambridge: Cambridge University Press.

James, J. (1976) 'Banking market structure, risk and the pattern of local interest rates in the US, 1893–1911', *Review of Economics and Statistics*, 58(4): 453–462.

Johnson, H.G. (1971) 'The Keynesian Revolution and the Monetarist Counter-Revolution', *American Economic Review*, 61(2): 1–14.

Jones, M.E.F. (1985) 'The regional impact of an overvalued pound in the 1920s', *Economic History Review*, 38(3): 393–401.

Jordan, J.L. (1986) 'The Andersen-Jordan approach after nearly 20 years', *Federal Reserve Bank of St. Louis Review*, 68(8): 5–8.

Judd, J.P. and Scadding, J.L. (1982) 'The search for a stable money demand function', *Journal of Economic Literature*, 20(3): 993–1023.

Kaldor, N. (1960) 'The Radcliffe Report', *Review of Economics and Statistics*, 60: 127–138.

Kaldor, N. (1986) *The Scourge of Monetarism*, Second edition, Oxford: Oxford University Press.

Kaldor, N. and Trevithich, J. (1981) 'A Keynesian perspective on money', in M. Sawyer (ed.) *Post Keynesian Economics: Schools of Thought in Economics*, Aldershot: Edward Elgar.

Kannan, R. (1987) 'Banking development and regional disparities', *Indian Economic Journal*, 35(2): 58–76.

Kareken, J.H. (1957) 'Lenders' preferences, credit rationing, and the effectiveness of monetary policy', *Review of Economics and Statistics*, 39: 292–302.

Karras, G. (1996) 'Is Europe an optimum currency area? Evidence on the magnitude and asymmetry of common and country-specific shocks in 20 European countries', *Journal of Economic Integration*, 11(3): 366–384.

Kashyap, A.K. and Stein, J.C. (1997a) 'Monetary policy and bank lending', in N.G. Mankiw (ed.) *Monetary Policy*, Chicago, IL: University of Chicago University Press for NBER.

Kashyap, A. and Stein, J. (1997b) The role of banks in monetary policy: a survey with implications for the European Monetary Union, *Federal Bank of Chicago, Economic Perspectives*, September/October, 2–18.

Kashyap, A.K., Stein, J.C. and Wilcox, D.W. (1993) 'Monetary policy and credit conditions: evidence from the composition of external finance', *American Economic Review*, 83(1): 78–98.

Keehn, R.H. (1974) 'A note on the cost of trade credit and the discriminatory effects of monetary policy', *Journal of Finance*, 29: 1581–1582.

Keleher, R.E. (1977a) 'Fundamental determinants of credit volume: a survey and regional application', Technical Papers, Federal Reserve Bank of Atlanta, Atlanta, GA.

Keleher, R.E. (1977b) 'A framework for examining the small, open regional economy: an application of the macroeconomics of open systems', Working Paper Series, Federal Reserve Bank of Atlanta, Atlanta, GA.

Keleher, R.E. (1979) 'Regional credit market integration: a survey and empirical examination', Technical Papers, Federal Reserve Bank of Atlanta, Atlanta, GA.

Kenen, P. (1969) 'The Theory of Optimum Currency Areas: an eclectic view', in R.A. Mundell and A.K. Swoboda (eds) *Monetary Problems of the International Economy*, Chicago, IL: University Press.

Kent, C. (2003) *Inflation and competitiveness. Country report: Italy*, Washington: International Monetary Fund.

Keran, M.W. (1970a) 'Monetary and fiscal influences on economic activity: The foreign influence', *Federal Reserve Bank of St. Louis Review*, 52(2): 16–28.

Keran, M.W. (1970b) 'Monetary and fiscal influences on economic activity. The historical evidence', *Federal Reserve Bank of St. Louis Review*, 52: 5–24.

Keran, M.W. (1970c) 'Selecting a monetary indicator. Evidence from the United States and other developed countries', *Federal Reserve Bank of St. Louis Review*, Vol. 52, No. 9.

Keynes, J.M. (1930/1971) *A Treatise on Money*, London: Macmillan (reprinted in D. Moggridge (ed.) (1971), The collected writings of John Maynard Keynes, vols. 5 and 6, London: Macmillan for the Royal Economic Society).

Keynes, J.M. (1936/1973b) *The General Theory of Employment, Interest, and Money*, London: Macmillan (reprinted in D. Moggridge (ed.) (1973b), The collected writings of John Maynard Keynes, vol. 7, London: Macmillan for the Royal Economic Society).

Keynes, J.M. (1937a/1973a) 'The general theory of employment', *Quarterly Journal of Economics*, 51: 209–23 (reprinted in D. Moggridge (ed.) (1973a), The collected writings of John Maynard Keynes, vol. 14, London: Macmillan for the Royal Economic Society).

Keynes, J.M. (1937b/1973a) 'Alternative theories of the rate of interest', *Economic Journal*, 47: 663–669 (reprinted in D. Moggridge (ed.) (1973a), The collected writings of John Maynard Keynes, vol. 14, London: Macmillan for the Royal Economic Society).

Khatkhate, D.R. and Short, B.K. (1980) 'Monetary and central banking problems of mini states', *World Development*, 8(12): 1017–1025.

Khatkhate, D.R. and Villanueva, D.P. (1978) 'Operation of selective credit policies in less developed countries: certain critical issues', *World Development*, 6: 979–990.

Kieler, M. (2003) *'Is inflation persistence higher in euro area than in the United States?*, Washington: International Monetary Fund.

Kieler, M. and Saarenheimo, T. (1998) 'Differences in monetary policy transmission? A case not closed', Economic Papers no. 132, European Commission, Directorate-General for Economic and Financial Affairs, Brussels.

King, M. (2002) 'No money, no inflation. The role of money in the economy', *Bank of England Quarterly Bulletin*, Summer, 162–177.

King, R.G. and Plosser, C.I. (1984) 'Money, credit, and prices in a real business cycle', *American Economic Review*, 74(3): 363–380.

Kleimeier, S. and Sander, H. (2001) 'European financial market integration: evidence on the emergence of a single eurozone retail banking market', Maastricht Research School of Economics of Technology and Organization, Research Memoranda no. 060.

Kouparitsas, M.A. (1999) 'Is the EMU a viable common currency area? A VAR analysis of regional business cycles', *Federal Reserve Bank of Chicago, Economic Perspectives*, 23: 2–20.

Kozicki, S. and Tinsley, P. (2002) 'Alternative sources of the lag dynamics of inflation', Proceedings of a Conference on 'Price Adjustment and Monetary Policy' held at the Bank of Canada, November 14–15.

Kozlowski, P.J. (1991) 'Integrating money into regional models of leading indicators', *Review of Regional Studies*, 21(3): 235–248.

Kregel, J.A. (1984–1985) 'Constraints on the expansion of output and employment: real or monetary?', *Journal of Post Keynesian Economics*, 7(2): 139–152.

Kresge, D.T. (1974) 'The impact of monetary policy on the allocation of bank credit', *National Bureau of Economic Research, Explorations in Economic Research*, 1(2): 205–257.

Kretzmer, P.E. (1992) 'Monetary vs. fiscal policy: new evidence on an old debate', *Federal Reserve Bank of Kansas City, Economic Review*, 77(2): 21–30.

Krugman, P.R. (1993) 'Lessons of Massachusetts for EMU', in F. Torres and F. Giavazi (eds) *Adjustment and Growth in the European Monetary Union*, Cambridge: Cambridge University Press.

Kwiatkowski, D., Phillips, P., Schmidt, P. and Shin, Y. (1992) 'Testing the null hypothesis of stationarity against the alternative of a unit root', *Journal of Econometrics*, 54: 91–115.

Kydland, F. and Prescott, E. (1982) 'Time to build and aggregate fluctuations', *Econometrica*, 50: 1345–1370.

Kydland, F. and Prescott, E. (1990) 'Business cycles: real facts and monetary myths', *Federal Reserve Bank of Minneapolis Quarterly Review*, 14(2): 1–16.

Laidler, D. (1966) 'The rate of interest and the demand for money: some empirical evidence', *Journal of Political Economy*, 74(6): 543–555.

Laidler, D. (1977) *The Demand for Money: Theories and Evidence*, second edition, New York: Dun-Donnelley.

Laidler, D. (1978) 'Money and money income: an essay on the 'transmission mechanism'', *Journal of Monetary Economics*, 4: 151–191.

Laidler, D. (1982) *Monetarist Perspectives*, Oxford: Philip Allan.

Laidler, D. (1989) 'Dow and Saville's Critique of Monetary Policy. A Review Essay', *Journal of Economic Literature*, 27(3): 1147–1159.

Laidler, D. (1990) *Taking Money Seriously*, New York: Philip Allan.

Laidler, D. (2001) 'The transmission mechanism with endogenous money', in P. Arestis, M. Desai and S.C. Dow (eds) *Money, Macroeconomics and Keynes, Essays in Honour of Victoria Chick*, vol. 1, London: Routledge.

Laidler, D. and Parkin, J.M. (1970) 'The demand for money in the United Kingdom 1956–67: preliminary estimates', *Manchester School*, 38: 187–208.

Latané, H.A. (1954) 'Cash balances and the interest rate: a pragmatic approach', *Review of Economics and Statistics*, 36: 456–461.

Latané, H.A. (1960) 'Income velocity and interest rates: a pragmatic approach', *Review of Economics and Statistics*, 42: 445–460.

Lavoie, M. (1984) 'The endogenous flow of credit and the Post Keynesian Theory of Money', *Journal of Economic Issues*, 18: 771–797.

Lavoie, M. (1992) *Foundations of Post Keynesian Economics Analysis*, Aldershot: Edward Elgar.

Lawrence, R.J. (1963) 'The regional impact of monetary policy', Ph.D. Dissertation, University of Michigan (Ann Arbor Mich.: University Microfilms), Michigan.

Lawson, T. (1989) 'Abstraction, tendencies and stylised facts: a realist approach to economic analysis', *Cyprus Journal of Economics*, 13: 59–78.

Lawson, T. (1997) *Economics and Reality*, London: Routledge.

Ledo, M., Sebastián, M. and Taguas, D. (2002) 'El diferencial de inflación entre España y la UEM', *Papeles de Economía Española*, 91: 13–25.

Leeper, E.M., Sims, C.A. and Zha, T. (1996) 'What does monetary policy do?', *Brookings Papers on Economic Activity*, 2: 1–78.

Lees, F.A. (1969) 'Interregional flows of funds through state and local government securities (1957–1962)', *Journal of Regional Science*, 9(1): 79–86.

Leeuw, F. de and Gramlich, E.M. (1969) 'The channels of monetary policy: a further report on the Federal Reserve-MIT Model', *Journal of Finance*, 24: 265–290.

Lettau, M., Ludvigson, S., and Steindel, C. (2002) 'Monetary policy transmission through the consumption-wealth channel', *Federal Reserve Bank of New York Economic Policy Review*, May, 117–133.

Lieberson, S. and Schiwirian, K.P. (1962) 'Banking functions as a index of inter-city relations', *Journal of Regional Science*, 4(1): 69–81.

Lindsey, D.E. and Wallich, H.C. (1998) 'Monetary policy', in J. Eatwell, M. Milgate and P. Newman (eds) *The New Palgrave: A Dictionary of Economics*, Vol. 3, pp. 508–515, New York: Palgrave Publishers Ltd.

Lo Cascio, I. (2001) 'Do labour markets really matter? Monetary shocks and asymmetric effects across Europe?', Ente per gli studi monetari, bancari e finanziari 'Luigi Einaudi', Termi di Ricerca no. 22.

Lombra, R.E. and Torto, R.G. (1973) 'Federal Reserve 'defensive' behaviour and the reverse causation argument', *Southern Economic Journal*, 40(1): 47–55.

Lombra, R.E. and Torto, R.G. (1974) 'Measuring the impact of monetary and fiscal actions: a new look at the specification problem', *Review of Economics and Statistics*, 56(2): 104–107.

Long, J. and Plosser, C. (1983) 'Real business cycles', *Journal of Political Economy*, (91): 39–69.

Long, J.B. and Summers, L.H. (1988) 'How does macroeconomic affect output?', *Brookings Papers on Economic Activity*, 2: 433–480.

Lösch, A. (1954) *The Economics of Location*, New Haven: Yale University Press.

Lucas, R.E. (1972) 'Expectations and the neutrality of money', *Journal of Economic Theory*, 4: 103–124.

Lucas, R.E. (1973) 'Some international evidence on output-inflation tradeoffs', *American Economic Review*, 63(3): 326–334.

Macesich, G. (1964) 'Liquidity preference. A southern banking tradition', in M.L. Greehut and W.T. Whitman (eds) *Essays in Southern Economic Development*, Chapel Hill: University of North Carolina Press.

Mackay, R.R. and Molyneux, P. (1996) 'Bank credit and the regions: a comparison within Europe', *Regional Studies*, 30(8): 757–763.

Maclennan, D., Muellbauer, J. and Stephens, M. (2000) 'Asymmetries in housing and financial market institutions and EMU', CEPR Discussion Paper no. 2062.

Magnifico, G. (1973) *European Monetary Unification*, London: Macmillan.

Mankiw, N.G. (1990) 'A quick refresher course in Macroeconomics', *Journal of Economic Literature*, 28: 1645–1660.

Marelli, E. (1985) 'Economic policies and their effects upon regional economies', *Papers of the Regional Science Association*, 58: 127–139.

María-Dolores, R. (2002) 'Asymmetries in the cyclical effects of monetary policy on output: some European evidence', Working Paper DEFI no. 02–04, FEDEA, Madrid.

Martin, R.L. (2001) 'EMU versus the regions: regional convergence and divergence in Euroland', *Journal of Economic Geography*, 1: 51–80.

Martínez Estévez, A. (1994) 'Implicaciones regionales de las políticas económicas', in A. Pulido and B. Cabrer (eds) *Datos, técnicas y resultados del moderno análisis económico regional*, Madrid: Ediciones Mundi-Prensa.

Martínez Estévez, A. and Pedreño Muñoz, A. (1990) 'Comunidad Valenciana: crecimiento y crisis exportadora', *Papeles de Economía Española*, 45: 379–397.

Mathur, V.K. and Stein, S. (1980) 'Regional impact of monetary and fiscal policy: an investigation into the reduced form approach', *Journal of Regional Science*, 20(3): 343–351.

Mathur, V.K. and Stein, S. (1982) 'The regional impact of monetary and fiscal policy: some further results', *Papers of the Regional Science Association*, 50: 67–74.

Mathur, V.K. and Stein, S. (1983) 'Regional impact of monetary and fiscal policy: a reply', *Journal of Regional Science*, 23(2): 263–265.

Mattesini, F. (1993) *Financial Markets, Asymmetric Information and Macroeconomic Equilibrium*, Aldershot: Edward Elgar.

Mauskopf, E. (1990) 'The transmission channels of monetary policy: how have they changed?', *Federal Reserve Bulletin*, 76(12): 985–1008.

Mazzola, F., Fazio, G. and Lo Cascio, I. (2002) 'Regional asymmetric reactions to shocks in EMU: an assessment of different approaches', paper presented at the conference 'Innovation and Growth: New Challenges for the Regions', Sophia Antipolis, France, January 18–19, 2002.

McAdam, P. and Morgan, J. (2001) 'The monetary transmission mechanism in the euro-area level: issues and results using structural macroeconomic models', Working Paper no. 93, European Central Bank, Frankfurt.

McCallum, B.T. (2001) 'Analysis of the Monetary Transmission Mechanism: Methodological Issues', in Deutsche Bank (ed) *The Monetary Transmission Process: Recent Developments and Lessons for Europe*, New York: Palgrave-Macmillan.

McCoy, D. and McMahon, M. (2000) 'Differences in the transmission of monetary policy in the Euro-area: an empirical approach', Irish Central Bank, TP-05/RT/00, June.

McKillop, D.G. and Hutchinson, R.W. (1990) *Regional Financial Sectors in the British Isles*, Aldershot: Avebury.

McKinnon, R. (1963) 'Optimum currency areas', *American Economic Review*, 53: 717–25.

McPheters, L.R. (1976) 'Banking system diffusion of open market operations', *Southern Economic Journal*, 43(2): 1009–1016.

Meiselman, D. and Simpson, T.D. (1971) 'Monetary policy and consumer expenditures: the historical evidence', in Federal Reserve Bank of Boston (ed.) *Consumer Spending and Monetary Policy: The Linkage*, Monetary (Conferences Series no. 5), Boston.

Meltzer, A.H. (1963) 'The demand for money: the evidence from the time series', *Journal of Political Economy*, 71: 219–246.

Meltzer, A.H. (1995) Monetary, credit and (other) transmission processes: a monetarist perspective, *Journal of Economic Perspectives*, 9(4): 49–72.

Messori, M. (1993) 'Banking and finance in the Italian Mezzogiorno: issues and problems', paper presented at International Congress 'The European Periphery Facing the New Century', 30 September–2 October 1993, Santiago de Compostela, Spain.

Meyer, L.H. (2001) 'Does money matter?' *Federal Reserve Bank of St. Louis Review*, 83(5): 1–15.

Meyer, L.H. and Hart, W.R. (1975) 'On the effects of fiscal and monetary policy: completing the taxonomy', *American Economic Review*, 65(4): 762–767.

Meyer, P.A. (1967) 'Price discrimination, regional loan rates and the structure of the banking industry', *Journal of Finance*, 22(1): 37–48.

Mihov, I. (2001) 'One monetary policy in EMU. Countries, regions, channels', *Economic Policy*, October, 369–406.

Miles, D.K. and Wilcox, J. (1991) 'The money transmission mechanism', in C.J. Green and D.T. Llewellyn (eds) *Surveys in Monetary Economics*, Oxford: Blackwell.

Miller, E. (1978) *Microeconomic Effects of Monetary Policy: The Fallout of Severe Monetary Restraint*, New York: St. Martin's Press.

Miller, R.J. (1978) *The Regional Impact of the Monetary Policy in the United States*, Lexington: Lexington Books.

Minsky, H.P. (1967) 'Money, other financial variables, and aggregate demand in the short run', in G. Horwich (ed.) *Monetary Process and Policy: a Symposium*, Homewood, Illinois: Richard D. Irwin Inc.

Minsky, H.P. (1969) 'Private sector asset management and the effectiveness of monetary policy: theory and practice', *Journal of Finance*, 24: 223–238.

Minsky, H.P. (1982) *Inflation, Recession and Economic Policy*, Brighton: Wheatsheaf.

Minsky, H.P. (1986) 'The evolution of financial institutions and the performance of the economy', *Journal of Economic Issues*, 20: 345–353.

Minsky, H.P. (1993) 'On the non-neutrality of money', *Federal Reserve Bank of New York, Quarterly Review*, 18(1): 77–82.

Mishkin, F.S. (1982) 'Does anticipated monetary policy matter? an econometric investigation', *Journal of Political Economy*, 90(1): 22–51.

Mishkin, F.S. (1995) 'Symposium on the monetary transmission mechanism', *Journal of Economic Perspectives*, 9(4): 3–10.

Mishkin, F.S. (1996) 'The channels of monetary transmission: lessons for monetary policy', NBER Working Paper no. 5464, National Bureau of Economic Research, Cambridge, Massachusetts, USA.

Mishkin, F.S. (2001) 'The transmission mechanism and the role of asset prices in monetary policy', NBER Working Paper no. 8617, National Bureau of Economic Research, Cambridge, Massachusetts, USA.

Modigliani, F. (1963) 'The monetary mechanism and its interaction with real phenomena', *Review of Economics and Statistics*, 45: 79–107.

Modigliani, F. and Miller, M.H. (1958) 'The cost of capital, corporation finance, and the theory of investments', *American Economic Review*, 48: 261–297.

Moggridge, D.E. and Hogdson, S. (1974) 'Keynes on monetary policy, 1910–1946', *Oxford Economic Papers*, 26(2): 226–247.

Mojon, B. and Peersman, G. (2001) 'A VAR description of the effects of monetary policy in the individual countries of the euro area', European Central Bank, Working Paper no. 92.

Molyneux, P. (1989) '1992 and its impact on local and regional banking markets', *Regional Studies*, 23(6): 523–533.

Moore, B.J. (1988a) *Horizontalists and Verticalists: The Macroeconomics of Credit Money*, Cambridge: Cambridge University Press.

Moore, B.J. (1988b) 'The endogenous money supply', *Journal of Post Keynesian Economics*, 10(3): 372–385.

Moore, B.J. (1988c) 'The endogeneity of money: a comment', *Scottish Journal of Political Economy*, 35(3): 291–294.

Moore, B.J. (1989a) 'The effects of monetary policy on income distribution', in P. Davidson and J. Kregel (eds) *Macroeconomic Problems and Policies of Income Distribution: Functional, Personal, International*, Aldershot: Edward Elgar.

Moore, B.J. (1989b) 'On the endogeneity of money once more', *Journal of Post Keynesian Economics*, 11(3): 479–497.

Moore, B.J. (1991) 'Money supply endogeneity: 'reserve price setting' or 'reserve quantity setting?', *Journal of Post Keynesian Economics*, 13(3): 404–413.

Moore, C.L. (1979) 'Banking and the regional income multiplier', *Northeast Regional Science Review*, 9: 1–7.

Moore, C.L. and Hill, J.M. (1982) 'Interregional arbitrage and the supply of loanable funds', *Journal of Regional Science*, 22(4): 499–512.

Moore, C.L. and Nagurney, A. (1989) 'A general equilibrium model of interregional monetary flows', *Environment and Planning A*, 21(3): 397–404.

Moore, C.L., Karaska, G.J. and Hill, J.M. (1985) 'The impact of the banking on regional analyses', *Regional Studies*, 19(1): 29–35.

Morgan, B. (1978) *Monetarists and Keynesians: Their Contribution to Monetary Theory*, London: Macmillan.

Morgan, D.P. (1993) 'Asymmetric effects of monetary policy', *Federal Reserve Bank of Kansas City, Economic Review*, 78(2): 21–34.

Morgan, E.V. (1973) 'Regional problems and common currencies', *Lloyds Bank Review*, 110: 19–30.

Mosser, P.C. (1992) 'Changes in monetary policy effectiveness: evidence from large macroeconometric models', *Federal Reserve Bank of New York, Quarterly Review*, 17(1): 36–51.

Mundell, R.A. (1961) 'A theory of optimum currency areas', *American Economic Review*, 51: 657–665.

Nelson, E. (2000) 'UK monetary policy 1972–1997: a guide using Taylor rules', Working Paper no. 120, Bank of England, London.

Nickell, S. (2003) 'A picture of European unemployment: success and failure', Discussion Paper no. 0577, Centre for Economic Performance.

Niggle, C.J. (1989a) 'Book-review of 'Horizontalists and verticalists': the macro-economics of credit money', *Journal of Economic Issues*, 23(4): 1181–1185.

Niggle, C.J. (1989b) 'Monetary policy and changes in income distribution', *Journal of Economic Issues*, 23(3): 809–822.

Niggle, C.J. (1990) 'The evolution of money, financial institutions, and monetary economics', *Journal of Economic Issues*, 24(2): 443–450.

Niggle, C.J. (1991) 'The endogenous money supply theory. An institutionalist appraisal', *Journal of Economic Issues*, 25(1): 137–151.

Obstfeld, M. (2002) 'Exchange rates and adjustment: perspectives from the new open-economy macroeconomics', *Monetary and Economic Studies*, 20: 23–46.

Obstfeld, M. and Peri, G. (1998) 'Regional non-adjustment and fiscal policy', in D. Begg, et al. (eds) *EMU: Prospects and Challenges for the Euro*, pp. 205–259, Oxford: Blackwell Publishers.

OECD (1975) *The Role of Monetary Policy in Demand Management: The Experience of Six Major Countries*, OECD Monetary Studies Series, Paris: OECD.

OECD (1999) *EMU: Facts, Challenges and Policies*, Paris: OECD.

Olivera, A. (2003) 'Tipos de cambio reales y diferenciales de productividad: impli-caciones para la UME', Documentos de Trabajos Conjuntos, DT 2003–04, Facultad de CCEE y EE, Universidad de La Laguna (ULL) and Universidad de Las Palmas de Gran Canaria (ULPGC).

Orphanides, A. and Williams, J.C. (2002) 'Robust monetary policy rules with unknown natural rates', Working Paper no. 2003-01, Federal Reserve Bank of San Francisco.

Ostas, J.R. (1977) 'Regional differences in mortgage costs: a re-examination', *Journal of Finance*, 32(5): 1774–1778.

Padoa-Schioppa, T. (2000) 'Is a euroland banking system already emerging?', Lecture given at Société Universitaire Européenne de Recherches Financiéres – SUERF, Vienna, 29 April 2000.

Palley, T.I. (1991) 'The endogenous money supply: Consensus and disagreement', *Journal of Post Keynesian Economics*, 13(3): 397–413.

Patinkin, D. (1998) 'Neutrality of money', in J. Eatwell, M. Milgate and P. Newman (eds) *The New Palgrave: A Dictionary of Economics*, Vol. 3, pp. 639–645, New York: Palgrave Publishers Ltd.

Pedreño, A. (1992) 'Comunidad Valenciana: hacia un nuevo modelo de crecimiento', *Papeles de Economía Española*, 51: 384–397.

Pedreño, A. and Pardo, G. (1990) 'El sector exterior de la economía valenciana: impacto de la política monetaria', *Economistas*, 45–46: 178–183.

Peersman, G. (2003) 'The transmission of monetary policy in the euro area' unpublished manuscript.

Peersman, G. and Smets, F. (2001) 'The Monetary transmission mechanism in the Euro area: more evidence from VAR analysis', Working Paper no. 91, European Central Bank, Frankfurt.

Peersman, G. and F. Smets (2002) 'The Industry Effects of Monetary Policy in the Euro Area', Working Paper no. 165, European Central Bank, Frankfurt.

Peterson, M. (1973) 'Some evidence on intra-regional differences in yields and costs of mortgage lending', *Land Economics*, 49: 96–99.

Phillips, P.C.B. and Perron, P. (1988) 'Testing for a unit root in time series regression', *Biometrika*, 75: 335–346.

Pollin, R. (1991) 'Two theories of money supply endogeneity: some empirical evidence', *Journal of Post Keynesian Economics*, 13(3): 366–396.

Poole, W. and Kornblith, E.B.F. (1973) 'The Friedman-Meiselman CMC paper: New evidence on an old controversy', *American Economic Review*, 63: 908–917.

Porteous, D.J. (1995) *The Geography of Finance*, Aldershot: Edward Elgar.

Radcliffe Report (1959) *Committee on the Working of the Monetary System*, London: HMSO.

Ramaswamy, R. and Sloek, T. (1998) 'The real effects of monetary policy in the European Union: What are the differences?', *IMF Staff Papers*, 45(2): 374–396.

Ramos, R., Clar, M. and Suriñach, J. (1999a) 'Specialisation in Europe and asymmetric shocks: potential risks of EMU', in M. Fischer and P. Nijkamp (eds) *Spatial Dynamics of European Integration*, Berlin: Springer-Verlag.

Ramos, R., Clar, M. and Suriñach, J. (1999b) 'EMU: *some unanswered questions*', paper presented at the ERSA Congress, August 1999, Dublin.

Rasche, R.H. (1972) 'A review of empirical studies of the money supply mechanism', *Federal Reserve Bank of St. Louis Review*, 54(7): 11–19.

Rasche, R.H. (1993) 'Monetary aggregates, monetary policy and economic activity', *Federal Reserve Bank of St. Louis Review*, 75(2): 1–35.

Raymond, J.L. (1990) 'El perfil coyuntural de las comunidades autónomas', *Papeles de Economía Española*, 45: 62–73.

Raymond, J.L. (1993) 'La evolución coyuntural de las comunidades autónomas', *Papeles de Economía Española*, 55: 31–41.

Richardson, H.W. (1973) *Regional Growth Theory*, London: Macmillan.

Roberts, R.B. and Fishkind, H. (1979) 'The role of monetary forces in regional economic activity: an econometric simulation analysis', *Journal of Regional Science*, 19(1): 15–29.

Robertson, N. (1985) 'The scope for an autonomous monetary policy for Scotland', paper presented to the SER Conference, Glasgow, 1985.

Rockoff, H. (1977) 'Regional interest rates and bank failures, 1870–1914', *Explorations in Economic History*, 14: 90–95.

Rodríguez-Fuentes, C.J. (1993) 'Dinero, política monetaria y economía regional: una aproximación', *Situación*, 2: 27–43.

Rodríguez-Fuentes, C.J. (1996) 'Una aproximación a la teoría monetaria post-keynesiana', *Información Comercial Española*, 758: 67–77.

Rodríguez-Fuentes, C.J. (1997a) 'El papel del sistema bancario en el desarrollo regional. ¿Reparto o creación de crédito?', *Revista de Estudios Regionales*, 47: 117–139.

Rodríguez-Fuentes, C.J. (1997b) *Política Monetaria y Economía Regional*, Madrid: Consejo Económico y Social.

Rodríguez-Fuentes, C.J. (1998) 'Credit availability and regional development', *Papers in Regional Science*, 77(1): 63–75.

Rodríguez-Fuentes, C.J. (2002) 'Dinero, regiones y políticas monetarias', *Perspectivas del Sistema Financiero*, 75: 19–32.

Rodríguez-Fuentes, C.J. (2004) 'Monetary Policies for Small Island Economies', in N. Karagiannis and M. Witter (eds) *The Caribbean Economies in an era of Free Trade*, Aldershot: Ashgate.

Rodríguez-Fuentes, C.J. and Dow, S.C. (2003) 'EMU and the regional impact of monetary policy', *Regional Studies*, 37(9): 973–984.

Rodríguez-Fuentes, C.J. and Hernández-López, M. (1997) 'Análisis de diferencias estructurales interregionales determinantes en el impacto regional de la política monetaria', *Estudios de Economía Aplicada*, 7: 141–157.

Rodríguez-Fuentes, C.J., Padrón-Marrero, D. and Olivera-Herrera, A. (2004a) 'Integración monetaria y segmentación regional de mercados bancarios', *Revista de Estudios Regionales*, 70: 41–61.

Rodríguez-Fuentes, C.J., Padrón-Marrero, D. and Olivera-Herrera, A.J. (2004b) 'Estructura financiera regional y política monetaria. Una aproximación al caso español', *Papeles de Economía Española*, 101: 252–265.

Rodríguez-Fuentes, C.J., Padrón-Marrero, D. and Olivera-Herrera, A.J. (2004c) 'La endogeneidad de la oferta monetaria: teoría y evidencia empírica para la economía española', *Revista Asturiana de Economía*, 29: 91–110.

Rogers, J.H. (2002) 'Monetary union, price level convergence and inflation: how close is Europe to the United States?', International Finance Discussion Paper no. 740, Board of Governors of the Federal Reserve System.

Rogers, J.H., Hufbauer, G.C and Wada, E. (2002) 'Price level convergence and inflation in Europe', International Finance Division, Federal Reserve Board.

Romer, C. and Romer, D. (1989) 'Does monetary policy matter? A new test in the spirit of Friedman and Schwartz', *NBER Macroeconomics Annual 4*, Cambridge: MIT Press.

Romer, C. and Romer, D. (1990) 'New evidence on the monetary transmission mechanism', *Brookings Papers on Economic Activity*, 1: 149–213.

Romer, D. (2000) 'Keynesian Macroeconomics without the LM curve', *Journal of Economic Perspectives*, 14(1): 149–169.

Rousseas, S. (1986) *Post Keynesian Monetary Economics*, London: Macmillan.

Rudebusch, G.D. (1998) 'Do measures of monetary policy in a VAR make sense?', *International Economic Review*, 39: 907–931.

Ruffin, R.J. (1968) 'An econometric model of the impact of open market operation on various bank classes', *Journal of Finance*, 23(4): 625–637.

Samolyk, K.A. (1989) 'The role of banks in influencing regional flows of funds', Working Paper 8914, Federal Reserve Bank of Cleveland.

Samolyk, K.A. (1991) 'A regional perspective on the credit view', *Federal Reserve Bank of Cleveland, Economic Review*, 27(2): 27–38.

Samolyk, K.A. (1994) 'Banking conditions and regional economic performance. Evidence of a regional credit channel', *Journal of Monetary Economics*, 34: 259–278.

Samuelson, P.A. (1964) 'Theoretical notes on trade problems', *Review of Economics and Statistics*, 46: 145–154.

Santomero, A.M. (1993) 'European banking post-1992: lessons from the United States', in J. Dermine (ed.) *European Banking in the 1990s*, second edition, Oxford: Blackwell.

Sargent, T.J. and Wallace, N. (1975) "Rational' expectations, the optimal monetary instruments, and the optimal money supply rule', *Journal of Political Economy*, 83(2): 241–254.

Schaaf, A.H. (1966) 'Regional differences in mortgage financing costs', *Journal of Finance*, 21: 85–94.

Schmidt, R.H. (1999) 'Differences between financial systems in European countries: consequences for EMU', paper prepared for the Conference 'The Monetary Transmission Process', organised by the Deutsche Bundesbank in Frankfurt, March 1999.

Scott, I.O. (1955) 'The regional impact of monetary policy', *Quarterly Journal of Economics*, 69(2): 269–284.

Seaks, T.G. and Allen, S.D. (1980) 'The St. Louis Equation: a decade later', *Southern Economic Journal*, 46(3): 817–829.

Selgin, G.A. (1986) 'Commercial banks as pure intermediaries: between 'old' and 'new' views', *Southern Economic Journal*, 56(1): 80–86.

Shackle, G.L.S. (1955) *Uncertainty in Economics*, Cambridge: Cambridge University Press.

Short, J. and Nicholas, D.J. (1981) *Money Flows in the UK Regions*, Farnborough: Gower.

Simpson, T.D. (1984) 'Changes in the financial system. Implications for monetary policy', *Brookings Papers on Economic Activity*, 1: 249–265.

Sims, C. (1972) 'Money, income and causality', *American Economic Review*, 62: 540–552.

Sims, C. (1992) 'Interpreting the macroeconomic time series facts. The effects of monetary policy', *European Economic Review*, 36: 975–1011.

Sofianos, G., Wachtel, P. and Melnik, A. (1990) 'Loan commitments and monetary policy', *Journal of Banking and Finance*, 14(4): 677–689.

Spencer, D.E. (1989) 'Does money matter? The robustness of evidence from vector autoregressions', *Journal of Money, Credit and Banking*, 21(4): 442–454.

Spencer, R.W. (1974) 'Channels of monetary influence: a survey', *Federal Reserve Bank of St. Louis Review*, 56(11): 8–26.

Stiglitz, J.E. (1989) 'Financial markets and development', *Oxford Review of Economic Policy*, 5(4): 55–68.

Stiglitz, J.E. (1993) 'Overview', in A. Giovannini (ed.) *Finance and Development: Issues and Experience*, Cambridge: Cambridge University Press.

Stiglitz, J.E. and Weiss, A. (1981) 'Credit rationing in markets with imperfect information', *American Economic Review*, 71(3): 393–410.

Straszheim, M.R. (1969) 'The Regional Dimension to Commercial Bank Markets and Counter Cyclical Monetary Policy', Discussion Paper no. 50, Program on Regional and Urban Economics, Harvard University.

Straszheim, M.R. (1971) 'An introduction and overview of regional money and capital markets', in J.F. Kain and J. Meyer (eds) *Essays in Regional Economics*, Cambridge: Harvard University Press.

Strotz, R.H. (1967) 'Evidence on the impact of monetary variables on aggregate expenditure', in G. Horwich (ed.) *Monetary Process and Policy: A Symposium*, Homewood, Illinois : Richard Irwin, Inc.

Struthers, J. (1984) 'Rational expectations: a promising research program or a case for monetarist fundamentalism?', *Journal of Economic Issues*, 18(4): 1133–1154.

Studart, R. (1995) *Investment Finance in Economic Development*, London: Routledge.

Suardi, M. (2001) 'EMU and asymmetries in the monetary policy transmission', Economic Papers no. 157, European Economy.

Surico, P. (2003) 'How does the ECB target inflation?', Working Paper no. 299, European Central Bank, Frankfurt.

Svensson, L. (1999) 'Monetary policy issues for the eurosystem', Seminar Paper no. 667, Institute for International Economic Studies.

Svensson, L. (2003) 'What is wrong with Taylor rules? Using judgment in monetary policy through targeting rules', *Journal of Economic Literature*, 41: 426–477.

Sylla, R. (1969) 'Federal policy, banking market structure and capital mobilization in the United States, 1863–1913', *Journal of Economic History*, 29: 657–686.

Tait, A. (1977) 'Financial institutions and monetary policy', in D. MacKay (ed.) *Scotland 1980. The Economics of Self-government*, Edinburgh: Q Press.

Taylor, J.B. (1993) 'Discretion versus policy rules in practice', *Carnegie-Rochester Conference Series on Public Policy*, 39: 195–214.

Taylor, J.B. (1995) 'The monetary transmission mechanism: an empirical framework', *Journal of Economic Perspectives*, 9(4): 11–26.

Taylor, J.B. (1999) 'The robustness and efficiency of monetary policy rules as guidelines for interest rate setting by the European Central Bank', *Journal of Monetary Economics*, 43(3): 655–679.

Teigen, R.L. (1964) 'A structural approach to the impact of monetary policy', *Journal of Finance*, 19: 284–312.

Thurston, T.B. (1976) 'Regional interaction and the reserve adjustment lag with the commercial banking sector', *Journal of History*, 31(5): 1443–1456.

Toal, W.D. (1977) 'Regional impacts of monetary and fiscal policies in the post war period: some initial tests', Technical Paper, Federal Reserve Bank of Atlanta, Atlanta, GA.

Tobin, J. (1947) 'Liquidity preference and monetary policy', *Review of Economics and Statistics*, 29: 124–131.

Tobin, J. (1956) 'The interest elasticity of transactions demand for cash', *Review of Economics and Statistics*, 38: 241–247.

Tobin, J. (1958) 'Liquidity preference as behaviour towards risk', *Review of Economics and Statistics*, 25: 65–86.

Tobin, J. (1963) 'Commercial banks as creators of money', in D. Carson (ed.) *Banking and Monetary Studies*, U.S. Treasury, Richard D. Irwin.

Tobin, J. (1970) 'Money and income: post ergo propter hoc?', *Quarterly Journal of Economics*, 84: 301–317.

Tobin, J. (1978) 'Monetary policies and the economy: the transmission mechanism', *Southern Economic Journal*, 44(3): 421–431.

Townsend, R.M. (1983) 'Financial structure and economic activity', *American Economic Review*, 73(5): 895–911.

Tsiang, S.C. (1978) 'The diffusion of reserves and the money supply multiplier', *Economic Journal*, 88: 269–284.

Tussing, A.D. (1966) 'Can monetary policy influence the credit availability?', *Journal of Finance*, 21: 1–13.

Van den Heuvel, S.J. (2002a) 'Does bank capital matter for monetary transmission?' *Federal Reserve Bank of New York Economic Policy Review*, 8(1): 259–265.

Van den Heuvel, S.J. (2002b) 'The bank capital channel of monetary policy', Department of Finance, The Wharton School, University of Pennsylvania.

van Els, P., Locarno, P., Mojon, B. and Morgan, J. (2002) 'New macroeconomic evidence on monetary policy transmission in the euro area', *Journal of the European Economic Association*, 1(2–3): 720–730.

von Hagen, J. and Brückner, M. (2002) 'Monetary and fiscal policy in the European Monetary Union', IMES Discussion Paper Series, no 2002-E-16, Bank of Japan.

Vrooman, J. (1979) 'Does the St. Louis Equation even believe in itself?', *Journal of Money, Credit and Banking*, 11(1): 111–117.

Waud, R.N. (1974) 'Monetary and fiscal effects on economic activity: a reduced form examination of their relative importance', *Review of Economics and Statistics*, 56(2): 177–187.

Weiss, L. (1988) 'Comment on Financial structure and aggregate economic activity: an overview', *Journal of Money, Credit and Banking*, 20(3): 594–596.

Whitman, M. (1967) 'International and interregional payments adjustment: a synthetic view', Princeton Studies in International Finance no. 19, Princeton University.

Williams, D., Goodhart, C.A.E. and Gowland, D.H. (1976) 'Money, income and causality: the UK experience', *American Economic Review*, 66(3): 417–423.

Williams, J. (2003) 'La competitividad de la banca regional en la Europa del euro', in J.B. Donges (coord.) *El sistema financiero en la Europa del Euro*, Madrid: Fundación ICO.

Williams, J. and Gardener, E.P.M. (2003) 'The efficiency of European regional banking', *Regional Studies*, 37(4): 321–330.

Wills, H.W. (1982) 'The simple economics of bank regulations', *Economica*, 49: 249–259.

Winger, A. (1969) 'Regional growth disparities and the mortgage market', *Journal of Finance*, 24: 659–662.

Winnett, A. (1992) 'Some semantics of endogeneity', in P. Arestis and V. Chick (eds) *Recent Developments in Post Keynesian Economics*, Aldershot: Edward Elgar.

Wojnilower, A.M. (1980) 'The central role of credit crunches in recent financial history', *Brookings Papers on Economic Activity*, 2: 277–339.

Wonnacott, P. (1967) 'The similarity of quantity theory and Keynesian policy prescriptions in recent years', in G. Horwich (ed.) *Monetary Process and Policy*, Illinois: Richard D. Irwin.

Worrell, D. (1991) 'Fiscal and monetary policies in small economies', in Yin-Kann Wen and Yayshree Sengupta (eds.) *Increasing the international competitiveness of exports from Caribbean countries*, Economic Institute of the World Bank.

Wray, L.R. (1989a) 'A Keynesian Theory of banking: a comment on Dymski', *Journal of Post Keynesian Economics*, 12(1): 152–156.

Wray, L.R. (1989b) 'Horizontalists and verticalists: the macroeconomics of credit money. Book-review', *Journal of Economic Issues*, 23(4): 1185–1189.

Wray, L.R. (1990) *Money and Credit in Capitalist Economies: The Endogenous Money Approach*, Aldershot: Edward Elgar.

Wray, L.R. (1992a) 'Alternative approaches to money and interest rates', *Journal of Economic Issues*, 26(4): 1145–1178.

Wray, L.R. (1992b) 'Alternative theories of the rate of interest', *Cambridge Journal of Economics*, 16: 69–89.

Wray, L.R. (1992c) 'Commercial banks, the central bank and endogenous money', *Journal of Post Keynesian Economics*, 14(3): 297–310.

Wray, L.R. (1993) 'Money, interest rates, and monetarist policy: some more unpleasant monetarist arithmetic?', *Journal of Post Keynesian Economics*, 15(4): 541–569.

Index

For Product Safety Concerns and Information please contact our EU
representative GPSR@taylorandfrancis.com Taylor & Francis Verlag GmbH,
Kaufingerstraße 24, 80331 München, Germany

Printed and bound by CPI Group (UK) Ltd, Croydon, CR0 4YY
08/05/2025
01864531-0001